The Future of the Social Investment State

Social investment is part of a strategy to modernize the European welfare states by focusing on human resource development throughout the life-course, while ensuring financial sustainability. The last decades have seen cost containment in areas such as pensions and health care, but also expansion in areas such as early childhood education, higher education and active labour market policies. This development is linked to a Social Investment (SI) approach, which should, ideally, promote a better reconciliation of work and family life, high levels of labour market productivity and strong economic growth, while also mitigating social inequality. However, institutionalization of policies that may mainly benefit the middle class has some unintended effects, such as perpetuating new inequalities and the creation of other Matthew effects. While research on the rise of the social investment state as a new paradigm of social policy-making for European welfare states has grown significantly, there are still important gaps in the literature. The chapters in this book address the controversies around social investment related to inequalities, individual preferences and the politics of social investment. This volume is therefore organized around policies, politics and outcomes. The contributing authors bring together expert knowledge and different perspectives on SI from several disciplines, with original path-breaking empirical contributions, addressing some key questions that thus far are unanswered, related to Matthew effects, inequalities, ambiguities of social investment and institutional complementarities. Furthermore, it is the first volume that covers the core policy areas of social investment: childcare, education and labour market policies.

The chapters in this book were originally published in a special issue of the *Journal of European Public Policy*.

Marius R. Busemeyer is a Professor of Political Science at the University of Konstanz, Germany. His research focuses on comparative political economy and welfare state research, education and social policy, public spending, theories of institutional change and, more recently, public opinion on the welfare state. His publications include a book, *Skills and Inequality* (Cambridge University Press, Winner of the 2015 Stein Rokkan Prize for Comparative Social Science Research), an edited volume (with Christine Trampusch), *The Political*

Economy of Collective Skill Formation (Oxford University Press), and a recently edited special issue of the *Socio-Economic Review*, 'The political economy of skills and inequality' (with Torben Iversen).

Caroline de la Porte is a Professor in European and Comparative Welfare Policy in the Department of International Economics, Government and Business at the Copenhagen Business School, Frederiksberg, Denmark. Her research focuses on the European Union (EU) and comparative welfare state reform, with a special interest in the Nordic countries. She has published widely on the EU's influence on labour market reform, pensions as well as anti-poverty policies. Recent publications include an edited special issue on the EU and welfare state reform under conditions of crisis (with Elke Heins, in *Comparative European Politics*, 2015), an analysis of European Court of Justice rulings regarding atypical work in the context of labour market dualization (with Patrick Emmenegger, in the *Journal of European Social Policy*, 2017) and an analysis of the development of active labour market policy across Europe before and after the Great Recession (with Mattias Bengtsson and Kerstin Jacobsson, in *Social Policy and Administration*, 2017).

Julian L. Garritzmann is a Senior Researcher at the University of Zurich, Switzerland. In his current research Julian analyses public opinion towards social investment vis-à-vis compensatory social policies, he develops new approaches to study political effects on public policy and he analyses the (higher) education-inequality nexus. Moreover, in a recent project – together with Silja Häusermann and Bruno Palier – Julian analyses the politics of social investment in democracies around the globe. Recent publications include 'Party politics and education spending: challenging some common wisdom' (with Kilian Seng, in the *Journal of European Public Policy*, 2016) and 'Attitudes towards student support: How positive feedback-effects prevent change in the Four Worlds of Student Finance' (in the *Journal of European Social Policy*, 2015, recipient of the JESP/Doctoral researcher prize 2014). Julian's book on the 'Political Economy of Higher Education Finance' (published with Palgrave Macmillan in 2016) received the Dissertation Award of the German Political Science Association.

Emmanuele Pavolini is a Full Professor in Economic Sociology and Social Policy at the University of Macerata, Italy. He is co-editor of JESP – *Journal of European Social Policy* – and he has extensively published in Italian and English on the Italian welfare state in comparative perspective, Southern European welfare states, specific social policies (such as childcare, pensions, education policies), inequalities in the access to welfare state provision, occupational welfare and welfare mix and third-sector organizations. Recent publications include an edited book, *The Italian Welfare State in European Perspective: A Comparative Analysis* (with Ugo Ascoli, 2015), gathering the best Italian welfare state scholars; an analysis of long-term care across Europe (with Costanzo Ranci, in the *Journal of European Social Policy*, 25(3): 2015); and a comparative analysis of welfare state reform in Italy and Spain in a context of permanent strain (with Margarita Leon, Ana Guillen and Ugo Ascoli, in *Comparative European Politics*, 2015).

Journal of European Public Policy Series

Series Editors
Jeremy Richardson is Emeritus Fellow at Nuffield College, Oxford University, UK,
and an Adjunct Professor in the National Centre for Research on Europe, University
of Canterbury, New Zealand.
Berthold Rittberger is professor and chair of International Relations at the
Geschwister-Scholl-Institute of Political Science at the University of Munich.

This series seeks to bring together some of the finest edited works on European Public Policy. Reprinting from Special Issues of the *Journal of European Public Policy*, the focus is on using a wide range of social sciences approaches, both qualitative and quantitative, to gain a comprehensive and definitive understanding of Public Policy in Europe.

Federal Challenges and Challenges to Federalism
Edited by John Erik Fossum and Markus Jachtenfuchs

Political Budgeting Across Europe
Edited by Christian Breunig, Christine S. Lipsmeyer and Guy D. Whitten

Ideas, Political Power, and Public Policy
Edited by Daniel Béland, Martin B. Carstensen and Leonard Seabrooke

The European Union as a Global Regulator
Edited by Alasdair Young

Differentiated Integration in the European Union
Edited by Benjamin Leruth and Christopher Lord

Legislative Lobbying in Context
The Policy and Polity Determinants of Interest Group Politics in the European Union
Edited by Jan Beyers, Caelesta Braun and Heike Klüver

The Future of the Social Investment State
Politics, Policies and Outcomes
Edited by Marius R. Busemeyer, Caroline de la Porte, Julian L. Garritzmann and Emmanuele Pavolini

For more information about this series, please visit: https://www.routledge.com/Journal-of-European-Public-Policy-Special-Issues-as-Books/book-series/JEPPSPIBS

The Future of the Social Investment State

Politics, Policies and Outcomes

Edited by
Marius R. Busemeyer, Caroline de la Porte, Julian L. Garritzmann and Emmanuele Pavolini

LONDON AND NEW YORK

First published 2019
by Routledge
2 Park Square, Milton Park, Abingdon, Oxon, OX14 4RN, UK

and by Routledge
52 Vanderbilt Avenue, New York, NY 10017, USA

First issued in paperback 2020

Routledge is an imprint of the Taylor & Francis Group, an informa business

© 2019 Taylor & Francis

British Library Cataloguing-in-Publication Data
A catalogue record for this book is available from the British Library

ISBN 13: 978-0-367-58715-4 (pbk)
ISBN 13: 978-1-138-31817-5 (hbk)

Typeset in Myriad Pro
by codeMantra

Publisher's Note
The publisher accepts responsibility for any inconsistencies that may have arisen during the conversion of this book from journal articles to book chapters, namely the possible inclusion of journal terminology.

Disclaimer
Every effort has been made to contact copyright holders for their permission to reprint material in this book. The publishers would be grateful to hear from any copyright holder who is not here acknowledged and will undertake to rectify any errors or omissions in future editions of this book.

Contents

CONTENTS

Citation Information

The chapters in this book were originally published in the Journal of European Public Policy, volume 25, issue 6 (June 2018). When citing this material, please use the original page numbering for each article, as follows:

Chapter 1
The future of the social investment state: politics, policies, and outcomes
Marius R. Busemeyer, Caroline de la Porte, Julian L. Garritzmann and Emmanuele Pavolini
Journal of European Public Policy, volume 25, issue 6 (June 2018) pp. 801–809

Chapter 2
Social investment as a policy paradigm
Anton Hemerijck
Journal of European Public Policy, volume 25, issue 6 (June 2018) pp. 810–827

Chapter 3
Agents of institutional change in EU policy: the social investment moment
Caroline de la Porte and David Natali
Journal of European Public Policy, volume 25, issue 6 (June 2018) pp. 828–843

Chapter 4
Public demand for social investment: new supporting coalitions for welfare state reform in Western Europe?
Julian L. Garritzmann, Marius R. Busemeyer and Erik Neimanns
Journal of European Public Policy, volume 25, issue 6 (June 2018) pp. 844–861

Chapter 5
The multidimensional politics of social investment in conservative welfare regimes: family policy reform between social transfers and social investment
Silja Häusermann
Journal of European Public Policy, volume 25, issue 6 (June 2018) pp. 862–877

Chapter 6

The Matthew effect in childcare use: a matter of policies or preferences?
Emmanuele Pavolini and Wim Van Lancker
Journal of European Public Policy, volume 25, issue 6 (June 2018) pp. 878–893

Chapter 7

Good intentions and Matthew effects: access biases in participation in active labour market policies
Giuliano Bonoli and Fabienne Liechti
Journal of European Public Policy, volume 25, issue 6 (June 2018) pp. 894–911

Chapter 8

Political participation in European welfare states: does social investment matter?
Paul Marx and Christoph Giang Nguyen
Journal of European Public Policy, volume 25, issue 6 (June 2018) pp. 912–943

Chapter 9

Pro-elderly welfare states within child-oriented societies
Róbert Iván Gál, Pieter Vanhuysse and Lili Vargha
Journal of European Public Policy, volume 25, issue 6 (June 2018) pp. 944–958

For any permission-related enquiries please visit:
http://www.tandfonline.com/page/help/permissions

Notes on Contributors

Giuliano Bonoli is a Professor for Social Policy at the University of Lausanne, Switzerland. His work has focused on pension reform, the labour market and family polices, with particular attention paid to the politics of welfare state transformation.

Marius R. Busemeyer is a Professor of Political Science at the University of Konstanz, Germany. His research focuses on comparative political economy and welfare state research, education and social policy, public spending, theories of institutional change and, more recently, public opinion on the welfare state.

Róbert Iván Gál is a Senior Researcher at the Hungarian Demographic Research Institute and an Affiliated Professor at Corvinus University of Budapest, Hungary. He researches life-cycle financing, intergenerational transfers and National Transfer Accounts.

Julian L. Garritzmann is a Senior Researcher at the University of Zurich, Switzerland. In his current research Julian analyses public opinion towards social investment vis-à-vis compensatory social policies, he develops new approaches to study political effects on public expenditure and he analyses the (higher) education-inequality nexus.

Silja Häusermann is a Professor of Political Science at the University of Zurich, Switzerland. She teaches classes on Swiss politics, comparative political economy, comparative politics and welfare state research. Her research interests are in comparative politics and comparative political economy.

Anton Hemerijck is a Professor of Political Science and Sociology at the European University Institute, Florence, Italy. His research interests include the social investment in Europe and beyond; the politics of inter-temporal policy choice; and open institutionalism as corrective to prevailing determinist account of policy legacies, political institutions and their socio-economic impact.

Fabienne Liechti is a PhD Candidate in the Department of Social Policy at the University of Lausanne, Switzerland. Her research interests include labour market policies and, more broadly, welfare state research, social policies, inequality and redistribution.

Paul Marx is a Professor of Political Science and Socio-Economics at the University of Duisburg-Essen, Germany. In addition, he is affiliated with the Danish Centre for Welfare Studies at the University of Southern Denmark, Odense, Denmark as a part-time Professor and to the IZA Institute of Labor Economics as a Research Fellow. His research interests are related to social and political inequality, political behaviour and comparative welfare state and labour market analysis.

David Natali is an Associate Professor in the Faculty of Political Science in Forli at the University of Bologna, Italy and an Associate Researcher at the European Social Observatory of Brussels, Belgium. His work deals with the comparative analysis of social protection reforms across Europe and the role of the European Union (EU) in the field.

Erik Neimanns is a Senior Researcher at the University of Konstanz, Germany. His research interests include social investment and the welfare state, and within this he focuses on public opinion of social investment.

Christoph Giang Nguyen is a Postdoctoral Researcher in the Department of German Politics at the Free University of Berlin, German and in the Department of Political Science and Public Management at Southern Denmark University, Odense, Denmark.

Emmanuele Pavolini is a Full Professor in Economic Sociology and Social Policy at the University of Macerata, Italy. He has extensively published in Italian and English on the Italian welfare state in comparative perspective, Southern European welfare states, specific social policies (such as childcare, pensions, education policies), inequalities in the access to welfare state provision, occupational welfare and welfare mix and third-sector organizations.

Caroline de la Porte is a Professor in European and Comparative Welfare Policy in the Department of International Economics, Government and Business at the Copenhagen Business School, Denmark. Her research focuses on the EU and comparative welfare state reform, with a special interest in the Nordic countries. She has published widely on the EU's influence on labour market reform, pensions as well as anti-poverty policies.

Pieter Vanhuysse is a Professor of Comparative Welfare State Research in the Department of Political Science and Public Management at the University of Southern Denmark, Odense, Denmark. He researches comparative social policy, political sociology and comparative political economy. Within these he focuses on intergenerational equity in public policy, Social Investment (SI) and human capital, macro-social resilience, generational politics and policies and demographic change.

Wim Van Lancker is an Assistant Professor in Social Work and Social Policy in the Centre for Sociological Research at the University of Leuven, Belgium, and he is affiliated with the Herman Deleeck Centre for Social Policy at the University of Antwerp, Belgium as a Postdoctoral Research Fellow of the Research Foundation Flanders (FWO).

Lili Vargha is a Junior Researcher at the Hungarian Demographic Research Institute and a PhD Candidate in the Doctoral School of Demography and Sociology at the University of Pécs, Hungary. She researches ageing, intergenerational transfers, economic life cycle, costs of childbearing and time use.

The future of the social investment state: politics, policies, and outcomes

Marius R. Busemeyer, Caroline de la Porte, Julian L. Garritzmann and Emmanuele Pavolini

ABSTRACT

In all advanced democracies, policies related to the welfare state are the largest part of public policy activity. Cross-pressured by globalization, deindustrialization, rising public debts, demographic changes, permanent austerity and the rise of 'new social risks', welfare states in post-industrial democracies have entered a new phase of consolidation and transformation since the 1980s. Against early fears, retrenchment has not been 'the only game in town'. Rather, many countries have expanded new welfare policies such as 'social investments'. This collection adds to the recent literature on the emergence of the 'social investment state' in several ways: (1) it assesses to what degree social investment policies have become established across countries and at the EU level; (2) it demonstrates that and why the politics of social investment are different from those of compensatory social policies on the micro and macro level; and (3) it points at important socio-economic effects of social investments.

Introduction

Across the advanced democracies, policies related to the welfare state are the largest part of public policy activity. After a long period of expansion in the post-war decades, welfare states in advanced post-industrial democracies entered a new phase of consolidation and transformation in the 1980s. Policy-makers simultaneously faced multiple challenges. On the one hand, globalization, rising public debt and demographic changes have led to 'permanent austerity' (Pierson 2001), which has required welfare retrenchment and cost containment. On the other hand, 'new social risks' (Bonoli 2007; Esping-Andersen 1999) related to and emerging from precarious

1

employment, labour market dualisation, youth unemployment, difficulties of reconciling work and family life, and single-parenthood have generated new public demands for welfare expansion.

Many policy-makers and academics have argued that focusing on social investments (SIs) rather than passive social transfers could become a key strategy to deal with these cross-pressures and to modernize European welfare states. Instead of, or in addition to, compensating citizens *ex post* for income or job losses as the 'old' welfare states have done, proponents of SI (Esping-Andersen 2002; Hemerijck 2013; Morel *et al.* 2012) have recommended the recalibration of social policy towards more future-oriented policies, centring on human capital development throughout the life-course. SI policies aim at 'creating, mobilizing, or preserving skills' (Garritz-mann *et al.* 2017: 37). These investment policies – such as active labour market policies, public childcare provision or education – are regarded by many as a 'magic bullet': ideally, they could simultaneously empower individuals, facilitate the reconciliation of work and family life, and thereby contribute to economic growth and social cohesion (Morel *et al.* 2012). However, the effects of SI on poverty and on different forms of inequality are not so clear (Cantillon 2011; Vandenbroucke and Vleminckx 2011). That said, SI has a distinct agenda, which focuses on capabilities. It is not seen as a replacement for health care or pensions, to name two of the most costly social protection policies. Investment in skills is integrated with many policies that have previously been associated with passive transfers, such as social assistance or labour market policy.

Research on the rise of the SI state has grown significantly in the 2000s. While its popularity has grown among policy-makers, academics and the general public, the discussion about its effectiveness and legitimacy has become more intense (Hemerijck 2017). Most existing research has traced the transformation of welfare states towards SI, or the lack thereof (Bonoli 2013; Morel *et al.* 2012; Hemerijck 2013). The contributions to this collection add new insights to this line of research, but also address two significant gaps in the literature: the *politics* of SI policies and the *effects* of SI policies on important outcomes. They study various kinds of SI policies (childcare, education, family and labour market policies) using a wide variety of theoretical and methodological approaches. While contributing to ongoing debates, they also open up a number of new themes by focusing, for example, on the important but neglected group of migrants or by connecting the SI debate to research in demography, political behaviour and political psychology. To foreshadow some of the key insights and cross-cutting themes, we have clustered the main findings around three central research questions.

Transformations towards social investment: innovation in a time of permanent austerity

How, and to what degree, is SI implemented in European welfare states and at the European Union (EU) level? Several contributions in this collection show that, even in times of 'permanent austerity' (Pierson 2001) and 'frozen landscapes' (Esping-Andersen 1996) for the welfare state, a significant number of countries have expanded SI policies. Furthermore, the SI approach has been prominent – at least rhetorically – at the EU level. Our collection's first contribution, by Anton Hemerijck, sets the scene by providing background on the conceptual and historical development of the SI paradigm, complemented with country examples of transformations of European welfare states towards this model. Hemerijck shows that in some cases these transformations have been successful, but often go along with political 'uphill' battles against the proponents of the traditional welfare state model – that is, SI reforms in the advanced welfare states imply serious policy and fiscal trade-offs. The fact that politics is often 'impatient' (Ferrera 2017) can be a further hindrance to the introduction of SI policies, which, by design, often generate benefits more in the long-term.

The contribution by Caroline de la Porte and David Natali shows that SI has been a feature of the EU approach to welfare state reform over recent decades, even if only through soft law. The EU 'social investment moment' in the 2011–2013 period, when a comprehensive EU SI framework was delineated, emerged owing to the role of three types of entrepreneur: intellectual; bureaucratic; and political. Despite this, there was little political support across EU institutions and member states for a strong EU SI, which explains why it was weakly institutionalized. The long-term perspective in their analysis shows that the core aims of the European Employment Strategy and the social open method of coordinations resurfaced with the EU SI. While scholars have highlighted that SI focuses on preparing rather than repairing, and on skills development, the EU SI frame is much broader. It also incorporates pre-existent EU initiatives around poverty and homelessness under the social inclusion OMC. The EU's 'social investment moment' has provided a broad narrative around EU social policy initiatives.

This example, as well as the country examples from Hemerijck's contribution, reveal the *ambiguity* of SI. On the one hand, SI aims to provide skills across the life-course and therefore contrasts with the passive focus of more traditional welfare transfers. However, it can be used to propose SI as a replacement for social protection. Nevertheless, there is consensus among scholars that it should be seen as a complement to social protection (including pensions), and as a means to modernize the welfare state.

The politics of social investment

Although SI policies have been studied for quite a while now, knowledge about the *politics* of SI remains limited (for a recent review, see Garritzmann *et al.* [2017]). Several contributions in this collection seek to address this gap, studying which political actors foster (what kind of) SI policies, and whether the political dynamics of SI reforms are similar to those in the more traditional fields of welfare state policy-making. Are the politics of SI distinct from those of other social policies? To what degree are SI policies special?

Julian L. Garritzmann, Marius R. Busemeyer, and Erik Neimanns start with citizens' preferences and engage in a comparative analysis of public opinion towards SI and social compensation policies. The study of public opinion on SI has been a relatively neglected field owing to limitations in publicly available survey data. Therefore, this contribution employs novel data from a representative survey in eight European countries. Factor analyses reveal that people's social policy preferences cluster along three distinct dimensions: (1) traditional social compensation policies, such as unemployment benefits and pensions; (2) SI policies (skills-oriented active labour market policies [ALMPs] and education); and (3) 'workfare' policies (setting stronger incentives for the unemployed to take up work). The contribution thus shows that SI indeed is 'special', as the preferences towards SI and social compensation are distinct, leading to different political dynamics.

Complementing this analysis, the contribution by Silja Häusermann studies the politics of SI reforms exemplarily for the crucial case of family policies in Germany, pointing out their multidimensional character. Häusermann shows how the supporting coalitions of social compensation and SI policies differ (and change) in important ways, focusing on the political positions of collective actors such as parties, unions and employers' associations. In Germany, new coalitions supporting progressive family policies have developed between the centre-left Social Democratic party centre-right Christian democrats, liberal politicians and employers. This mirrors the micro-level findings in the study of policy preferences by Garritzmann, Busemeyer, and Neimanns. They find that SI policies are supported the most by individuals with higher levels of education, who also subscribe to economically left-wing and/or to more egalitarian social values; in contrast, the coalitions supporting policy reforms expanding income protection and traditional forms of social compensation comprise (male) individuals with lower incomes and education levels. These differences highlight potential tensions in the electoral constituencies of mainstream left-wing parties: younger, left-libertarian individuals demand SI policies, whereas the traditional working class voters tend to be more in favour of income protection policies.

In sum, there is strong evidence that the political dynamics of SI reforms indeed differ from those of traditional welfare state policies. This is a challenge, but also a chance for political parties seeking welfare reform, and offers interesting new dimensions regarding party competition and citizens' preferences and voting behaviour.

Social investment outcomes: social stratification and social inequalities

The third theme in this collection evaluates the consequences of SI policies for different kinds of inequalities. The starting point here is the notion that – compared to more traditional social policies, such as unemployment benefits or health care – the redistributive effects of SI policies are likely to be very different. A prominent criticism of SIs is that they are less effective in reducing poverty compared to traditional social policies (Cantillon 2011) as they are rather focused on the middle-class, particularly in corporatist-type welfare states. In this sense, SIs might in fact contribute to rising inequalities.

Two contributions in our collection study these 'Matthew effects' – that is, whether those that are already better off benefit the most from SI. Both contributions offer a more nuanced and differentiated look at the phenomenon. On the one hand, the magnitude of Matthew effects varies across policy fields: Matthew effects are stronger in childcare than in active labour market policies. Emmanuele Pavolini and Wim Van Lancker find that access to formal childcare is partially mediated by different social and cultural norms on motherhood. The likelihood of using formal childcare tends to be lower in countries with more traditional norms and, within countries, for those households that subscribe to more traditional views on motherhood. However, they find that Matthew effects are more the result of constraints on the 'supply side' of formal child care by the state (policy design and insufficient levels of spending), rather than on the demand side (individual preferences and norms associated with usage patterns of formal childcare). This implies that a significant part of the (often criticized) 'Matthew effect' of SI can be attributed to how, and how much, states invest in and regulate social policies, although benefit recipients' preferences also play a significant role.

On the same theme, Giuliano Bonoli and Fabienne Liechti investigate active labor market policies (ALMPs) and provide evidence that Matthew effects are present only in some active labour market programmes, but not in others. In particular, Matthew effects have the strongest negative impact for programmes that require a given level of cognitive skills, such as training, and for those that are closest to the labour market, such as wage subsidies. In contrast, job creation programmes do not show particular signs of Matthew effects, at least for non-migrant, low-skilled workers. Again, this result is worrisome, because it indicates that particularly those ALMPs that have stronger SI elements produce more Matthew effects.

Both contributions show that the extent of Matthew effects also varies across countries. In general, in Scandinavian countries, where SI policies are well-established alongside compensation policies, the benefits of the former are more equally distributed across socioeconomic classes compared to Continental and Anglo-Saxon countries. Moreover, the contributions of this collection shed light on an emerging but crucial issue, which remains understudied in current research on SI – that is, to what extent can SI policies promote the inclusion of migrants? The contributions are a first step towards mitigating this research gap, revealing results that are worrying from a social inclusion perspective. For instance, Bonoli and Liechti underline that migrants are more exposed to Matthew effects in ALMPs compared to other disadvantaged social groups. As a result, they are more likely to be excluded from labour market programmes. Put differently, while SIs might decrease some inequalities, they also seem to create and reinforce new types of inequalities, such as those between migrants and non-migrants. Going one step further, this implies that the more the advanced welfare states 'turn' towards SI, the bigger the inequality between native citizens and migrants might become (unless the policy design is adapted accordingly as well).

Extensions: new directions for research on social investment and beyond

Finally, this collection contains two contributions that open up new perspectives for research on SI policies. The first, by Paul Marx and Christoph Nguyen, connects welfare state research with literature on political behaviour. Marx and Nguyen analyse the extent to which SI policies contribute to political empowerment and participation at the micro-level. They find that SI indeed enhances political engagement among several socioeconomically disadvantaged groups. More specifically, they demonstrate that in countries that invest significantly in SIs (education, childcare and ALMPs), the 'political efficacy gap' is less pronounced for several risk groups than in other countries. That said, however, the contribution also shows that this increased efficacy does not translate into higher participation rates. More generally, Marx and Nguyen's contribution highlights the benefits of bringing together the SI literature with research on political behaviour and political psychology.

The second extension is the contribution by Róbert Gál, Pieter Vanhuysse, and Lili Vargha, which connects the SI debate with approaches in demography research. It represents an important expansion of the conventional perspective in public policy research, because it provides new data on the specific contribution of public policies relative to the broader contributions from individuals in society to well-being and redistribution efforts. The contribution shows that many European welfare states are indeed characterized by a strong bias in public spending in favour of the elderly. It presents new original data on monetary transfers, as well as time transfer across different types of welfare states. The findings suggest that the rather strong and well-known differences in welfare states in terms of redistribution become blurred when considering resources and time. Thus, as welfare *societies*, parents invest twice as many resources – both time and monetary – in their children compared to in older people. This suggests that policy-makers and academics should consider these investments when designing public policy and considering labour market policy.

Conclusion

Taken together, the contributions to this collection show that the notion of SI comes along with a high degree of *ambiguity*. This ambiguity relates to the concept of SI itself, its normative implications, and the empirical effects of SI policies on inequality. In politics, ambiguity can turn into a political asset, as different actors may use the notion of SI for different reasons (Jenson 2010; Morel *et al.* 2012). Several contributions in our collection find that policy actors exploit this ambiguity in the development of SI policies. De la Porte and Natali, in relation to the European Commission, as well as Häusermann, on the German case, show that SI policies have been introduced because the same policy can be supported by different actors, often for different reasons, resulting in heterogeneous coalitions promoting SI. For example, cross-class coalitions could form between the new educated middle class, represented by new left parties, liberal parties, skill-focused employers and white-collar trade unions to promote SIs, whereas a coalition of old left and conservative parties, blue-collar unions and low-skill firms could oppose these reforms, instead protecting the more traditional, compensatory welfare state. Hence, theoretical ambiguity has been useful in order to foster hybrid policy reforms, combining, for example, workfare policies with training subsidies and policies promoting the reconciliation of work and family life. In this sense, the politics of SI differ from those of more traditional compensatory redistributive social policies. Exploration of the link between ambiguity of SI and the political dynamics of reforms should receive further attention in future research. This is all the more true for non-Western democracies, where policy-makers have also begun to establish SI, but with different policy contents and politics, and at different points in time (Garritzmann *et al.* 2017).

Moreover, ambiguity also prevails when it comes to studying the effects of SI reforms on socioeconomic and political outcomes. On the one hand, some SI policies can, at least in theory, effectively promote the integration of labour market outsiders, the reduction of inequalities, and the universal provision of early childhood education to enhance equality of opportunities. On the other hand, there are concerns about Matthew effects and new kinds of inequalities emerging from SI, such as the exclusion of parents with traditional values from formal childcare and discrimination against migrants in active labour market policies. As is often the case, the institutional and political context matters. So far, we know that – as confirmed by the contributions in this collection – in universal-type welfare states where SIs and social compensation are used as complements, Matthew effects are less prevalent and the societies are more equal.

The future of the SI state is open. The current period can be regarded as a critical juncture for welfare state recalibration: On the one hand, SI is losing momentum at the supranational level and in many European countries, particularly against the background of right-wing (radical) populist parties gaining strength across Europe and favouring more traditional family structures and welfare state policies. In fact, right-wing populist parties might become the most important opposition to a 'social investment turn' in the near future. On the other hand, (new) political coalitions might (be able to) continue expanding SI. They also need to consider the quality of SI, which is crucial for it to be a success for those individuals towards whom SI is aimed. This seems economically and politically more viable in countries where SIs complement social compensation. Economically, more traditional social policies might be better able to mitigate poverty and economic inequality; however, SI seems better equipped to address the development of capabilities throughout the life-course. Politically, combining social compensation and SI is the most viable option, as it could be fostered by broader cross-class and intergenerational coalitions.

Disclosure Statement

No potential conflict of interest was reported by the authors.

Funding

The research by Marius R. Busemeyer and Julian L. Garritzmann was supported by the European Research Council (ERC) [grant number 311769].

References

Bonoli, G. (2007) 'Time matters: postindustrialization, new social risks, and welfare state adaptation in advanced industrial democracies', *Comparative Political Studies* 40(5): 495–520.

Bonoli, G. (2013) *The Origins of Active Social Policy: Labour Market and Childcare Policies in a Contemporary Perspective*. Oxford: Oxford University Press.

Cantillon, B. (2011) 'The paradox of the social investment state: growth, employment and poverty in the Lisbon era', *Journal of European Social Policy* 21(5): 432–49.

Esping-Andersen, G. (1996) 'After the golden age? Welfare state dilemmas in a global economy', in G. Esping-Andersen (ed.), *Welfare States in Transition: National Adaptations in Global Economies*, London: Sage, pp. 1–33.

Esping-Andersen, G. (1999) *Social Foundations of Postindustrial Economies*, Oxford: Oxford University Press.

Esping-Andersen, G. (2002) *Why we Need a New Welfare State*, Oxford: Oxford University Press.

Ferrera, M. (2017) 'Impatient politics and social investment: The EU as 'policy facilitator'', *Journal of European Public Policy* 24(8): 1233–51.

Garritzmann, J.L., Häusermann, S., Palier, B. and Zollinger, C. (2017) 'WOPSI: The World Politics of Social Investment', *LIEPP Working Paper*, no 64. Paris: SciencesPo.

Hemerijck, A. (2013) *Changing Welfare States*, Oxford: Oxford University Press.

Hemerijck, A. (2017) *The Uses of Social Investment*, Oxford: Oxford University Press.

Jenson, J. (2010) 'Diffusing ideas for after neoliberalism. The social investment perspective in Europe and latin America', *Global Social Policy* 10(1): 59–84.

Morel, N., Palier, B. and Palme, J. (2012) *Towards a Social Investment State? Ideas, Policies and Challenges*, Bristol: Policy Press.

Pierson, P. (2001) 'Coping with permanent austerity: welfare state restructuring in affluent Democracies', in P. Pierson (Ed.), *The New Politics of the Welfare State*, Oxford: Oxford University Press, pp. 410–56.

Vandenbroucke, F. and Vleminckx, K. (2011) 'Disappointing poverty trends: Is the social investment state to blame?' *Journal of European Social Policy* 21(5): 450–71.

Social investment as a policy paradigm

Anton Hemerijck

ABSTRACT
This contribution delineates the *sui generis* paradigmatic portent of the social investment perspective. After theoretically defining the notion of a policy paradigm in welfare state analysis, the substantive core of the social investment paradigm is presented in two consecutive steps. First, the substantive core of the social investment policy paradigm is exemplified in terms of three core policy functions, relating to: raising and maintaining human capital 'stock' throughout the life course; easing the 'flow' of contemporary labour market transitions; and upkeeping strong minimum-income universal safety nets as social protection and economic stabilization 'buffers'. To drive home the conjecture of social investment as a policy paradigm in its own right, this will, in the final section, be compared with two preceding hegemonic ideal-typical policy paradigms: the demand-oriented Keynesian-Beveridgean welfare compromise of the post-war era; and its anti-thesis, the neoliberal supply-side critique of the welfare state of the 1980s, along a number of institutionally relevant dimensions.

1. Taking social investment seriously

More than a quarter century ago, in the early 1990s, the Organisation for Economic Co-operation and Development (OECD) received a mandate to examine the labour market performance of its member countries. The *OECD Jobs Study*, published in 1994, exposed the 'dark side' of double-digit unemployment of many of its West European members (OECD 1994, 1997). Hovering around 10 per cent, with few signs of improvement, unemployment rates in France, Germany and Italy were twice as high as in the United States of America (US), while their employment rates were about 12 points below that of the US. The Paris-based think tank argued that Europe's comprehensive welfare states faced a dire trade-off between equity and employment. The central policy recommendations that followed for the *OECD Jobs Study* included wage bargaining decentralization, lowering minimum wages, reducing non-wage labour costs, restricting the duration of unemployment insurance, lower taxes and loosening employment protection to allow for an expansion of fixed-term contracts. By so doing, West European countries would be able to raise employment figures to American levels. The price to be paid was to lessen the generosity of the welfare state and thus allow for greater wage and income inequality in order to improve effective labour market allocation by 'making work pay' (OECD 1997).

Fast forward 20 years to the 2015 OECD report on inequality, *In It Together. Why Less Inequality Benefits All*, and we are confronted with a sea change in perspective. The imperative of 'making work pay' by social retrenchment and market deregulation is replaced by a 'capacitating' approach, whereby activating poverty relief, family and gender policy, education, training and employment services and public health, are understood to 'crowd in', rather than 'crowd out', private economic initiative, productivity, employment and growth, while containing inequality much better than the retrenchment-deregulation recipe of the earlier *Jobs Study*. The reappraisal of social policy as contributing to higher employment levels in a more inclusive labour market is strongly echoed in the 2017 edition of the OECD Employment Outlook (2017).

As quite a few European countries, including Denmark, Finland, Sweden, Austria, Germany and the Netherlands, at far higher rates of employment today than the US, feature prominently in OECD studies as the closest approximations of the new 'goodness of fit' between efficiency, employment and equity, it is no surprise that the European Union has been championing the new welfare edifice, most assertively in the *Social Investment Package for Growth and Social Cohesion*, published in February 2013, urging member states to advance post-crisis welfare reform strategies that help 'prepare' individuals, families and societies to respond to the changing nature of social risks in advanced economies, by investing in human capabilities from early childhood through old age, rather than pursuing policies that merely 'repair' social misfortune after moments of economic or personal crisis (European Commission 2013).

The EU's turn to social investment and the OECD's departure from a 'one-size-fits-all' welfare retrenchment and labour market deregulation drive toward an agenda of 'inclusive growth', begs the question of whether we are seeing the emergence of a distinctly novel welfare paradigm. I believe we are. But in spite of the strong lip-service given to social investment by the European Commission, the 'default' neoliberal paradigm of market liberalization, balanced budgets, hard currency and welfare retrenchment also remains with us. As the Single European Act (SEA) of 1986 and the Economic and Monetary Union (EMU) of 1999 were negotiated at a time when the 'supply side' revolution in economic theory was riding high, the architects of the single market and the single currency believed that the Maastricht

Treaty would discipline member states to keep their 'wasteful' welfare states in check. The consequence under current EMU rules is that social investment reform has yet to live up to its full potential (see De la Porte and Natali 2018).

The purpose of this contribution to this collection is to provide a conceptual reflection of the social investment perspective as a distinct policy paradigm, anchored in: (1) politically salient policy objectives; (2) a causal policy theory, specifying in how social risks impact on citizen life-chances; (3) expedient policy instruments mitigating social vulnerability in the knowledge economy under conditions of adverse demography; (4) governance prerequisites for effective implementation; in correspondence with (5) more overriding normative convictions.

The remainder of this contribution proceeds in three steps. Section 2 theoretically delineates the notion of a policy paradigm in comparative welfare state analysis. Section 3 presents the core of the social investment paradigm in terms of three complementary policy functions, relating to: (1) raising and maintaining human capital 'stock' throughout the life course; (2) easing the 'flow' of contemporary labor market transitions; and (3) the upkeeping strong minimum-income universal safety nets as social protection and economic stabilization 'buffers'. To drive home the conjecture of social investment as a welfare paradigm in its own right, Section 4 expounds a typological comparion with the two earlier, more widely accepted, policy paradigms of the Keynesian–Beveridgean welfare state and the neoliberal critique of the welfare state. Section 5 concludes.

2. Policy paradigms in motion

Boundedly rational' authorities, steering through complex and ambiguous and – at times – turbulent environments, rely on 'cognitive maps', 'interpretive frames', 'causal beliefs', 'common understandings' or 'worldviews' and 'rules of thumb' in their policy-making endeavours (Blyth 2002; Fleckenstein 2011; Hall 1989; Hemerijck and Schludi 2000; Simon 1957). Once cognitive templates align with normative beliefs, they amass paradigmatic portent by transforming understandings into 'taken-for-granted' mindsets through policy makers make sense of inherently ambiguous policy environments, and help guide them to attain political goals through the policy process (Beland and Cox2010). Inevitably, when policy paradigms gain general currency, they bolster and entrench policy routines in a path-dependent fashion.

In the world of welfare provision, policy paradigms are ever present. Notwithstanding, they are notoriously difficult to observe, precisely because of their 'taken-for-granted' properties. An exemplary case of the staying power of the ordo-liberal idea of the welfare state as a burden on economic growth can be found in the speech of German Chancellor Angela Merkel rendered at the World Economic Forum on 5 January 2013, held in Davos. In her address, Merkel dramatized the European predicament by underscoring that the crisis-prone continent 'has around 7% of the world population … almost 25% of global [gross domestic product (GDP)]. Yet Europe also accounts for nearly 50% of global social spending', intimating that Europe's generous welfare provision undermines competitiveness (Merkel 2013). On closer inspection, the EU's share of global welfare spending is a little less than 40 per cent and broadly in synch with the US and Japan in the OECD area (Begg *et al.* 2015). More erroneous is that Merkel's conjecture of generous welfare provision as hampering growth does not stand up to empirical scrutiny. Four out of the ten most successful economies around the globe, according to the Global Competitiveness Index of the World Economic Forum (2014), are European high-spending welfare states, including Germany, with levels of social spending hovering around 20 per cent of GDP. Should we therefore not consider the causal arrow running in reverse with high-spending – social-investment-oriented – welfare states contributing to the long-run economic prowess of Finland, Sweden, the Netherlands and Germany, with above average spending levels on child and family policy, female-friendly parental leave, good education and high-quality training systems and pro-active labour market policies (Hemerijck 2013; Morel *et al.* 2012)? At a minimum, the finding that high social spending does not *per se* hurt competitiveness presses us to consider the *quality* rather than the *quantity* of social spending for a better understanding of the relation between welfare provision and economic prosperity in rich democracies.

Hegemonic paradigms inadvertently expose themselves when established policy routines in line with prevailing doctrines are no longer fully consistent with empirical indicators and observations. Observed discrepancies can trigger – with delay – a process of rethinking and re-imagining policy by seeing policy prolems in a 'new light' and solutions in 'new ways'. Questioning taken-for-granted assumptions and biases is at the heart of paradigm change. Protracted policy failures often politicize the policy process. Seeing problems in a 'new light' is a painful process, as it destabilizes revered causal beliefs, normative convictions and policy-making routines. Policy-makers, socialized by extant paradigms are, initially, likely to resist new evidence, alternative explanations and novel justifications for policy reform that challenge the validity of cherished assumptions. This is what Peter Hall observed in his seminal 1993 article on macroeconomic policy paradigm change in Britain in the late 1970s. The disruptive political U-turn from Keynesian policy priorities to monetarism in British macroeconomic management was galvanized by a severe crisis of stagflation, which could not be adequately explained, nor resolved, within the prevailing Keynesian framework. Labour and the Conservative Party, led by Margaret Thatcher, entered an virulent struggle over policty objectives and substance. This ultimately opened up the discursive space for a novel, or perhaps forgotten, (neo)classical supply-side macro- and microeconomic ideas to compete for public attention. For his magistral analysis of macroeconomic paradigm change in Britain, Hall theoretically distinguished, between three key constitutive variables: (1) the principal political goals that guide policy; (2) the policy instruments employed to attain privileged goals; and (3) the precise settings of instruments. Together these three components add up to a policy paradigm, defined by Hall as the 'overarching set of ideas specifying how the problems facing (policy-makers) are to be perceived, which goals must be attained through policy and what sort of techniques can be used to reach those goals' (Hall 1993: 279).

A distinct welfare policy paradigm, it should be emphasized, is more than a competing macroeconomic belief system. Welfare states are made up of normatively charged portfolios of interdependent policy areas, including social security, wage bargaining, labour market policy and regulation, family benefits and services, public health, education and training, and also macroeconomic policy, which jointly affect of citizen life chances, (un-)employment, (in-)equality, relative poverty, gender (im-)balance, social mobility and stratification. A welfare policy paradigm is therefore best understood as a common cognitive and normative frame of reference, shared by boundedly rational policy-makers, that informs their understandings of salient policy problems, guides policy prescription and reform, across a range of range interdependent social policy provisions, in relatively coherent directions.

3. The theoretical core of the social investment paradigm

At the heart of a policy paradigm lies a problem-oriented *policy theory* that can serve as an explanation of past policy experience and as a compass for selecting policy instruments and their governance prerequisites. The *policy theory* of the social investment paradigm was given explicit impetus with the publication of the collective book, directed by Gøsta Esping-Andersen, *Why We Need a New Welfare State* (Esping-Andersen *et al.* 2002), commissioned by the Belgian Presidency of the European Union in 2001. The core empirical diagnosis of *Why We Need a New Welfare State* is that economic internationalization, technological innovation, demographic ageing and changing family structures in the post-industrial age increasingly foster suboptimal life chances for large parts of the population. Esping-Andersen *et al.* not only took issue with the neoliberal axioma that generous welfare provision inevitably implies a loss of economic efficiency. Perhaps, the volume was even more critical about the staying power of male-breadwinner, pension-heavy and insider-biased welfare provision in many European countries, reinforcing stagnant employment and long-term unemployment, in-work poverty, labour market exclusion, family instability, high dependency ratios and below-replacement fertility rates. Four core features stand out in the policy theory of social investment, bearing on the question of 'redistribution', the welfare state's 'carrying capacity', the 'gendered family life-course', and the critical importance of aligning 'institutional complementaries' across in-kind capacitating and income-benefit compensating policies in practical delivery.

3.1. Beyond redistribution and social insurance

Social policy scholars from various disciplines conventionally analyse welfare provision through the (re-) distributive lense of 'decommodifying' taxes and transfers. By so doing, they easily overlook the increasing importance of in-kind benefits in the areas of childcare and family policy, training and education and active labour market policies, and such 'capacitating social services', a term coined by Sabel (2012), contribute to the resilience – both in terms of employment and poverty relief – of the welfare state. Because social risks of the life course and the labour market are increasingly difficult to predict, they are in the process of becoming uninsurable in actuarially neutral terms through ex-post *compensating* social insurance. As such, there is an obvious need to introduce cost-efficient ex-ante *preventive* capacitating interventions, alongside traditional social security. This is not to replace the insurance logic *per se*, but rather to complement and bolster the effectiveness of passive social security in the competitive knowledge-economy (see also Schmid 2017). Thus, by reframing the welfare conundrum away from a redistributive bargain in the 'here and now', and by conceptualizing how popular benefits and services can be sustained for future generations under more adverse demographic conditions, Esping-Andersen *et al.* radically transcended the distributive political frames of juxtaposing 'contributors' and 'beneficiaries' of the welfare state as distinct cleavages.

3.2. The welfare state's carrying capacity

Central to the sustainability of advanced welfare states is the number (*quantity*) and productivity (*quality*) of current and future workers and taxpayers. To the extent that social policies are geared towards maximizing employment and productivity of present and future workers, they effectively contribute the 'carrying capacity' of the welfare state and, by implication, economic progress. Employment and employability are central objectives behind the more overarching social investment aim of breaking the intergenerational transmission of social disadvantage. A larger, more productive and less socially scarred workforce is fundamental to a costly but potentially productive social investment strategy. Faced with the increased volatility in post-industrial labour markets, most people find themselves in between different jobs and caring obligations at various stages in their lives, with the risk of falling behind after precarious transitions. On the other hand, the vast majority of youngsters in schools will become productive workers, most ill people return to the labour market after medical intervention, young mothers more easily find work if supported by good daycare and generous parental leave provision, and also the (short-term) unemployed usually resume paid work after spells of remedial training and activation while being supported by social security (Hills 2014).

3.3. The work–family life course

The *work–family life course* is very much the 'lynchpin' of the social investment policy paradigm (Kuitto 2016). More flexible labour markets and skill-biased technological change, but also higher divorce rates and lone-parenthood, make female economic independence an important prerequisite for curbing child poverty. Absent possibilities of externalizing child and elderly care, a rising numbers of female workers face 'broken careers' and postponed motherhood, with low fertility intensifying the ageing burden in pensions and healthcare in the medium term (Esping-Andersen 2009). Most worrysome is the rise of marital homogamy in the new era of high female employment. Chances are that highly educated and dual-earning households, with easy access to high quality childcare, race ahead while low-skill and low-work intensity households fall behind (Cantillon and Van Lancker 2013). For a better work–life balance, *Why We Need a New Welfare State* urged for social investment policies for improved resilience over the family life course. The orientation on the life course is crucial. Lengthier, more diverse and volatile working lives harbour important implications for social policy. People are most vulnerable over critical transitions in the life course: (1) when they move from education into their first job; (2) when they aspire to have children; (3) when they – almost inevitably – experience spells of labour market inactivity; and, finally, (4) when they move to retirement. To the extent that policy-makers are able to identify how economic wellbeing and social problems at such transitions in the life course impinge on later conditions, preventive policies should be advanced to forestall cumulative social risk and poverty reproduction, with the eradication of child poverty taking pride of place together with more continuous female careers.

3.4. Stocks, flows and buffers in 'institutional complementarity'

Like any notion of 'investment', the concept of social investment begs the question of measurable welfare 'returns' (Begg 2017; Burgoon 2017; De Deken 2017; Verbist 2017). Wellbeing returns on social investment hinge fundamentally on the synergy effects across complementary – capacitating and compensatory – policy interventions. In recent years, I have developed an operational taxonomy of three interdependent and complementary social investment policy functions: (1) easing the 'flow' of contemporary labour-market and life-course transitions; (2) raising and upkeeping the quality of the 'stock' of human capital and capabilities; and (3) maintaining strong minimum-income universal safety net 'buffers' for micro-level income protection and macro-economic stabilization in support of high employment levels in aging societies, for further empirical analysis and assessment (Hemerijck 2015, 2017). In this taxonomy, the 'buffer' function is about securing adequate and universal minimum income protection, thereby also stabilizing the business cycle and buffering economic shocks. Next, the 'stock' function, including cognitive and non-cognitive and physical and apprenticeship training and on-the-job professional skills. The 'stock' function of social investment has wider bearings relating to the provision of 'capacitating social services', bringing under one roof adjustable bundles of professional assistance from from child- to elderly care, including skill enhancement and training services in case of unemployment, health, family and housing support. The 'flow' function, finally, is about efficient and optimal allocation of labour and employment over the lifespan, making sure that unemployment workers can return to work as fast as possible through active labour market policies and job matching. In this context, Guenther Schmid (2015) aptly speaks of a shift from 'making work pay' to 'making transitions pay'.

In everyday policy practice there is ample overlap between the policy functions of 'stocks', 'flows' and 'buffers'. Policy provisions that seemingly focus on one of the three functions, often back up the others in an interconnected fashion and need to do so (Dräbing and Nelson 2017). For example, poverty alleviation is principally a 'buffering' policy, but adequate financial security can facilitate smoother labour market 'flow' as a consequence of mitigated pressure to accept any job on offer, with the potential overall benefit of better job matching and less skill erosion. Portable pension 'buffers' also contribute to better labor market 'flow' for older workers. As Europe's workforce is shrinking, measures to improve labor market 'flow' must be accompanied with effective 'stock' and 'buffer' policies to make sure that a more mobile workers receive the training and skills and measures of income protection that effective support and empower them to make successful transitions. In recent reports of inequality, OECD experts argue that any reduction of inequality between the rich and poor citizens today requires the mobilization of a whole range of policies, from turning female employment into good quality careers ('flow'), to proactive early childhood development, youth and adult training policies ('stock'), and the expansion of effective and efficient activating tax-and-transfer systems ('buffers') in times of dire need (OECD 2008, 2011, 2015, 2017). This evidence on how effective 'stock', 'flow', and 'buffer' policies reinforce the proficiency of each other, allows us to conjecture the operation of a social investment 'life-course multiplier' effect, whereby high quality early childhood care over time contribute to higher levels of educational attainment, which in turn, together with more tailor-made vocational training, can spill over into higher and more productive employment in the medium term. To the extent that employment participation is furthermore supported by effective work-life balance policies, including adequately funded and publicly available childcare, higher levels of (female) employment with lower gender pay and employment gaps can be foreseen. More opportunities for women – and men – to combine partenting with paid labour is, in addition, likely to have a dampening effect on the so-called 'child gap', the difference between the desired number of children per couple (aspirational fertility) and the actual number of children (realized fertility) (Bernardi 2005). A final knock-on effect is a higher effective retirement age, provided the availability of active ageing policies, including portable and flexible pensions, for older cohorts (see Figure 1).

4. The social investment paradigm by typological comparison

Reference to the Keynesian–Beveridgean welfare state and the neoliberal critique of the interventionist welfare state, as representing distinct policy paradigms, has gained widespread acceptance in the literature on the modern welfare state. This is not the case for the social investment edifice. In

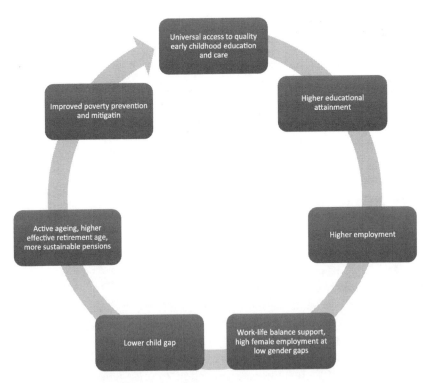

Figure 1. Social investment life-course multiplier.

academia, reference to social investment is decidedly on the increase. The index of 2010 *Oxford Handbook of the Welfare State* counts nine references to the Keynesian–Beveridgean consensus and 18 entries to the neoliberal critique of the welfare state, but none to social investment (Castles *et al.* 2010). The recently published *Handbook of European Social Policy* includes 28 references to social investment, compared with 20 entries to neoliberalism, and suprisingly none to Keynes, Beveridge and the post-war welfare compromise (Kennett and Lendvai-Bainton 2017).

After having exemplified the policy theory of the social investment paradigm, for the final section I now venture to make a conceptual comparison with the two more generally accepted welfare paradigms along a number of salient dimensions. Beyond the core policy theory, there are the obvious dimensions of salient problems, political objectives and privileged policy instruments (and their settings) highlighted by Hall. I add four attributes of key relevance to welfare provision. Inherent to the interdependent nature welfare provision, first and foremost, a wide variety of governance modes and social actors, beyond central bankers and fiscal authorities in macroeconomic management, are engaged in the formulation, implementation and delivery of social policies. A crisis in welfare provision, from this perspective, is not only likely to trigger contestation over substantive policy (re-)direction; it could just as well inspire political discord with prevailing governance structures and institutional actors, unleashing a search for novel rules, responsibilities and stakeholder (non-)involvement. Second, as welfare interventions cater after particular social groups, it is imperative to consider the target population, especially concerning gender. In the third place, there is the time horizon. Social policy interventions can bring immediate poverty relief, akin to Keynesian stimuli, but the timelines for the return to work after retraining and for early childhood care to pay off in terms of long-term productivity gains at higher levels of employment are much longer. Finally, as welfare provision is politically legitimated with reference to normative conception of fairness and the 'good life', justice, life, work, family and liberty, value orientations should be also be taken into considered, independently of expedient political problems (Jenson 2010).

4.1. Salient problems and political objectives

The experience of mass unemployment, unleashed by the Great Depression and the atrocities that followed in Word War Two, inspired post-war élites to single out full employment and the introduction of social citizenship rights to unemployment, sickness and old age insurance, together with universal access to education, housing, health care as the overriding objectives of welfare state expansion. The neoliberal critique of the post-war welfare state, by contrast, was rooted in the 1970s and 1980s crisis of stagflation. In response, non-inflationary economic growth, balanced budgets, and undistorted labour market allocation were singled out core objectives, to be achieved by rolling back the welfare state. The political objective of the social investment paradigm is generally framed in terms of breaking the inter-generational cycle of social disadvantage in an era of volatile and heterogeneous life course and labour market risks (Esping-Andersen *et al.* 2002). But perhaps the more mundane political objective concerns the very viability of popular welfare states, for which high levels of family-friendly employment are *sine qua non* in terms of its 'carrying capacity'.

4.2. Policy theory and instrumentation

The policy theory of the post-war welfare state is rooted in the Keynesian revolution in macroeconomics. In his *General Theory* (1936), John Maynard Keynes exemplified how the political objective of full employment can be upheld by countercyclical macroeconomic demand management. William Beveridge proposed compulsory social insurance as an 'automatic stabilizers' in times of recession, thereby protecting families from cyclical unemployment crises and economic hardship (Beveridge 1942, 1944).

If Keynesian macroeconomics was the brainchild of the Great Depression, the revival of the 'new' classical microeconomics and rational-expectation macroeconomic theory and monetarism are intellectual products of the 1960s' experience cost-push price inflation and the rise of structural unemployment in the 1970s and 1980s. Following 'new' classical economics, recessions are best understood – contra Keynes – as the outcomes of exogenous shocks – the oil shock of the 1970s being a case in point – as a consequence of market imperfections produced by the welfare state, ranging from 'moral hazard' distortions related to compulsory social insurance, to 'unemployment hysteresis' and 'deadweight loss' problems, resulting from heavy taxation, overprotective job security, high minimum wages, and inefficient public employment services (Blanchard and Summers 1987). An additional predicament is the conjecture of low (public) service productivity, associated with the so-called 'Baumol cost disease' (Baumol 1967). To boost non-inflationary economic growth, consistent with the neoliberal consensus, a slimmed-down welfare state, labour market deregulation, collective bargaining decentralization, public service liberalization, low taxation, balanced budgets, and monetarism, enforced by independent central banks, gained prominence in the policy repertoires of a majority of OECD economies since the 1980s.

Theoretically, the social investment paradigm places the Baumol cost predicament in a entirely different light. Publicly financed social investments can create extra private output at relatively low social costs, as parenting services, education, active labour market, health and long-term care interventions contribute to higher employment and long-term productivity gains across all economic sectors, to service and protect Europe's ageig populations (Atkinson 2015; Wren 2017). But, in contrast to the 'general (economic) theoretical' premises and assumptions of both the Keynesian–Beveridgean welfare state and its neoliberal anti-thesis, social investment diagnosis is more 'contextualized' in its understanding of the contingent – both positive and perverse – interaction effects of family demography, labour market dynamics and technological change, in relation to critical institutional differences across welfare regimes. Likewise, 'contextualization' also features prominently in social investment policy instrumentation, relating to specific mixes of 'stock', 'flow' and 'buffer' policies for mitigating gender-, family- and labour-market contingencies and how effective policy mixes, 'crowding in' employment and family-friendly inclusive growth have to differ across welfare regimes (Hemerijck *et al.* 2016; Kvist 2015).

4.3. Institutional governance

Based on a general diagnosis of *market failures* in financial markets and the cyclical nature of industrial capitalism, securing effective demand and protection against unemployment have been emancipated as prime responsibilities of the modern *state* in the post-war era. Although Beveridge argued that wage bargaining should remain the prerogative of trade unions and employers' associations, he believed that, under conditions of full employment, wage co-ordination between the social partners and public authorities was required for mitigating inflation. Social partnership in the administration of social insurance provision, he thought, could contribute to 'public regarding' collective action in management of the post-war welfare state.

In the neoliberal critique, based on a general diagnosis of *state failure*, social partnership, social partnership wage co-ordination and social security administration are primarily understood as *rent-seeking* 'distributive coalitions', producing strong 'insider–outsider' cleavages in the labour market, to the detriment of job opportunies for the young, women, the old, the low skilled and migrants (Lindbeck and Snower 1989). A rule based fiscal policy, prescribing balanced budgets, together with an anti-inflationary monetary policy, under the jurisdiction of an independent central bank, are presumed to discipline public officials to adopt liberalizing market-conforming 'structural' reforms.

The social investment paradigm is, like the Keynesian–Beveridgean consensus, rooted in a positive understanding of public policy and the role of state. However, the welfare state in the social investment paradigm is more appreciated as a complex interacting system, where feedback loops can foster positive wellbeing synergies as well as unintended negative consequences, such as Matthew effects (discussed by Pavolini and Van Lancker 2018 in this volume). What therefore stands out in institutional terms is the high level of professional discretion attributed to decentralized levels of public administration for tailoring person-centred service provision to the disabled, youngsters with learning difficulties and families with young children, by aligning capacitating in-kind benefits and protective cash-transfers, in an integrated fashion, to support livelihood independence. The institutional preconditions are thus far more demanding than both centralized social security state of the post-war era and the market-oriented minimalist welfare state of neoliberal descent. Effective social investment governance requires national administrations to render ample backing and discretionary policy space to regional and local authorities and civil society user-led organizations to bundle 'stock', 'flow' and 'buffer' policy mixes (Sabel *et al.* 2017).

4.4. Target population and gender

In principle, the target population of the Keynesian–Beverdigean welfare state, based on social citizenship rights, is highly inclusive. But given its central ojective to eradicate mass unemployment, the post-war welfare state developed a strong bias toward the working age population and the old-aged poor. Moreover, as full employment policy and social insurance against industrial-biographical risks were conscripted to male breadwinners only, the expansion of the Keynesian–Beveridgean welfare state entrenched traditional familyhood, making women as homemakers and children entirely dependent on male breadwinner employment, their wages and deferred social security benefit rights.

Like its Keynesian precursor, the target population of the neoliberal paradigm is principally the working-age population. Novel is that dependent pensioner cohorts are increasingly understood as a cost burden, as their growing volume and high benefits conjure uprising fiscal outlays to be borne by shrinking future working-age populations. With respect to gender, the neoliberal consensus is in principle 'gender-neutral', but in *modus operandi* 'gender-blind' is the more appropriate depiction. Although neoliberalism gained political momentum with the expansion of the service economy in the 1980s, which opened up job opportunities for women, right-conservative coalitions in power at the time left problems of maternal employment with ongoing family care responsibilities largely unaddressed.

As the social investment welfare paradigm is directly linked heterogeneous vulnerabilities related to labour-market and family life-course transitions, rather than to traditional biographical risks, its target population is highly inclusive from early childhood to long-term care. In an era of rising child and in-work poverty, the social investment paradigm seemingly privileges investments in early childhood and social service support for working parents. The shift in policy orientation from older to younger age cohorts, however, does not belie the commitment of sustainable pension provision in times of adverse demography. On the contrary, to the extent that quality childcare and preschool provision, alongside effective parental leaves and other family benefits, supported active labour market policies and vocational rehabilitation programmes enable (more) parents to engage in gainful employment without (gendered) career interruptions, health care and pension provision are effectively placed on a more sustainable fiscal footing. With its strategic emphasis on work–life balance and reconciliation, the social investment paradigm radically transcends the *male* bias in the Keynesian welfare state and *gender-blind* neoliberal labour market deregulation (Leon 2014).

4.5. Time horizon

Keynesian–Beveridgean welfare interventions are essentially *reactive*, with compulsory social insurance operating as *ex-post* shock absorbers during demand-deficient recessions with the medium-term intent to restore *medium-term* (male) full employment and macroeconomic stability. The neoliberal time horizon is essentially *ahistorical*: understorted market competition, monetary stability, budget consolidation and institutional liberalization should prevail under all circumstances. What stands out in the social investment paradigm is the central focus on life course dynamics and risks, from which *ex ante* and preventive family training and employment interventions naturally follow in a *future-oriented* manner.

4.6. Normative orientations and political discourse

At the normative core of the post-war welfare state lies Beveridge's inclusive resolve to eradicate the 'Great Social Evils of Want, Disease, Ignorance, Idleness and Squalor' (Beveridge 1944: 31). Neoclassical economists and political philosophers often present their justification for welfare state retrenchment in amoral terms, by conjecturing an inescapable 'big trade-off' between equality and efficiency as an unintended consequence of generous welfare provision (Okun 1975). From this reading, 'there-is-no-alternative' (TINA) to privileging *'negative freedom'* and individual responsibility over *'positive freedom'* as the latter inadvertently harms economic efficiency by undermining, at the micro-level, individual responsibility, self-reliance and liberty. In an open economy, therefore, relatively high levels of income inequality at market-clearing levels of full employment have to be accepted as fair, and a price worth paying for liberty (Friedman 1962; Hayek 1976, 2001 [1944]).

At the normative heart of the social investment paradigm lies a reorientation away from both Beveridge's notion of *freedom from want* and neoliberal predilection for *negative freedom* towards a richer understanding of human development in terms of *freedom to act*, taking inspiration from the 'capability

Table 1. Welfare regime paradigms compared, but then leave out name in first quadrant.

Welfare paradigm typologies compared	Keynesian–Beveridge	Neoliberal critique	Social investment
Policy problem and political objective	Demand deficient mass unemployment and poverty Full employment and social citizenship in industrial societies	Stagflation and labour market hysteresis Non-inflationary growth and undistorted labour market allocation in the service economy	Inter-generational reproduction of social disadvantage Human development (to sustain popular welfare states under adverse demography in the knowledge economy
Policy theory	Volatile capitalism (market failures) requires macro-economic steering through counter-cyclical demand management and fine tuning	Insurmountable 'big trade-off' between equity and efficiency: welfare (state failure) 'crowds out' private economic initiative ('moral hazard', 'deadweight loss', 'collective rent-seeking' and 'Baumol cost disease'	Social investments 'crowd in' private economic initiative, growth and competitiveness through higher employment, improved human capital use and economic security over the life course
Policy instrumentation	Income-replacing social insurance and (industrial) job protection, to help restore full employment (alongside fiscal stimulus)	Benefit curtailment, deregulation, liberalization, (public) pension privatization, undergirded by anti-trust legislation, non-discretionary rules-based fiscal discipline and hard currency monetary policy, to enforce 'structural reform'	Capacitating bundles of human capital 'stock', labour-market 'flow' and activating social security 'buffer' policies to address life-course contingencies *ex ante*
Governance prerequisites	Strong state, national accounting, efficient social security administration, progressive taxation and social partnership concertation to mitigate inflation (macro-level discretion)	Contracting out public services and new public management to pre-empt organized 'rent-seeking' and bureaucratic 'capture' by 'distributive coalitions' (no discretion)	Provision of integrated personalized services and benefits in 'institutional complementarity' (bottom–up discretion with strong central-level backing)
Target population and gender	Male breadwinners and (indirectly) dependent family, reinforcing female homemaking	Working age population dependent pensioner cohort (as a burden). Gender neutral in principle, but gender blind qua caring family support	All age cohorts, with a gender-equitable emphasis on vulnerable families, working parents and children
Time horizon	*Ex-post* medium-term macroeconomic restoration of full employment equilibria	General (ahistorical) imperative to reinforce permanently enforce *laissez-faire* market 'level-playing field' equilibria	*Ex-ante*, future-oriented and preventative mixes of 'stock', 'flow' and 'buffer' policies to sustain the 'carrying capacity' of popular welfare states with a focus on human development over risky transitions
Normative commitment	A free society without want, disease, idleness, squalor and ignorance	'There-is-no-alternative' to privileging 'negative' over 'positive' freedom to secure life and liberty (inequality to be accepted as 'fair')	Capacitating (life- course contingent) social justice

approach' of Amartya Sen (2001, 2009; see also Morel and Palme 2017). The normative foundation of the social investment edifice remains anchored in the Rawlsian principle favouring of the least well-off as a precondition effective social investment, but no longer in a decommodifying manner, but rather in terms of enhancing citizens' capabilities to flourish over the life course, by constantly scrutinizing and correcting unequal market and non-market opportunity structures, including those produced – interactively – by the welfare state itself (Table 1).

Acknowledgements

The author wishes to thank two anonomous reviewers for their constructive comments, and Frank Vandenbroucke and Jim Mosher for insisting on keeping the argument focused on the social investment paradigm.

Disclosure statement

No potential conflict of interest was reported by the authors.

References

Atkinson, A.B. (2015) *Inequality: What Can Be Done?*, Cambridge, MA: Harvard University Press.

Baumol, W.J. (1967) 'The macroeconomics of unbalanced growth', *American Economic Review* 57(3): 415–26.

Begg, I. (2017) 'Social investment and its discount rate', in A. Hemerijck (ed.), *The Uses of Social Investment*, Oxford: Oxford University Press, pp. 174–183.

Begg, I., Mushoevel, F. and Niblett, R. (2015) 'The welfare state in Europe – visions for reform', in B. Stiftung (ed.), *Vision Europe Summit. Redesigning European Welfare States – Ways Forward*, Guetersloh: Bertelsmann Stiftung, pp. 12–37.

Beland, D. and Cox, R.H. (2010) *Ideas and Politics in Social Science Research*, Oxford: Oxford University Press.

Bernardi, F. (2005) 'Public policies and low fertility: rationales for public intervention and a diagnosis for the spanish case', *Journal of European Social Policy* 15(2): 123–38.

Beveridge, W.H. (1942) *Social Insurance and Allied Services, Presented to Parliament as Command Paper 6404. Report by Sir William Beveridge [The Beveridge Report]*, London: HMSO.

Beveridge, W.H. (1944) *Full Employment in a Free Society: A Report*, London: Allen & Unwin.

Blanchard, O. and Summers, L. (1987) 'Hysteresis in unemployment', *European Economic Review* 31: 288–95.

Blyth, M. (2002) *Great Transformations: Economic Ideas and Institutional Change in the Twentieth Century*, Cambridge: Cambridge University Press.

Burgoon, B. (2017) 'Practical pluralism in the empirical study of social investment: examples from active labour market policy', in A. Hemerijck (ed.), *The Uses of Social Investment*, Oxford: Oxford University Press, pp. 161–73.

Cantillon, B. and Van Lancker, W. (2013) 'Three shortcomings of the social investment perspective', *Acta Sociologica* 55(2): 125–42.

Castles, F.G., Leibfried, S., Lewis, J., Obinger, H. and Pearson, C. (eds.) (2010) *The Oxford Handbook of the Welfare State*, Oxford: Oxford University Press.

De Deken, J. (2017) 'Conceptualising and measuring social investment', in A. Hemerijck (ed.) *The Uses of Social Investment*, Oxford: Oxford University Press, pp. 184–93.

De la Porte, C. and Natali, D. (2018) 'Agents of Institutional Change in EU Policy: The Social Investment 'Moment'', *Journal of European Public Policy*. doi:10.1080/13501763.2017.1401110

Dräbing, V. and Nelson, M. (2017) 'Addressing human capital risks and the role of institutional complementarities', in A. Hemerijck (ed.), *The Uses of Social Investment*, Oxford: Oxford University Press, pp. 128–39.

Esping-Andersen, G. (2009) *The Incomplete Revolution: Adapting to Women's New Roles*, Cambridge: Polity.

Esping-Andersen, G., Gallie, D., Hemerijck, A. and Myles, J. (2002) *Why We Need a New Welfare State*, Oxford: Oxford University Press.

European Commission (2013) *Towards Social Investment for Growth and Cohesion – Including Implementing the European Social Fund 2014-2020*, COM(2013) 83 final, Brussels, 20.02.2013.

Fleckenstein, T. (2011) 'The politics of ideas in welfare state transformation: Christian democracy and the reform of family policy in Germany', *Social Politics International Studies in Gender, State & Society* 18(4): 543–71.

Friedman, M. (1962) *Capitalism and Freedom*, Chicago: University of Chicago Press.

Hall, P.A. (1989) *The Political Power of Economic Ideas: Keynesianism Across Nations*, Princeton, NJ: Princeton University Press.

Hall, P.A. (1993) 'Policy paradigms, social learning, and the state: the case of economic policy-making in Britain', *Comparative Politics* 25(3): 275–93.

Hayek, F.A. (1976) *Law, Legislation, and Liberty, ii. The Mirage of Social Justice*, London: Routledge & Kegan Paul.

Hayek, F.A. (2001 [1944]) *The Road to Serfdom*, London: Routledge.

Hemerijck, A. (2013) *Changing Welfare States*, Oxford: Oxford University Press.

Hemerijck, A. (2015) 'The quiet paradigm revolution of social investment', *Social Politics: International Studies in Gender, State & Society* 22(2), 242–56. doi:10.1093/sp/jxv009

Hemerijck, A. (ed.) (2017) *The Uses of Social Investment*, Oxford: Oxford University Press.

Hemerijck, A. and Schludi, M. (2000) 'Sequences of policy failures and effective policy responses', in F.W. Scharpf and V. Schmidt (eds.), *Welfare and Work in the Open Economy, i. From Vulnerability to Competitiveness*, Oxford: Oxford University Press, pp. 125–228.

Hemerijck, A., Burgoon, B., Dipietro, A. and Vydra, S. (2016) *Assessing Social Investment Synergies (ASIS), A Project to Measure the Returns of Social Policies*, Report for DG EMPL, Brussels: European Commission.

Hills, J. (2014) *Good Times, bad Times: The Welfare Myth of Them and Us*, Bristol: Policy Press.

Jenson, J. (2010) 'Diffusing ideas for after-neoliberalism: the social investment perspective in Europe and latin America', *Global Social Policy* 10(1): 59–84.

Kennett, P. and Lendvai-Bainton, N. (2017) *Handbook of European Social Policy*, Basingstoke: Edward Elgar Publishing.

Keynes, J.M. (1936 [1973]) *The General Theory of Employment, Interest and Money*, London: Macmillan for the Royal Economic Society.

Kuitto, K. (2016) 'From social security to social investment? Compensating and social investment welfare policies in a life-course perspective', *Journal of European Social Policy* 26(5): 442–59.

Kvist, J. (2015) 'A framework for social investment strategies: integrating generational, life course and gender perspectives in the EU social investment strategy', *Comparative European Politics* 13(1): 131–49.

Leon, M. (ed.) (2014) *Care Regimes in Transitional European Societies*, Basingstoke: Palgrave.

Lindbeck A., and Snower, D. J. (1989) *The Insider-Outsider Theory of Employment and Unemployment*, Cambridge, MA: MIT Press.

Merkel, A. (2013) *Speech by Federal Chancellor Merkel at the World Economic Forum Annual Meeting* 2013, Davos, 24 January, available at https://www.bundesregierung.de/ … /2013-01-24-merkel-davos.ht

Morel, N. and Palme, J. (2017) 'Social investment and capabilities: a normative foundation', in A. Hemerijck (ed.), *The Uses of Social Investment*, Oxford: Oxford University Press, pp. 150–157.

Morel, N., Palier, B. & Palme, J. (eds.) (2012) *Towards a Social Investment Welfare State? Ideas, Policies, Challenges*, Bristol: Policy Press.

OECD (1994) *The OECD Jobs Study: Facts, Analysis, Strategies*, Paris: OECD.

OECD (1997) *The OECD Jobs Strategy: Making Work Pay: Taxation, Benefits, Employment and Unemployment*, Paris: OECD.

OECD (2008) *Growing Unequal*, Paris: OECD.

OECD (2011) *Doing Better for Families*, Paris: OECD.

OECD (2015) *In It Together; Why Less Inequality Benefits All*, Paris: OECD.

OECD (2017) *Employment Outlook 2017*, Paris: OECD.

Okun, A.M. (1975) *Equality and Efficiency: The Big Trade Off*, Washington, DC: The Brookings Institution.

Sabel, C. (2012) 'Individualized service provision and the new welfare state: are there lessons from Northern Europe for developing countries?', in C. Luiz de Mello and M.A. Dutz (eds.), *Promoting Inclusive Growth, Challenges and Policies*, Paris: OECD, pp. 75–111.

Sabel, C., Zeitlin, J. and Quack, S. (2017) 'Capacitating services and the bottom-up approach to social investment', in A. Hemerijck (ed.), *The Uses of Social Investment*, Oxford: Oxford University Press, pp. 140–49.

Schmid, G. (2015) 'Sharing risks of labour market transitions: towards a system of employment insurance', *British Journal of Industrial Relations* 53(1): 70–93.

Schmid, G. (2017) 'Towards life course insurance', in A. Hemerijck (ed.), *The Uses of Social Investment*, Oxford: Oxford University Press, pp. 108–17.

Sen, A. (2001) *Development as Freedom*, Oxford: Oxford University Press.

Sen, A. (2009) *The Idea of Justice*, Cambridge, MA: Harvard University Press.

Simon, H. (1957) *Models of Man: Social and Rational*, New York: John Wiley & Sons.

Verbist, G. (2017) 'Measuring social investment returns: do publicly provided services enhance social inclusion?', in A. Hemerijck (ed.), *The Uses of Social Investment*, Oxford: Oxford University Press, pp. 194–204.

WEF (World Economic Forum) (2014) *Global Competitiveness Report 2013–2014*, www3.weforum.org/docs/WEF_GlobalCompetitivenessReport_2013-14

Wren, A. (2017) 'Social investment and the service economy trilemma', in A. Hemerijck (ed.), *The Uses of Social Investment*, Oxford: Oxford University Press, pp. 97–107.

Agents of institutional change in EU policy: the social investment moment

Caroline de la Porte and David Natali

ABSTRACT

The contribution addresses – through actor-centred historical institutionalism – why and how social investment (SI) emerged at the European Union (EU) level. SI policies built on the institutional basis of the policy co-ordination processes in employment and social inclusion, which originated in the late 1990s and early 2000s. The pre-existent processes represented the necessary but not sufficient condition for the EU SIP to materialise. The decisive factor was the activity of three types of entrepreneurs – intellectual, bureaucratic and political – that enabled the crystallization of the EU Social Investment package (SIP) through issue-framing, institutional alignment and consensus-building. Despite this, the SIP of 2013 ended as a 'social investment moment' that rapidly lost momentum because no additional measures such as indicators or funds were integrated with SIP. Furthermore, the Commission's political priorities changed and the key entrepreneurs that had been active for the materialisation of the SIP were no longer centre stage. The continued presence of former influential entrepreneurs in the EU policy arena, although in different roles, may enable integration of EU SI into new EU social policy initiatives.

Introduction

In 2013, the European Union (EU) adopted a 'Social Investment Package' (SIP) centred on policies to invest in human capital throughout the life-course. This contribution is interested in why and how social investment (SI) policy developed at EU level, focusing on the role of agents of institutional change. In the literature, such actors are referred to as 'policy entrepreneurs' (Kingdon 1995), or 'ideational leaders' (Stiller 2010), who create policy agendas and make decisions on new policy. This study unpacks this broad range of actors, identifying three ideal-type agents that mobilize different power resources during the policy process. The first type is the 'intellectual entrepreneur', whose resource is knowledge and who is typically active prior to and in the early phases of agenda-setting. The second type is the 'bureaucratic entrepreneur', whose resource is access to institutional opportunities, and who is central between agenda-setting and decision-making in transposing knowledge to a particular institutional setting. The third type is the 'political entrepreneur', whose resource is political power, and who is directly or indirectly involved in decision-making.

Applying this actor-based historical institutional framework, we found that SIP, consisting of soft-law initiatives, was adopted owing to the combined activity of the three types of entrepreneurs. However, SI lost momentum when the entrepreneurs involved in its development were no longer centrally present in the EU social policy arena. Even so, the former institutional base of SI, rooted in the European Employment Strategy (EES) from the late 1990s and the social inclusion Open Method of Co-ordination (OMC) from the early 2000s, is still present. Furthermore, the persistent activism of some leading figures, although no longer as central entrepreneurs, contributes to maintaining some focus on SI in the context of the European Pillar of Social Rights (EPSR).

The remainder of this contribution is organized as follows: the following section presents a literature review, the theoretical and analytical actor-based analytical framework, as well as the methodology. The subsequent section consists of the analysis of SI institutionalization, in four temporal stages. The final section discusses and concludes.

Literature review, theory and analytical framework

Literature review

The EU's initial response to the crisis – including a Memoranda of Understanding for countries unable to repay their debt without financial support – was one of austerity. The countries under such coercive arrangements have been forced to 'implement pretty much the same deeply unpopular … austerity package' (Armingeon and Baccaro 2012: 275). In parallel, the EU socio-economic governance was revised, emphasizing cost containment and budgetary control, in order to prevent sovereign debt crises in the future (de la Porte and Heins 2015). Governance of both economic and social policies is now centralized in the European Semester.

While considerable attention has been paid to alterations in the governance of the EU (Scharpf 2013; Verdun 2015), there have been fewer contributions on EU employment and social policy (Crespy and Menz 2015). Some scholars have argued that SI emerged as a positive narrative in a context marked by austerity (Ferrera 2016; Hemerijck 2015). Indeed, trust in the EU decreased rapidly following the EU's austerity policy: it was 32 per cent in 2012 (compared to 57 per cent in 2007). Similarly, the percentage of Europeans that had a positive image of the EU in the first half of 2007 was 52 per cent, contrasting with 30.5 per cent in 2012 and in 2013 (EU 2016). In this vein, Hemerijck (2015: xiii) underscored that: 'The paramount importance of the 2013 Social Investment Package is that it officially endorses a socially inclusive and economically robust alternative to the less coherent fiscal austerity orthodoxy cum monetarist heterodoxy policy mix.' Ferrera (2016) analysed the discursive and capacity-building potential of SI, concluding that the discourse has not been influential at national level following the adoption of the EU's Social Investment Package. Zeitlin and Vanhercke (2017) examined the 'socialization' of the European Semester through a framework based on learning in the Commission. Their findings suggest that the EU's social dimension is very strong.

While these works have made important contributions, they have not considered the role of agents in a longitudinal and institutional analysis of the genesis of SI at EU level. This contribution analyses why, how, under which political conditions, and in which institutional setting, the SIP emerged. The agency-based historical institutionalist perspective highlights that SIP emerged because there was a pre-existent institutional base, but also because various entrepreneurs mobilized through a combination of different power resources. It also shows the limit of entrepreneurial activity: even when consensus is obtained that enables a decision on a policy, it can quickly disappear from the agenda again, when political conditions are not favourable. This is particularly the case for soft law – such as SI – that is not strongly institutionalized. From a theoretical-analytical perspective, our study shows why, when and how agents matter in institutional change. It also conceptualizes 'policy entrepreneurs' precisely, enabling applicability of this framework to other studies of policy alteration.

Theory, analytical framework and methodology

This contribution develops a theory to capture when agents are influential in a longer process of bounded institutional change (Mahoney and Thelen 2010; Pierson 1996). Time is conceptualized in inductively derived temporal 'stages', during which there is significant institutional development (de la Porte 2008). For our case, institutional change (in 'stages') can be located in Commission communications and recommendations, European Council Conclusions, treaty changes, changed governance structures, or core quantitative indicators representing a policy frame. In each stage, change is gradual, through displacement, layering, drift and conversion (Streeck and Thelen 2005).

In this contribution, we do not *ex ante* associate agents with a type of change (Mahoney and Thelen 2010). Instead, the analytical approach ties in the role of actors with institutional change dynamically, by building on 'policy entrepreneurship'. Thus, two main shortcomings in the literature are addressed – that is, the vague definition of actors and of their activities. Policy entrepreneurs are crucial in a process of institutional change, as they are capable, *inter alia*, of identifying problems and finding solutions, advocating new ideas and mobilizing political support and public opinion. They are considered as a broad category of actors who are 'in or out of government, in elected or appointed positions, in interest groups or research organizations' (Kingdon 1995). In Table 1, we specify three types of entrepreneur according to the arena in which they operate and, by implication, their main power resources. We also present the different types of activities in which they can engage.

A 'political entrepreneur' is a politically appointed or politically elected individual who has a legal mandate to directly or indirectly engage in decision-making. A 'bureaucratic entrepreneur' is located in the bureaucracy, such as in the European Commission or in a ministry, where policies are prepared. While bureaucrats undertake and organize preparatory work around an issue, bureaucratic entrepreneurs mobilize resources to enable the adoption of policy, in close collaboration with decision-makers. Bureaucratic entrepreneurs can also mobilize external input to increase the likelihood of a decision on a particular policy issue. This includes appointing academics and others to provide policy advice and input. An 'intellectual entrepreneur' is a prominent academic or expert, who is appointed to undertake an analysis or to provide policy recommendations on specific issues.[1]

Concerning the types of activities actors can engage in, Heclo (1974) focused on 'puzzling' and 'powering'; Mintrom and Norman (2009) considered activities such as problem-definition and team-building; while Stiller (2010) explored ideational, as well as communicative and relational, activities. The literature on policy decisions has typically focused on the stages of the policy cycle, from agenda-setting through to decision-making. Building on this, this contribution works with three broad categories of activities that entrepreneurs engage in: 'issue-framing'; 'institutional alignment'; and 'consensus-seeking'. Issue framing includes activities that frame a policy problem, locating

Table 1. Policy entrepreneurs and their activities.

Entrepreneur activities	Type of entrepreneur		
	Intellectual	Bureaucratic	Political
Issue-framing	+++	++	+
Institutional alignment	+	+++	+++
Consensus-seeking	+	+	+++

Source: Author's own elaboration.
+++ Strong activity.
++ Some activity.
+ Little activity.

evidence to support a particular frame, developing indicators, and envisaging policy solutions. Institutional alignment consists of adapting a policy solution to the relevant institutional setting, including team-building. Consensus-seeking involves seeking alliances, 'powering', as well as decision-making. The timing of issue-framing, institutional alignment, and consensus-building may partially overlap, and various entrepreneurs may be involved in different activities. Moreover, entrepreneurs may persist in the broad arena – here, EU social policy – over long time periods. This often happens through 'revolving doors' that allow actors to move from one position and affiliation to another within a particular policy arena.

Methodologically, the examination involves process-tracing; that is, speci-fying the 'process whereby relevant variables have an effect' within a case (Hall 2008: 23). This combines an inductive approach – for identifying signifi-cant moments of institutional change – with a causal–analytical framework – to analyse which constellations of actors are involved in institutional change. The contribution identifies key variables or combinations of variables, focus-ing on activities of actors, that explain a case (here stage). In each 'stage' we follow the activities of entrepreneurs. Thereby, we intend to shed light on the conditions under which their role is significant for institutional change (Trampusch and Palier 2016: 15). In our conceptualization, the role of three distinct, individual entrepreneurs is analysed. Political conditions are crucial intervening variables for the persistence and strength of insti-tutional change.

For each stage, data sources are triangulated to provide a cross-data val-idity check. The primary data comprises official documentation from the Commission, minutes of meetings of relevant expert groups and conclusions of the European Council, all of which are publicly available. In addition, 10 in-depth semi-structured expert interviews with key actors involved in the genesis of EU SI have been conducted. The interviewees were selected to represent intellectuals, bureaucrats, and political actors involved in the process under scrutiny. This includes six actors that we have identified as pol-itical, intellectual or bureaucratic entrepreneurs, as well as four actors involved in the political and bureaucratic context, but that did not have an entrepreneurial role.

Analysis

Each stage examines the issue-framing, institutional alignment, and consen-sus-building activities of the relevant entrepreneurs in institutional change. Stages 1 and 2 respectively present the emergence and drift of SI initiatives in EU social policy. Stage 3 – which covers a shorter time period – analyses the activities related to SI itself in detail. Stage 4 provides a preliminary analy-sis of how SI is integrated into the EPSRs.

Stage 1: 1997–2003: institutional creation of employment and social inclusion co-ordination

Stage 1 comprises the institutional creation of the EES and the social inclusion OMC in terms of policy aims and governance procedure. This is the basis on which SI was later built, during stage 3. Allan Larsson was influential in the creation of the EES, first as a political entrepreneur and then as a bureaucratic entrepreneur. Larsson's ideas were shaped by those of Meidner and Rhen, Nordic economists who highlighted the role of labour market policies as a bridge between social and economic policies that should contribute to economic growth and fair distribution In the early 1990s, Larsson had mobilized a common employment policy for Europe in the party of European socialists when he was head of the Swedish socialist party – that is, as a political entrepreneur. He became director general for the directorate general of employment and social affairs (DG EMPL) – becoming a central figure in the EU's bureaucracy – in 1995, which enabled him to adapt his policy vision to the EU institutional setting. When he was a bureaucratic entrepreneur, he framed 'social protection as a productive factor', which formed the basis for developing a common European approach to employment and social policy, in DG EMPL. He also obtained agreement on this notion with the directorate general of economic and financial affairs (DG ECFIN), facilitated by his own background as finance minister. He worked closely with Odile Quintin and Jerome Vignon, long-term high-level civil servants in DG EMPL who supported Larsson's efforts in developing the institutional base for the EES. Under the directorship of Allan Larsson, in 1996 an employment committee comprising member state representatives from ministries of labour and an employment indicator sub-committee with technical experts to agree on EU indicators for employment policy was created (de la Porte 2008).

Jean-Claude Juncker, prime minister of Luxembourg and President of the European Council (during the second half of 1997), and Wim Kok, a Dutch social-democratic politician, were key political entrepreneurs who gained consensus among member states, enabled by a social-democratic majority among EU member states, on the EES (Interview 2017a). This facilitated agreement on the 'Employment Title' in the Amsterdam Treaty (1997), which provided a legal base for EU activity in employment policy. Employment policy was addressed by the EU through policy co-ordination to support member states in modernizing their employment policies. The aims of EES were agreed at a summit initiated by Juncker at the end of 1997. The policies agreed in the EES supported the monetarist paradigm defining the Economic and Monetary Union (EMU), favouring labour market flexibility, but were more comprehensive, including policies related to areas such as work–life balance and life-long learning, which are also central in SI (de la Porte 2011).

Following this, the Commission, with the involvement of intellectual entre-preneurs, aimed to develop EU policy for social inclusion and social protec-tion. The Commission, particularly Odile Quintin, engaged in preparatory work. Concerning social protection, Maurizio Ferrera, Anton Hemerijck and Martin Rhodes, as intellectual entrepreneurs, prepared a publication for the Portuguese Presidency in the first half of 2000. The volume was on the future of the welfare states, calling for recalibration, rather than retrenchment, of social and employment policies (Ferrera *et al.* 2000). The high-level report had a strong impact on the policy framework that was being developed during the Portuguese Presidency of the European Council in 2000.

During the Portuguese Presidency of the European Council in 2000, Antonio Guterres, then prime minister, and Maria Rodrigues, his advisor, engaged as political entrepreneurs in brokering and persuasion on a common EU social policy, with ideas and knowledge from the report on the future of welfare states. Guterres and Rodrigues wanted social policy to be on an equal footing with economic and employment policy. To mark this, they launched, for the first time, a spring summit, where the economic and social ministers were to meet to discuss and agree on the EU's socioeconomic strategy. At the first summit in Lisbon, the social inclusion process was launched and a statistical database – EU Statistics on Income and Living Con-ditions (EU-SILC) – was developed in parallel. This summit has continued since then on an annual basis. Formally (legally), the Ecofin Council had most weight in the Council, but politically – supported by a strong representation of social democratic governments in the Council – the employment and social affairs council had considerable weight at the time. A social protection committee and an indicators sub-group were created to support the social inclusion and social protection processes, similar to the committees estab-lished to work with the EES (de la Porte 2008). The political momentum in support of economic growth with strong social protection continued for several years. The Belgian minister of social affairs at the time, Frank Vanden-broucke, was keen on strengthening social protection policy at EU level during the Belgian Presidency. Thus, in 2001, he commissioned Gøsta Esping-Ander-sen, an intellectual entrepreneur, to write a report about a new welfare archi-tecture for Europe. It was published as a book advocating SI, especially focusing on investing in children from a young age (Esping-Andersen 2002). The academic work by Esping-Andersen was influential because it reinforced Larsson's idea of 'social protection as a productive factor', but with more evi-dence, as well as policy recommendations on how to reform social protection and develop SI.

Political and bureaucratic entrepreneurs in the Commission and the Council were key movers in issue-framing, institutional alignment and consen-sus-building for EU co-ordination in employment policy and in social inclusion policy. Intellectual entrepreneurs provided research-based input to the debate. The institutional base of SI policies – issue-specific committees and technical sub-committees, objectives, legal and/or political commitment, indicators – was created during stage 1.

Stage 2: 2004–2010: policy and institutional drift

Stage 2 resulted in institutional and policy drift (that is, altered effect of an institution owing to changed circumstances) of the aims related to human capabilities in the EES and to the rights-based and anti-poverty aims of the social inclusion OMC. The political context among member states changed in 2004 in conjunction with the eastward enlargement of the EU. The discourse on stable economic growth, coupled with comprehensive employment and social policy, was replaced with concerns about low growth and the social impact of enlargement in the member states Attention to the social dimension of Europe was no longer central because the left-leaning political parties in the Council had lost ground and the Commission had become more centre-right in its orientation.

André Sapir, an intellectual entrepreneur, contributed to shifting the political debate at that time. The Sapir Reports 1 and 2 emphasized the need to strengthen competitiveness (Sapir 2003). This issue-framing resonated well with member state political priorities at the time. The focus on competitiveness in the Sapir reports is reflected in the report that fed into the assessment of the Lisbon strategy in 2004/5. The 'Jobs, jobs, jobs', report initiated by Wim Kok, a political entrepreneur who had also been a pivotal figure in stage 1, altered the debate from growth, employment and social cohesion towards competitiveness, growth and jobs. It recommended that the link between economic and employment policies (EMU co-ordination and the EES) be strengthened, while social inclusion OMC was to continue alongside, but without the same political weight. These changes represent policy drift concerning the social dimension of the EU, which was endorsed by member states during the mid-term review of the Lisbon Strategy in 2005.

Following this, Barrosso planned to further revise the Lisbon Strategy in his second term, including centralization of all co-ordination procedures (Interview 2017b). Furthermore, the centre-right political majority among member states in the European Council and in the European Parliament were favourable to this agenda (Interview 2017c). Following the financial crisis of 2008, the economies of the periphery countries suffered, leading to sovereign debt crises whereby these countries were at risk of not being able to pay back their public debt without financial aid. Thus, when the second Barroso Commission took office, in 2009, the main issue on the EU agenda was regaining stability in the eurozone. The emphasis at EU level was on fiscal consolidation, to contain the effects of the crisis in the eurozone and to prevent sovereign debt crises in the peripheral economies. At the same time, the plans already made for revising the Lisbon Strategy were pursued. Preparations for Europe 2020, which was to narrow the focus of the EES and OMCs to better support competitiveness and jobs, were already underway.

Laszlo Andor, who became commissioner for employment and social affairs under the Barroso Commission in 2009, wanted to move beyond the fiscal consolidation agenda that was dominant at the time. When he entered office, most of Europe 2020 had already been planned, although the relative weight of employment and social policy had not been settled. Andor was a key political entrepreneur who wanted to enhance the EU's attention to social policy. He worked on maintaining focus on the poverty issue. He engaged in consensus-building, first in the Commission, where DG ECFIN and the Secreteriat-General (SECGEN) had to be convinced, and then in the Council. The Commission accepted the anti-poverty policy of Europe 2020 because it built on the existing institutional framework. The Commission even accepted a new anti-poverty aim: to reduce the number of people at risk of poverty by 20 million by 2020. The member states reluctantly endorsed the anti-poverty policy and numerical aim. It was endorsed only because it was lightly institutionalized and involved a weak core benchmark (reducing poverty across the EU by 20 million persons by 2020). Employment policy, including a benchmark to reach a 75 per cent employment rate by 2020, was consistent with the EU's growth strategy. Both aims were endorsed in 2010 as key pillars of the 'Europe 2020' strategy (Interview 2017a, 2017d). However, by the time Europe 2020 was adopted it had a low status politically, as it had mostly been developed prior to the financial crisis.

Europe 2020 was integrated into the centralized European Semester governance procedure. With the European Semester, DG ECFIN's role for stable finances and consolidation was strengthened legally, and also in terms of staffing; thus, there was virtually no room for social policy initiatives. Significant dossiers, such as labour markets, were shifted to DG ECFIN from DG EMPL. This signified that the aims for employment rates and flexibilization, linked closely to the EMU, were prioritized, whereas quality in work and quality learning were de-emphasized (Interview 2017b, 2017c, 2017d, 2017e).

The institutionalization of Europe 2020 and the European Semester were well underway and virtually decided when Andor took office. His influence on EU social initiatives was limited during this time. In the following period, Andor wanted a stronger a vision for social policy during the eurozone crisis. He became familiar with key academics involved in the SI debate and, in parallel, envisaged the development of a European unemployment insurance system (Interview 2017b, 2017d).

Stage 3: 2011–2013: the SI 'moment'

Stage 3 consists of the adoption of SI policy, comprising investment in human capital throughout the life-course, in line with the intellectual conceptualization about SI, but also other initiatives, such as anti-poverty policy. EU SI represents an instance of institutional displacement, whereby changes occur through the rediscovery of previously suppressed or suspended alternatives. Throughout this stage, various intellectual, political and bureaucratic entrepreneurs mobilized in issue-framing, institutional alignment and consensus-building on an EU SI policy. Numerous academic publications emphasized a life-course perspective of learning and skills development, highlighting the need to develop cognitive capabilities in early childhood, and on updating skills throughout the life-course (Morel *et al.* 2012). Building on this knowledge, intellectual entrepreneurs were first-movers in issue-framing of EU SI policy. In 2011, Bruno Palier, Frank Vandenbroucke and Anton Hemerijck wrote an opinion paper, entitled 'The EU needs a Social Investment Pact', intended to influence policy-makers (Vandenbroucke *et al.* 2011). These three academics were also very active in advocating SI as a policy frame in the European Commission and in the European Parliament. Hemerijck presented the 'SI Pact' to the European Parliament that debated the issue and later adopted a resolution on this topic (European Parliament 2013).

Andor appointed high-level staff in DG EMPL in order enable progress with his social policy ambitions. In 2011, he appointed Lieve Fransen, a central bureaucratic entrepreneur in framing and adapting SI to the Commission context, as director of social policy and Europe 2020. She became leader of the *ad hoc* SI expert group, to which she recruited various academics, including Vandenbroucke and Ferrera (European Commission 2017a). Fransen has been characterized as Andor's 'right hand' in the issue-framing of SI in the Commission. She chaired the meetings of the SI Expert Group and set the agenda, with a clear ambition to reach consensus on a strong narrative about social investment, accompanied by indicators. Fransen hoped SI would contribute to adding a social dimension to the European Semester, like the EES and OMC in inclusion had added a strong social dimension to the Lisbon Strategy (Interview 2017f, 2017g; Social Investment Expert Group 2013a, 2013b).

The SI Expert Group developed an SI narrative, strongly influenced by the ideas of intellectuals via the SI expert group and from the SI Pact (Vandenbroucke *et al.* 2011) More specifically, the bureaucratic leadership of Fransen enabled a transposition of knowledge from academics to the European Commission. The SIP was adopted in February 2013. The central pillar of this was a communication on SI stressing ' the need to invest in human capital throughout life and ensure adequate livelihoods' (European Commission 2013).[2] It identified policies with a higher SI orientation, including: policies targeted at children; active labour market policies; education; training and lifelong education; housing support; rehabilitation; healthcare; and long-term care services. These aims were not new, but SI as an overarching frame-work was novel compared to the EES and the social inclusion OMCs. The SI communication remarried the EES and the social inclusion OMC, which had decoupled in the mid-term revision of the Lisbon Strategy in stage 2. SI was framed as a complement to social protection (Interview 2017f, 2017g, 2017h; Social Investment Expert Group 2013a). This countered fears among some academics that SI was merely a neoliberal policy frame in disguise (Nolan 2013). One expert suggested that SI represented 'a new "acquis" on the intellectual level' (Interview 2017g), while another assessed that the SIP aimed to make the European Semester 'more likeable' (Interview 2017f). Com-pared to the EES and social inclusion OMC – the antecedents to EU SI – there is more emphasis on starting investment in human capital very early. Indeed, the Commission recommendation that is part of the SIP focuses on children's rights and investment in children (Interview 2017g). The life-course perspec-tive that is the backbone of the SI approach developed by the EU places special emphasis on SI directed towards individuals and women, rather than families (Social Investment Expert Group 2013a).

Following issue-framing of SI and decision-making that resulted in the SIP, the debate in the SI expert group turned to indicators, measurement and implementation of SI. Fransen, as the key bureaucratic entrepreneur, hoped SI indicators would be adopted so that DG ECFIN would take account of SI in the European Semester. In the SI expert group there was extensive debate about the efficiency and effectiveness of SI and welfare states in general, but it was not conclusive. The debate on indicators was rather limited (Interview 2017g, 2017h, 2017i; Social Investment Expert Group 2013b). In terms of iden-tifying core quantitative indicators, the group fell short of its ambitions. Our interviewees noted that while the immediate explanation is technical – that is, there are no indicators to assess SI – the underlying reason is political[3] (Inter-view 2017f; Social Investment Expert Group 2013a, 2013b).

One interviewee concluded that: 'It was not the right time. Member states were not open to EU recommendations related to SI, such as investing more in child-care, and thus, the potential of SI was not fully exploited' (Interview 2017e). SI was largely ignored among member states, which contrasts with the high political engagement among member states with EU social policy during stages 1 and 2 (Ferrera 2016).

Since the political momentum for EU SI was not strong, it was weakly insti-tutionalized. SIP is loosely integrated in the European Semester and the struc-tural funds, it does not stipulate precise targets, and it does not have a strong legal base to require changes in member states. Analytically, we see a limited SI 'moment', rather than a shift to a strongly institutionalized SI policy. An expert close to the SI working group said that 'Andor should be credited for coming up with SI in the context of a neo-liberal/right-wing Commission', but that at the time 'the EU was more strongly committed to being a fiscal consolidation master than a SI cheerleader' (Interview 2017h). After the SI moment that culminated in the SIP it became 'lost in translation' in the shift from ideational consensus to indicators and political commitment. The other social policy issue which Andor had mobilised for as political entrepreneur, a European Unemployment Insurance system, stopped in the tracks before decision-making, owing to the redistributive implications for member states. Our findings regarding this stage imply that even if the combined issue-framing and consensus-building of intellectual, bureaucratic and political entrepreneurs lead to activity, a decision to endorse a policy, and some output, if the political context is not favourable, the possibilities for significant policy change are limited.

Stage 4: 2014–2018: from SI to the European pillar of social rights

After Andor's term in the Commission terminated, there were no strong SI entrepreneurs in the Commission. The SI working group was dissolved, Fransen left the Commission, and the main intellectual entrepreneurs of SI were no longer active in the EU arena. The social agenda of the new Juncker Commission in 2014 focused on strengthening social rights (Interview 2017a, 2017d, 2017j). Stage 4 starts with the Commission preparing this new agenda, the EPSR.

At the time of writing, SI policies, rooted back in the EES and the social OMCs, and extended with the SI communication, are integrated in discussions on the emergent pillar of social rights. Policy priorities of the EPSR include 'equal access to labour markets and skills development, tackling poverty and fair working conditions' (European Commission 2017b: 27). The European Parliament report on the EPSR concludes that it 'will not deliver without SI, especially in available and affordable high-quality infrastructure for caring for children and other dependent persons and also measures to combat discrimination between women and men' (European Parliament 2016: para 37). SI is integrated throughout the report, and is framed as a productive factor, following on from the initial framing by Allan Larsson in the 1990s, but including a broader range of areas (Interview 2017g).

The presence of SI can be partially explained by the fact that some of the central individuals involved in the EPSR have been key entrepreneurs in the previous moments of institutionalization of EU social policy. Fransen, now in a think-tank, reiterates and builds on the intellectual framing of SI (Dheret and Fransen 2017). Rodrigues, a key political entrepreneur behind the Lisbon Strategy and the social inclusion OMC, has mobilized for the EPSR, and with it SI, in the European Parliament (European Parliament 2016). Allan Larsson, a political and bureaucratic entrepreneur involved in the EES, is advising the European Commission on the pillar of social rights. While the pillar has many interesting social policy initiatives, the specification of instruments for SI is weak. Thus far, the result is not conclusive, but the presence of key entrepreneurs from the previous stages suggests that momentum for SI may at the very least be maintained, and perhaps even strengthened.

Concluding discussion

This contribution has considered, through an actor-based historical institutionalist analysis, why and how SI emerged in EU social policy governance in the aftermath of the economic and financial crisis. While SI has been described as a game changer in EU social policy, we have shown that it is more accurate to see it as a 'moment' in a longer time period of gradual institutional change. The 'SI moment' materialized owing to the combined activity of intellectual, bureaucratic and political entrepreneurs. It represents the partial reactivation of latent initiatives from the late 1990s and early 2000s, but providing a broad policy narrative – in fact broader than the SI narrative among academics that focuses on skills development throughout the life course – to join separate processes.

Building on the literature on policy entrepreneurs, this study shows that three categories of entrepreneurs – intellectual, bureaucratic, and political – are movers in gradual institutional change. The findings of the study suggest that historical institutionalists should focus on entrepreneurs even more than they currently do. These actors engage in a variety of issue-framing, institutional alignment, and consensus-building activities. Intellectual actors, mobilizing knowledge for problem-definition and solutions, are crucial in the early part of the policy cycle. They are important in exposing their ideas – and framing policy problems and solutions – over a longer time period, in relevant bureaucratic and political institutions. Bureaucratic entrepreneurs are crucial in setting up and managing expert groups, drawing in intellectual entrepreneurs, and transposing this knowledge to the relevant context through institutional alignment. Finally, political entrepreneurs are decisive in consensus-building related to the decision on a policy. Entrepreneurs engage in issue framing and consensus-building during a limited period of time, a window of opportunity, when their activity is likely to result in a decision, which may comprise institutional change. In addition to strong entrepreneurial activity during a short period of time, the analysis in this contribution shows that the *continuous* involvement of some actors in policy shaping is crucial, particularly for areas with a weak legal base, such as EU SI. Some of the entrepreneurs that supported EU social governance in the late 1990s continued to be involved in the EU arena for two decades, although not necessarily as entrepreneurs.

However, this study also suggests that political conditions are a crucial intervening variable that shapes the extent of institutional change. In stage 3 of our case study, political conditions in the Commission, with a very strong and reluctant DG ECFIN, were a hindrance to a more robust lasting presence of SI at EU level. The result is therefore that EU SI is weakly integrated in the European Semester, where economic and public policy is centrally co-ordinated at EU level. Furthermore, member states, with the presence of populist parties from the left and the right of the political spectrum, were not keen on accepting EU advice on SI. Compared to previous stages, stage 3 is marked by a lack of strongly engaged national politicians willing to trans-pose EU SI to national contexts. This contrasts with the strong political momentum from member states during stages 1 and 2, when the EES, OMC inclusion, and Lisbon strategy were debated among prominent politicians in some member states. Following counter-factual reasoning, if the 'SI moment' had not occurred then the policies in the EES and OMC inclusion would probably have remained as background ideas, rather than resurfacing during stage 3. EU SI did enable the various policy initiatives to be joined into one overarching policy narrative. Furthermore, although the political agenda has changed to an EPSR during stage 4, the continued presence of actors that made significant contributions in previous stages, although in different roles, may enable integration of EU SI into the EPSR.

Notes

1. While entrepreneurs among stakeholders may also be relevant to consider, they rarely have a formal role in the policy process. This differentiates them from the other actors under examination in this contribution.
2. The SIP also included a Recommendation on 'Investing in Children: Breaking the cycle of disadvantage' and a series of Staff Working Documents.
3. Various international organizations' work on indicators that could be considered to assess some aspects of SI. However, DG ECFIN and member states are reluc-tant to adopt and use such indicators at EU level, while DG EMPL is favourable to such indicators.

Acknowledgements

We would like to thank three anonymous referees, the participants of the October 2017 Work-in-progress seminar of the Department of Business and Politics, CBS and Margarita Leon for helpful comments on earlier versions of this paper.

Disclosure statement

No potential conflict of interest was reported by the authors.

References

Armingeon, K. and Baccaro, L. (2012) 'Political economy of the sovereign debt crisis: the limits of the internal devaluation', *Industrial Law Journal* 41(3): 254–75.

Crespy, A. and Menz, G. (2015) 'Commission entrepreneurship and the debasing of social Europe before and after the Eurocrisis', *JCMS: Journal of Common Market Studies* 53(4): 753–68.

de la Porte, C. (2008) 'The evolution and influence of the open method of coordination: the cases of employment and social inclusion', *Phd thesis, Social and Political Science Department*, Florence, European University Institute.

de la Porte, C. (2011) 'Principal–agent theory and the open method of co-ordination: the case of the European employment strategy', *Journal of European Public Policy* 18(4): 485–503.

de la Porte, C. and Heins, E. (2015) 'A new era of European integration? Governance of labour market and social policy since the sovereign debt crisis', *Comparative European Politics* 13(1): 8–28.

Dheret, C. and L. Fransen (2017) 'Social investment first! A precondition for a modern social Europe', *Issue Paper No. 82*, European Policy Center, March 2017.

Esping-Andersen, G. (ed) (2002) *Why we Need a new Welfare State*, Oxford: Oxford University Press.

European Commission (2013) *Towards Social Investment for Growth and Cohesion – Including Implementing the European Social Funds 2014–2020*, Brussels, COM(2013), 83 final.

European Commission (2017a) *Expert group on social investment for growth and cohesion*, available at http://ec.europa.eu/transparency/regexpert/index.cfm?do=groupDetail.groupDetail&groupID=2819 (accessed January 2017).

European Commission (2017b) *The European Pillar of Social Rights: Going Forward Together*, draft programme for meeting on 23 January 2017.

European Parliament (2013) *Resolution of 12 June 2013 on the commission communication 'towards social investment for growth and cohesion — including implementing the European social fund 2014–2020'* (2013/2607(RSP)).

European Parliament (2016) *Report on a European pillar of social rights*, 20 December, Employment and Social Affairs Committee, ref. 2016/2095.

European Union (EU) (2016) *Standard Eurobarometer 86, Public Opinion in the European Union: First Results*, Brussels.

Ferrera, M. (2016) 'Impatient politics and social investment: the EU as "policy facilitator"', *Journal of European Public Policy* 24: 1233–1251. doi:10.1080/13501763.2016.1189451.

Ferrera, M., Hemerijck, A. and Rhodes, M. (2000) *The Future of Social Europe, Recasting Work and Welfare in the New Economy*, Oeiras: Celta Editora.

Hall, P.A. (2008) 'Systematic process analysis: what it is and how to use it', *European Political Science* 7(3): 304–17.

Heclo, H. (1974) *Modern Social Politics in Britain and Sweden: From Relief to Income Maintenance*, New Haven, CT: Yale University Press.

Hemerijck (2015) 'The quiet paradigm revolution of social investment', *Social Politics: International Studies in Gender, State & Society* 22(2): 242–56.

Interview (2017a) Official, DG EMPL, 5 May (Bureaucrat).

Interview (2017b) Former member of Cabinet of Laszlo Andor, DG EMPL, Lukas Vesely, 4 May (Political).

Interview (2017c) Official, DG ECFIN, 4 May (Bureaucrat).

Interview (2017d) Member of Cabinet of Jean-Claude Juncker, 5 May (Political).

Interview (2017e) Laszlo Andor, 22 May (Political Entrepreneur).

Interview (2017f) Former academic member of ad-hoc Social Investment Expert Group (2017), 26 January (Academic Entrepreneur).

Interview (2017g) Former academic member of ad-hoc Social Investment Expert Group, 29 January (Academic Entrepreneur).

Interview (2017h) Former academic member of ad-hoc Social Investment Expert Group, 10 January (Academic Entrepreneur).

Interview (2017i) Former academic member of ad-hoc Social Investment Expert Group, 5 April (Academic Entrepreneur).

Interview (2017j) Lieve Fransen, former director responsible for Europe 2020 in Directorate-General Employment, Social Affairs and Inclusion of the European Commission, 10 May (Bureaucratic Entrepreneur).

Kingdon, J.W. (1995) *Agendas, Alternatives and Public Policies*, New York: Harper Collins.

Mahoney, J. and Thelen, K. (eds) (2010) *Explaining Institutional Change: Agency, Ambiguity and Power*, Cambridge: Cambridge University Press.

Mintrom, M. and Norman, P. (2009) 'Policy entrepreneurship and policy change', *Policy Studies Journal* 37(4): 649–67.

Morel, N., Palier, B. and Palme, J. (2012) 'Beyond the welfare state as we knew it?', in N. Morel, B. Palier and J. Palme (eds.), *Towards a Social Investment Welfare State? Ideas, Policies and Challenges*, Bristol: Policy Press, pp. 1–30.

Nolan, B. (2013) 'What use is 'social investment'?', *Journal of European Social Policy* 23 (5): 459–68.

Pierson, P. (1996) 'The path to European integration. A historical institutionalist analysis', *Comparative Political Studies* 29(2): 123–63.

Sapir, A. (2003) *An agenda for a growing Europe: making the EU system deliver*, Report of an Independent High Level Group established at the initiative of the President of the European Commission.

Scharpf, F. (2013) 'Monetary union, fiscal crisis and the disabling of democratic accountability', in A. Schäfer and W. Streeck (eds.), *Politics in the Age of Austerity*, Cambridge: Polity Press, pp. 108–42.

Social Investment Expert Group (2013a) Minutes of 06/03/2013.

Social Investment Expert Group (2013b) Minutes of 18/06/2013.

Stiller, S. (2010) *Ideational Leadership in German Welfare State Reform. How Politicians and Policy Ideas Transform Resilient Institutions*, Amsterdam: Amsterdam University Press.

Streeck, W. and Thelen, K. (2005) *Beyond Continuity: Institutional Change in Advanced Political Economies*, Oxford: Oxford University Press.

Trampusch, C. and Palier, B. (2016) 'Between X and Y: how process tracing contributes to opening the black box of causality', *New Political Economy* 21:1–17, doi:10.1080/13563467.2015.1134465.

Vandenbroucke, F., Hemerijck, A. and Palier, B. (2011) 'The EU needs a social investment pact', *OSE Opinion Paper No. 5*, May.

Verdun, A. (2015) 'A historical institutionalist explanation of the EU's responses to the euro area financial crisis', *Journal of European Public Policy* 22(2): 219–237.

Zeitlin, J. and Vanhercke, B. (2017) 'Socializing the European semester: EU social and economic policy co-ordination in crisis and beyond', *Journal of European Public Policy*, 1–12. doi:10.1080/13501763.2017.1363269.

Public demand for social investment: new supporting coalitions for welfare state reform in Western Europe?

Julian L. Garritzmann, Marius R. Busemeyer and Erik Neimanns

ABSTRACT

Social investment has recently received much attention among policy-makers and welfare state scholars, but the existing literature remains focused on policy-making on the macro level. We expand this perspective by studying public opinion towards social investment compared to other welfare policies, exploiting new public opinion data from eight European countries. We identify three latent dimensions of welfare state preferences: 'social investment'; 'passive transfers'; and 'workfare' policies. We find that social investment is far more popular compared to the other two. Furthermore, we identify distinct supporting groups: passive transfer policies are most supported by low-income, low-educated people, by individuals leaning towards traditional social values and by those subscribing to left-wing economic attitudes. Social investment policies are supported by a broad coalition of individuals with higher educational backgrounds and left-libertarian views from all economic strata. Workfare policies are most popular with high-income individuals and those subscribing to economically conservative and traditional authoritarian values.

Introduction

The topic of social investment has recently received much attention among policy-makers and welfare state scholars (Bengtsson *et al.* 2017; Bonoli 2007; Esping-Andersen 2002; Morel *et al.* 2012; see Hemerijck (2018) in this collection). While there are many different definitions and conceptions of the social investment model in this literature, the core idea of this rising 'paradigm' (Hemerijck 2015) is to transform contemporary welfare states from more passive, transfer-oriented institutional regimes towards systems centred on the development of human capital and skills at different stages of the life-course from early childhood education via schooling up to post-secondary

---

ⓑ Supplemental data for this article can be accessed https://doi.org/10.1080/13501763.2017.1401107.

education and lifelong learning. Social investment policies aim at 'creating, mobilizing, and preserving' skills (Garritzmann *et al.* 2017: 36ff.; see also: Busemeyer *et al.* 2018). Even though the literature is increasingly paying more attention to the politics of reform, the bulk of existing literature focuses on the role of *collective* actors such as parties, unions and employer associations in the development of social investment policies. In contrast, we hardly have any knowledge on what citizens think about social investment (we discuss exceptions below), also because of a lack of survey data on this issue so far.

This contribution addresses this significant research gap by analysing public opinion towards social investment policies. We pose and answer three research questions. First, do citizens have coherent preferences towards various policies associated with the social investment model (e.g., childcare, active labour market policies [ALMPs], or higher education) and do these preferences differ systematically from those towards compensatory policies? Second, how extensive is popular support for social investment compared to demand for compensatory social transfer policies? And finally, what are the individual-level determinants of people's preferences towards social investment, i.e., are the supporting coalitions similar to those of more traditional welfare policies?

Empirically, we study public opinion towards social investments using a new representative survey recently conducted in eight European countries: the Investing in Education in Europe (INVEDUC) survey (Busemeyer *et al.* 2017). As the existing comparative social surveys (e.g., European Social Survey (ESS), International Social Survey Program (ISSP), Eurobarometer) hardly include questions on social investment, the advantage of the INVEDUC survey is that it for the first time allows studying people's social investment preferences empirically (but see Fossati and Häusermann [2014] analysing Swiss data).

We report three core findings. First, principal component factor analyses reveal that respondents' welfare policy preferences indeed cluster along two dimensions, a social investment and a social compensation dimension. In other words, citizens hold rather coherent preferences towards social investment in general. The partial exception is one form of ALMPs, namely 'workfare' (King 1995) or 'incentive reinforcement' (Bonoli 2010), which forms a distinct, third dimension. Like most social investment scholars (Bonoli 2010; Hemerijck 2015), citizens do not seem to connect workfare policies as part of the social investment approach. Second, a comparison between support for social investment and social compensation policies shows that social investments are much more popular among the European public than passive transfer-oriented policies. Finally, multivariate regressions show that the supporting groups for social investment indeed vary in important ways from those of more traditional welfare policies (see also Häusermann (2018) in this collection). Overall, our contribution seeks to add to welfare state research and public policy scholarship more generally by offering the first comparative empirical analysis of public opinion on social investment.

Public opinion towards social investment: theoretical perspectives

The literature on the politics of social investment has so far focused on causes and effects of (specific) social investment policies on the macro level (Bonoli 2007, 2013; Esping-Andersen 2002; Garritzmann et al. 2017; Hemerijck 2013; Morel et al. 2012; cf. also this collection's introduction: Busemeyer et al. (2018)). In contrast, citizens' preferences on social investments have received much less attention.

There is a significant amount of scholarship on preferences towards individual social investment policies, but they have usually been analysed separately from other policies. For instance, a few studies have analysed attitudes towards early childhood education and childcare (ECEC) (e.g., Busemeyer and Neimanns 2017; Goerres and Tepe 2010; Henderson et al. 1995; Mischke 2014), finding high popular support for the expansion of ECEC, but also some variation within and across countries. Individual preferences are largely determined by materialist self-interest related to variables such as income, educational background and age, as well as by ideological predispositions. Similar findings have been obtained in studies on attitudes towards education policy (Ansell 2010; Busemeyer 2012; Busemeyer and Garritzmann 2017a; Garritzmann 2015, 2016). Still others analysed preferences towards active labour market policies. For example, Kananen et al. (2006) used cross-sectional Eurobarometer data, finding that respondents' labour market situation affects their preferences, while income hardly matters. Rueda (2005) investigated preferences towards active and passive labour market policies, studying differences between labour market insiders and outsiders.

Yet, even though there is a significant amount of research on individual social investment policies, there is hardly any work on how these are related and whether they are sufficiently coherent to allow identifying distinct and different supporting coalitions for the social investment vs the transfer-oriented welfare state model. A noteworthy exception is Fossati and Häusermann's (2014) analysis of Swiss survey data. Their factor analyses show that Swiss citizens' welfare policy preferences are two-dimensional, as preferences towards social compensation and social investment clearly form distinct clusters, and that these preferences are good predictors of voting behaviour. The few existing studies on social investment attitudes for a broader set of countries (Häusermann et al. 2015; Häusermann and Kriesi 2015) provide first comparative insights, but suffer from shortcomings resulting from the use of existing comparative social surveys (ESS, ISSP, Eurobarometer), which we discuss below.

Inspired by this literature, our *first research question* is whether people indeed have coherent preferences towards social investment policies and whether these differ systematically from attitudes towards compensatory social policies. There are good theoretical reasons why this should be the case. First, the social investment literature (Hemerijck (2018) in this collection) emphasizes the importance of *complementarities* between different social investment policies. These complementarities arise from the fact that the social investment strategy aims at promoting the creation, mobilization and preservation of human skills across different stages of the life-cycle from early childhood education to lifelong learning (Garritzmann *et al.* 2017). Second, as we substantiate below, the beneficiary groups supporting social investment are different from those of social compensation, which could eventually encourage parties to mobilize different supporting coalitions for their policies. Young, well-educated middle-class parents, for example, benefit not only from the expansion of childcare facilities, but also from more investment in education and labour market training. Vice versa, the primary beneficiaries of social transfers – the poor, the ill, and the long-term unemployed – might be less (or not at all) interested in the expansion of social investment. On a more conceptual level, proponents of the social investment perspective point out that it represents a distinct justification for government involvement, which is complementary to the classical social insurance and redistributive functions of the welfare state (Barr 2012). In comparison to the latter two, social investment policies are geared towards preventing the emergence of social risks in a proactive manner, whereas typical social insurance and redistributive policies compensate *ex post*.

That said, the concept of the social investment state remains elusive and ambivalent in many ways (see Busemeyer *et al.* (2018) in this collection). In the political realm, it has been used by different political actors for different purposes, which was possible owing to the ambiguity of the concept. The 'third way' approach (Giddens 1998), partly implemented by the Blair and Schröder governments, might be considered as precursor to the social investment debate of the 2000s. However, these earlier policies often contained strong elements of 'incentive reinforcement' (Bonoli 2010) or 'workfare' (King 1995), promoting new kinds of ALMPs that strongly and often negatively incentivize the unemployed to get back into employment rather than engaging in retraining. In contrast, this workfare approach had not been a strong component of the universalist welfare model in Scandinavia, which is upheld as a role model of the social investment state among supporters because of its early expansion of social services complementing generous transfer schemes.

Rather than addressing – let alone solving – these ambiguities on the theoretical level, we adopt an empirical approach in this contribution. We are interested to what extent attitudes towards different social investment policies correlate with each other. We want to understand whether the public identifies distinct 'policy packages' and whether these are different from the packages promoted by policy-makers of different stripes. For instance, even though workfare-style policies are often discussed in the context of activation policies by policy-makers, individual support for these policies might not be associated with support for other social investment policies because of their emphasis on negative incentives. Also, depending on the particular political context, there might be some cross-national variation in how policy packages are reflected on the level of public opinion. In sum, we expect:

> Citizens' preferences towards different social investment policies cluster along a distinct dimension, whereas attitudes for social transfer policies cluster along a second dimension (Hypothesis 1).

Our second research question is – assuming two-dimensional preferences for now – how popular social investment is *vis-à-vis* compensatory policies. There are empirical indications that individual social investment policies such as education and childcare are popular, but there is no solid evidence on the popularity of the social investment model in its entirety (but see Busemeyer *et al.* 2017; Busemeyer and Garritzmann 2017b). Still, it is plausible to expect that social investment policies are highly popular (see also Bonoli 2013), because they create benefits for large parts of the electorate, in particular the well-educated (and politically active) middle class. The social investment model might also receive considerable political support, because it is – partly also because of its ambiguity – appealing to people with different ideological predispositions, taking up a 'middle-ground' between state- and market-based solutions. In other words, social investment could be a valence issue, which is difficult to oppose politically. Thus, we hypothesize:

> Social investment is highly popular among the European public, particularly *vis-à-vis* compensatory social policies (Hypothesis 2).

Our third research question relates to the determinants of people's preferences. We are particularly interested in whether and how the supporting coalitions of social investment policies differ from those of compensatory policies (cf. also Beramendi *et al.* [2015] for this relationship on the macro level). We argue that while preferences towards social investment and towards compensation are related to a certain degree, they differ in several important respects.

First, we expect that the traditional 'class conflict' identified for compensatory social policies is less important when it comes to social investment. The main reason is that whereas compensatory social policies are often strongly redistributive, the redistributive effects of social investment policies are much more complex as these often benefit the wealthier middle classes (see Bonoli and Liechti (2018) and Pavolini and Van Lancker (2018) in this collection). Thus, we expect that income is an important (negative) determinant of respondents' preferences towards compensatory policies, but not so for social investment. Second, we expect the effect of age to be different. The bulk of social transfer spending (particularly pensions) benefits the elderly, whereas social investments are geared towards the young: children; young adults; and parents. Hence, age should have a positive effect on respondents' compensation policy preferences, but a negative effect on their support for social investment (Busemeyer *et al.* 2009).

The third factor we emphasize is the role of ideological positions. In the literature on welfare state preferences it is common to measure respondents' position on a uni-dimensional left–right scale as a proxy for their underlying political preferences. However, a related literature on political behaviour, which tends to be neglected in welfare state research, argues that the ideological space is two-dimensional, distinguishing an 'economic' and a 'social' left–right dimension (for many: Häusermann and Kriesi 2015; Hooghe *et al.* 2002; Kitschelt 1994). The economic dimension concerns orientations towards the state-market relationship with people on the left supporting a strong role of the state and people on the right supporting market solutions. The social dimension relates to new political issues that have emerged during the post-materialist revolution since the 1970s. This dimension ranges from 'green/alternative/libertarian' (GAL) values, on the one hand, to 'traditional/authoritarian/nationalist' (TAN) orientations, on the other. We find this differentiation helpful because it has important implications for the study of social investment and social compensation policies (cf. also Beramendi *et al.* 2015; Häusermann and Kriesi 2015).

We hypothesize a positive association between a left-wing position on the economic dimension and support for both compensatory and social investment policies, because both are essentially public policy programmes. However, the association should be stronger for compensatory policies, because these are more aligned with the classical redistributive left–right conflict, as argued above. Regarding the GAL–TAN dimension, we expect significant differences between compensatory and social investment policies: Respondents with GAL views should favour social investments but be relatively opposed to compensation policies, because they are more in favour of equality of opportunities, gender equality and socioeconomic upward mobility (all of which the social investment paradigm seeks to achieve). In contrast, compensatory policies are often built upon a logic of status maintenance and were established in a time when the male-breadwinner model was dominant. Thus, egalitarian, post-materialist individuals can be assumed to support future-oriented social investments, but to be relatively opposed to traditional welfare policies. Vice versa, citizens with more TAN views should favour social transfers, but oppose social investments.

Taken together, we expect:

The determinants of respondents' preferences towards social compensation and social investment differ in important ways. Social investment and social compensation have very distinct supporting coalitions (Hypothesis 3). (See also contribution Häusermann (2018) in this collection).

Empirical analysis

Data

In order to test our arguments, we need country-comparative data on people's preferences on social investment policies and compensatory welfare policies. Unfortunately, the existing international comparative surveys (e.g., ESS, ISSP, or Eurobarometer) do not include questions that allow operationalizing our dependent variable in a valid way.[1]

Therefore, we conducted an original representative survey in eight Western European countries: the 'Investing in Education in Europe' (INVEDUC) survey (Busemeyer *et al.* 2017). The eight countries were chosen to cover the variety of welfare state regime traditions across Western Europe to increase the generalizability of the results: Denmark; Sweden; Germany; France; Spain; Italy; the United Kingdom (UK); and Ireland. The fieldwork was conducted by a professional survey company in April–May 2014, following a set of pre-tests in the countries. Interviews were conducted by native speakers, using computer-assisted telephone interviewing (CATI) techniques. The total number of observations is 8,905 with about 1,000 to 1,500 cases per country, depending on population size. The average response rate was 27 per cent, which is satisfactory for this kind of survey (see Busemeyer *et al.* (2017)). In the Online Appendix we present further information on the response rates by country (Table A1) and summary statistics of our variables (Table A2).

Operationalization of the dependent variables

In order to study respondents' attitudes towards social investment policies, we confronted respondents with a number of potential welfare state policy reforms, which the governments in the respective countries might pursue. These reform proposals were inspired by policy instruments discussed in the literature on social investment and welfare state reform (Bonoli 2013; Hemerijck 2013; Morel *et al.* 2012). One of the advantages of our survey is that we do not have to rely on proxies such as people's preferences towards different kinds of public spending (the common practice in other surveys) to understand their policy preferences (cf. Fossati and Häusermann 2014). Instead, we have much more direct, realistic, and concrete measures of respondents' support for social investment and other welfare policies. More specifically, respondents were asked:

> Governments and political leaders like to propose new policy reforms in order to address important social issues. Please indicate whether you would strongly agree, agree, neither agree nor disagree, disagree or strongly disagree with the following reform proposals:

1. Giving the unemployed more time and opportunities to improve their qualification before they are required to accept a job.
2. Expanding access to early childhood education and improving its quality.
3. Investing more money in university education and research at universities.
4. Forcing unemployed to accept a job quickly, even if it is not as good as their previous job.
5. Increasing old age pensions to a higher degree than wages.
6. Lowering the statutory retirement age and facilitating early retirement. [2]

In administering the survey, the order of items was randomized to avoid spurious relations. We designed the first three items to capture different key aspects of the social investment paradigm: The first item alludes to ALMPs that place emphasis on (re-)training in order to improve the individuals' job perspectives rather than their quick re-integration into the labour market – 'upskilling' in Bonoli's (2010) terms. Upskilling is a decisive part of the social investment agenda (Bonoli 2010) and has become a widely used policy tool in many European countries. The second item proposes the expansion of childcare (in terms of access and quality), which also is a core component of investment-oriented social policy reforms (Esping-Andersen 2002). The third item proposes expanding investments in universities and research, i.e., forms of human capital that are more relevant in later stages of the life-course with a more direct connection to the labour market (Garritzmann 2016). The first three items thus cover key aspects of the social investment approach. Even though these items all relate to the formation of human skills, they do not simply capture preferences for education policies as they refer to different policies with potentially distinct supporters (the unemployed in the first case, young families in the second, and students and researchers in the third).

The fourth item also follows an activation logic, but refers to the notion of 'workfare' policies (King 1995), i.e., ALMPs that set incentives to force unemployed persons back into the labour market. Bonoli (2010) termed these kinds of ALMPs 'incentive reinforcements': they have a strong employment orientation, but lack a social investment component. We are interested in how respondents' attitudes towards this policy relate to their attitudes towards the other policies. Finally, the fifth and the sixth items capture support for more traditional, transfer-oriented social policy reforms. The fifth item proposes to increase pensions more than wages, i.e., to shift resources to old-age pensions above and beyond what would be expected on the background of general wage increases. The sixth proposal is to allow individuals to retire earlier by lowering the statutory retirement age and expanding opportunities for early retirement. These aspects thus focus on social transfer policies and – more importantly – do not contain any social investment aspects.

Admittedly, as we study two policy reforms in the area of pensions, we can only make limited claims about passive transfer policy preferences in general. Space constraints in the survey prevented us from including a larger set of social transfer policies. Yet, we chose to focus on pensions because, compared to other social transfers, which are more redistributive in nature, pensions are likely to be supported by larger parts of the population. Hence, measuring support for social investment policies relative to the 'high benchmark' of equally popular pension policies is a conservative test for the general popularity of the former relative to the latter. Furthermore, we conducted an additional factor analysis of preferences for public spending using a different question from the survey. This allows us to compare preferences for spending on three different passive transfer and four different education policy fields (Online Appendix, Table A6). These comparisons confirm the existence of two different latent dimensions of welfare state (spending) preferences, as support for more pension spending is highly correlated with support for additional spending on unemployment benefits and health care, but not with support for education spending.

Findings: the multidimensionality of welfare policy preferences

Addressing the first research question, we performed a principal component factor analysis in order to ascertain whether our presumed classification of policy reforms is supported empirically (Hypothesis 1).[3] We find three factors with an Eigenvalue greater than 1, which is commonly used as a cut-off point for identifying factors. Table 1 displays the Eigenvalues and

Table 1. Rotated factor loadings and Eigenvalues after principal-component factor analysis, pooled sample.

Item	Factor 1: 'Social investment'	Factor 2: 'Passive transfers'	Factor 3: 'Workfare'
Labour market training	**0.4179**	0.1502	**−0.5922**
Expand early childcare	**0.7657**	0.0799	0.0796
Universities and research	**0.7623**	0.0094	−0.0662
Accept job quickly	0.0808	0.0257	**0.8807**
Pension increase	0.0828	**0.7891**	0.1015
Early retirement	0.0111	**0.7660**	−0.1424
Eigenvalues	1.5900	1.1092	1.0631

Note: Numbers are printed in bold to facilitate readability by emphasizing the high factor loadings.

the rotated factor loadings. The results clearly reveal that citizens' welfare policy preferences cluster along three dimensions. The factor loadings indicate how strongly the individual variables/items correlate with the respective factor. The analysis shows that – as expected – respondents' preferences towards labour market training, expansion of early childcare and higher education policies are strongly associated. They load on the same factor, which we label as a latent 'social investment' dimension. Secondly, preferences towards pension increases and early retirement strongly load on a second factor, which we label 'passive transfers'. Finally, we identify a third factor ('workfare'), which is strongly associated with the 'workfare' proposal, as well as – negatively – with the 'upskilling' proposal. This shows that the supporters of the positively activating social investment approach are different from the ones supporting negative incentive structures in labour market policies. Put differently, like social investment scholars (Bonoli 2010; Hemerijck 2018) citizens do not connect negative reinforcements with a social investment approach. In sum, the factor analysis shows that – as hypothesized – respondents have rather coherent preferences towards social investments on the one hand and transfer-oriented consumption policies on the other.

Country-specific factor analyses (see Table A3 in the Online Appendix) show that this finding does not only hold for the pooled sample, but also for the individual countries. The partial exception to this pattern is the third 'workfare'-dimension, where we detect some cross-country variation. In Denmark and the UK, this item loads negatively on the social investment dimension; in Sweden, it is correlated with the items about passive transfers.[4] These findings suggest that in countries with a relatively long tradition of social investment and active labour market policies (Hemerijck 2013), citizens understand workfare more as a policy in conflict with more generous approaches to social investment. In line with this, Ireland differs from the UK in that respect. The Swedish case is indicative of a situation where proponents of the social investment model are pitted against supporters of the traditional welfare state model, which in this case includes support for higher social transfers *as well as* a tighter stance on incentive reinforcement (see also the next section on support levels by country).

How popular is social investment?

Our second research question regards the overall popularity of the social investment model (Hypothesis 2). Figure 1 displays support levels for social investment, passive transfers and workfare policies (survey weights are applied, cf. Busemeyer *et al.* [2017] for details). It shows the share of respondents who 'agree' or 'strongly agree' with the respective reforms in each dimension. The figure clearly shows that in all countries expanding social investment is the most popular reform proposal. In the pooled sample

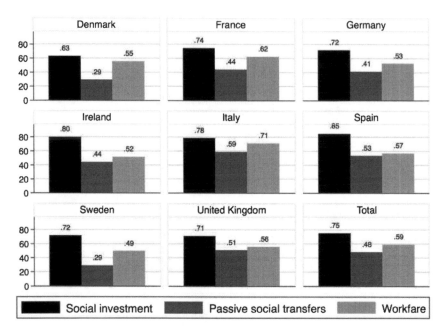

Figure 1. Share of respondents supporting social investment, passive transfers, and workfare policy reforms across countries.

about 75 per cent of respondent (strongly) agree with these reforms, whereas policy reforms aimed at expanding passive transfers receive much less support (48 per cent). Interestingly, reforms to strengthen (negative) incentives for unemployed persons to accept jobs actually receives higher levels of support (59 per cent) than expanding passive transfer policies. Figure 1 reveals some variation across countries, but overall we observe the same pattern: we find the highest popular support for reforms that expand social investment and the lowest support for expanding social transfers; workfare policies take an intermediate position.

The general popularity of social investment policies is underscored by the fact that even where social investment policies are already well-established (e.g., Denmark and Sweden), citizens are much more in favour of further expanding social investment policies than supporting policy reforms that would increase the generosity of transfers. This relative popularity of social investment appears to reflect the strong expected benefits associated with social investment rather than to represent a simple catch-up process towards the levels of established passive transfers.

Determinants of multidimensional welfare policy preferences

Finally, our third research question focuses on the determinants of respondents' preferences (Hypothesis 3). As explained above, the goal is to identify potential differences in patterns of support for these different policy approaches. The dependent variables are the three factors identified above. More specifically, we use the predicted values of the rotated factor scores (based on the regression method) for each of the three factors identified in the first part of the empirical analysis. Since the factor analysis transforms the initial variables coded in a five-point scale into a continuous variable with a mean of zero and a standard deviation of 1, we apply ordinary least square (OLS) regressions. In order to take into account the multilevel nature of the data (individuals nested within countries), we include country dummies and calculate country-clustered robust standard errors.[5]

We include several independent variables in the analysis. First, *educational background*, measured as respondents' highest achieved educational degree from basic to tertiary higher education. Second, respondents' net monthly *household income* (using individual net income yields the same results), given in county-specific income quintiles. Third, *gender* (female = 1) and, fourth, whether the respondent has *small children living in his/her household* (small children is here defined as children below the age of 10, since this is the age when children usually finish primary school). Fifth, age categories are included to test for non-linear age effects (robustness tests indeed reveal that this is the preferred specification). We use those aged 30–39 as the reference category, because they are in their prime working-age and should have the most coherent preferences in comparison to the other age-groups. Those aged 60 and above are further separated into a *retired* and a *non-retired* group to allow assessing whether retirement status has an influence on preferences independent of age. Finally, we include two variables measuring the two-dimensional left-right positions laid out above. Both of these scales are derived from a factor analysis of responses to a set of items asked in the survey (see the Online Appendix for details). Higher values on the *economic left–right scale* indicate support for a strong role of the market. Higher values on the *social values scale* imply a more positive orientation towards TAN values.

Figure 2 graphically shows our regression results by plotting point estimates and confidence bands (the full models are available in Table A4, Models 1–3 in the Online Appendix).[6] Most importantly, the analysis reveals clear differences in the determinants of public support across these different models, which indicates that – in line with our expectations – the composition of groups supporting these policy reform proposals does vary. First of all, social investment reforms are supported by individuals with higher levels of education, and by those who subscribe to economically left-wing and to more egalitarian social values. Neither individuals' income position, nor their gender, nor having small children are associated with support for social investment, which – together with the descriptive evidence displayed above – can be interpreted as indicating a broad base of support for social

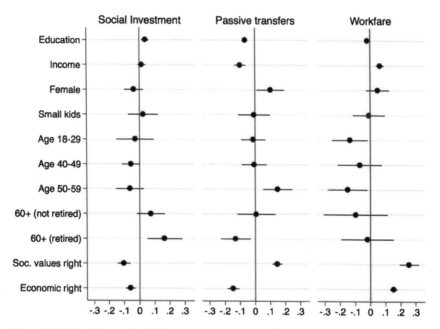

Figure 2. Determinants of social investment, passive transfer, and workfare policy proposals.
Note: Coefficients and 95% confidence bands are plotted; OLS regressions, pooled sample, country fixed effects, robust country-clustered standard errors.

investment reforms. Surprisingly, we also find a strong and robust positive association between being retired and support for social investment policies. This is clearly at odds with conceptions of the elderly being opposed to welfare state reforms that mainly benefit the young (Busemeyer *et al.* 2009). Yet, because this effect is limited to those in retirement, it might be that the transition from being a net taxpayer to becoming a welfare recipient leads to less concerns about taxes that need to be raised to finance social investment or that the elderly do in fact care about working conditions of younger generations and the provision of high-quality childcare for their grandchildren. In any case, this remains an interesting finding to be studied in future research.

Secondly, the characteristics of respondents supporting policy reforms expanding passive transfers are more reminiscent of the classic class cleavage: we find strong negative effects of income, educational background and male gender, as well as a positive association for economically left-wing ideological orientation. Different from social investment but in line with our expectation, supporters of passive transfers tend more towards the right on the social values dimension. Again, the effect of age on support is puzzling, since retired respondents oppose more generous passive transfers, but support is highest in the age group of those in their 50s. Analyses disaggregated by policy proposal, which we present in the Online Appendix (Figure A2), reveal that this effect is driven by the item of early retirement. Contrary to the proposal of pension increases (where we observe a positive linear effect of age), those in retirement would not benefit from more generous early retirement regulation. Furthermore, they might be concerned about negative side effects on the sustainability of pension payments. Support is highest among those that are close to reach the statutory retirement age.

Finally, support for 'workfare' policies is concentrated among those with higher incomes (educational background seems to matter less in this case), who also tend towards more TAN values and subscribe to an economically right-leaning position. This confirms that the characteristics of the group supporting workfare reforms – while also being smaller in size compared to social investment policies – are different, as it tends to be more concentrated in the 'upscale' groups. Since labour market risk is partly correlated with income, these groups are less likely to experience unemployment spells themselves and therefore are more supportive of reforms promoting stringent use of 'their' taxes. This is also reflected by the effects of age: the reference group of those in their 30s are in their prime labour market age and probably find it relatively easy to change jobs and therefore are more in favour of workfare compared to the other age groups.

Summing up, our analysis reveals distinct differences in the patterns of support for different policy reforms, which could become the foundation for efforts of parties to mobilize political coalitions in support of their proposed policy packages: First, supporting the existing literature on compensatory social policies and redistribution more generally, we find that passive transfer policies are most supported by low-income and low-educated people and individuals leaning towards TAN values, while also subscribing to left-wing economic attitudes. In contrast, we find that social investments are supported by individuals with a higher educational background and those expressing left-libertarian views. This coalition is also relatively broad in terms of size and includes individuals from different socioeconomic backgrounds (captured by income) and, surprisingly, also some pensioners. Finally, workfare policies are most popular with high-income individuals as well as those subscribing to economically conservative positions and traditional authoritarian values. In the Online Appendix, we present and discuss a number of robustness tests, which demonstrate that the findings hold across model specifications and different variable operationalizations.

Conclusion

The debate about the social investment model remains a rather élite-centred discourse, as most of the existing literature has focused on politics and policy-making on the macro level. Our contribution expands this perspective by studying individual preferences. Using a new public opinion survey on social investment and welfare state policies, we found that Europeans' welfare state preferences indeed cluster along three dimensions, related to social investment, passive transfers and workfare policies. We found that social investments are by far the most popular social policies across countries, and we identified different and distinct potential supporting groups for the individual policy 'packages'.

Our findings have important implications for the social investment debate: contrasting the somewhat mixed assessments of the success of the social investment model on the level of policy-making (see de la Porte and Natali (2018) in this collection), our analysis shows that from citizens' perspective, social investment policies remain highly attractive. This is because they appeal both normatively as well as economically to large parts of the electorate. Put differently, contrary to social compensatory policies, social investments find support even among the high-skilled and richer individuals. But the analysis also revealed that the supporting coalitions for social investment reforms and more traditional social policies are distinct, hinting at potential trade-offs, political struggles and conflicts over the transformation of existing welfare states. These struggles have already been apparent in the fate of social democratic parties in the last decades, as they are torn between the interests of their erstwhile core electoral constituencies in the working classes and new left-libertarian constituencies in the well-educated middle classes (Beramendi *et al.* 2015; Häusermann and Kriesi 2015; Kitschelt and Rehm 2015). The same can increasingly be said about right-wing parties trying to appeal to the urban middle classes by expanding social services such as childcare. From the perspective of public opinion, there is considerable potential for centrist policies focusing on human skills and social investment.

Notes

1. The ESS includes some questions on childcare and the ISSP Role of Government modules include a question on public education spending. But hitherto these surveys do not cover a broader range of social investment policies.
2. While the wording of some of the items is relatively complex, our pretests indicated that respondents understood the logic of the reform proposal sufficiently well. Thus they should provide valid measures. Most items mention several reform measures simultaneously. This has the drawback that respondents might value the individual components of the reform measures differently. But the question wording reflects our aim to present realistic reform proposals that are comparable across countries and avoid getting lost in specific reform details. The first and fourth item are replications from the Eurobarometer 56.1 (e.g., Kananen *et al.* 2006).
3. If we treat responses on the five-point Likert scales as ordinal rather than continuous and use a polychoric correlation matrix as input for the principal component factor analysis (Welkenhuysen-Gybels *et al.* 2003), the findings remain unchanged.

4. Sweden also stands out because early retirement loads *negatively* on the 'passive transfers' dimension. We discuss the particularities of the issue of early retirement, which help to make sense of this outlying value, in more detail below.
5. As an alternative, one could run multilevel/hierarchical random-effects models. These models yield the same coefficient estimates as the specification we use, but slightly larger standard errors. As the number of level 2 observations is relatively small $(N_j = 8)$, we chose the common standard.
6. In the Online Appendix, Figures A1–A2 and Table A4, Models 4–9, we present additional models estimated separately for each policy proposal.

Acknowledgements

We wish to thank participants of the workshop 'The Future of the Social Investment State', at the University of Lausanne, at the Workshop 'Aktivierend - investiv - prädistributiv: Neue Paradigmen in der Sozialpolitik(forschung)?' of the DVPW Working Group "Vergleichende Wohlfahrtsstaatenforschung" at the University of Kassel, and at the CES conference in Glasgow. We also thank the anonymous reviewers and the editors for helpful suggestions.

Disclosure statement

No potential conflict of interest was reported by the authors.

Funding

We gratefully acknowledge financial support by an European Research Consortium (ERC) 'Starting Grant', Grant No. 311769.

References

Ansell, B.W. (2010) *From the Ballot to the Blackboard: The Redistributive Political Economy of Education*, New York: Cambridge University Press.

Barr, N. (2012) *Economics of the Welfare State*, Fifth Edition, Oxford, New York: Oxford University Press.

Bengtsson, M., de la Porte, C. and Jacobsson, K. (2017) 'Labour market policy under conditions of permanent austerity: any sign of social investment?', *Social Policy & Administration* 51(2): 367–388.

Beramendi, P., Häusermann, S., Kitschelt, H. and Kriesi, H. (2015) *The Politics of Advanced Capitalism*, Cambridge: Cambridge University Press.

Bonoli, G. (2007) 'Time matters: postindustrialization, new social risks, and welfare state adaptation in advanced industrial democracies', *Comparative Political Studies* 40(5): 495–520.

Bonoli, G. (2010) 'The political economy of active labor-market policy', *Politics and Society* 38(4): 435–457.

Bonoli, G. (2013) *The Origins of Active Social Policy: Labour Market and Childcare Policies in a Comparative Perspective*, Oxford: Oxford University Press.

Bonoli, G. and Liechti, F. (2018) 'Good intentions and Matthew effects: access biases in participation in active labour market policies', *Journal of European Public Policy* 25(6): 894–911.

Busemeyer, M.R. (2012) 'Inequality and the political economy of education: an analysis of individual preferences in OECD countries', *Journal of European Social Policy* 22(3): 219–240.

Busemeyer, M.R. and Garritzmann, J.L. (2017a) 'Academic, vocational, or general? An analysis of public opinion towards education policies with evidence from a new comparative survey', *Journal of European Social Policy* 27(4): 373–386.

Busemeyer, M.R. and Garritzmann, J.L. (2017b) 'Public opinion on policy and budgetary trade-offs in European welfare states: evidence from a new comparative Survey', *Journal of European Public Policy* 24(6): 871–889.

Busemeyer, M.R., and Neimanns, E. (2017) 'Conflictive preferences towards social investments and transfers in mature welfare states: The cases of unemployment benefits and childcare provision', *Journal of European Social Policy*. doi:https://doi.org/10.1177/0958928716684302.

Busemeyer, M.R., Goerres, A. and Weschle, S. (2009) 'Attitudes towards redistributive spending in an era of demographic ageing: the rival pressures from age and income in 14 OECD countries', *Journal of European Social Policy* 19(3): 195–212.

Busemeyer, M.R., Garritzmann, J.L., Neimanns, E. and Nezi, R. (2017) 'Investing in education in Europe: evidence from a new survey of public opinion', *Journal of European Social Policy*. doi:10.1177/0958928717700562.

Busemeyer, M.R., de la Porte, C., Garritzmann, J.L. and Pavolini, E. (2018) 'The future of the social investment state: politics, policies, and outcomes', *Journal of European Public Policy* 25(6): 801–809.

de la Porte, C. and Natali, D. (2018) 'Agents of institutional change in EU policy: the social investment moment', *Journal of European Public Policy* 25(6): 828–843.

Esping-Andersen, G. (2002) 'A child-centred social investment strategy', in G. Esping-Andersen (ed.), *Why we Need a New Welfare State*, Oxford: Oxford University Press, pp. 26–65.

Fossati, F. and Häusermann, S. (2014) 'Social policy preferences and party choice in the 2011 Swiss elections', *Swiss Political Science Review* 20(4): 590–611.

Garritzmann, J.L. (2015) 'Attitudes towards student support: how positive feedback-effects prevent change in the four worlds of student Finance', *Journal of European Social Policy* 25(2): 139–158.

Garritzmann, J.L. (2016) *The Political Economy of Higher Education Finance. The Politics of Tuition Fees and Subsidies in OECD Countries 1945–2015*, Basingstoke: Palgrave Macmillan.

Garritzmann, J.L., Häusermann, S., Palier, B. and Zollinger, C. (2017) 'WoPSI - the world politics of social investment: an international research project to explain variance in social investment agendas and social investment reforms across countries and world regions', LIEPP working paper: 64, SciencesPo, Paris.

Giddens, A. (1998) *The Third Way: The Renewal of Social Democracy*, New York: John Wiley & Sons.

Goerres, A. and Tepe, M. (2010) 'Age-based self-interest, intergenerational solidarity and the welfare state: a comparative analysis of older people's attitudes towards public childcare in 12 OECD countries', *European Journal of Political Research* 49 (6): 818–851.

Häusermann, S. (2018) 'The multidimensional politics of social investment in conservative welfare regimes: family policy reform between social transfers and social investment', *Journal of European Public Policy* 25(6): 862–877.

Häusermann, S. and Kriesi, H. (2015) 'What do voters want? dimensions and configurations in individual-level preferences and party choice', in P. Beramendi, S. Häusermann, H. Kitschelt, and H. Kriesi (eds), *The Politics of Advanced Capitalism*, Cambridge: Cambridge University Press, pp. 202–230.

Häusermann, S., Kurer, T. and Schwander, H. (2015) 'High-skilled outsiders? labor market vulnerability, education and welfare state preferences', *Socio-Economic Review* 13(2): 235–58.

Hemerijck, A. (2013) *Changing Welfare States*, Oxford: Oxford University Press.

Hemerijck, A. (2015) 'The quiet paradigm revolution of social investment', *Social Politics: International Studies in Gender, State & Society* 22(2): 242–256.

Hemerijck, A. (2018) 'Social investment as a policy paradigm', *Journal of European Public Policy* 25(6): 810–827.

Henderson, T.L., Monroe, P.A., Garand, J.C. and Burts, D.C. (1995) 'Explaining public opinion toward government spending on child care', *Family Relations* 44(1): 37–45.

Hooghe, L., Marks, G. and Wilson, C.J. (2002) 'Does left/right structure party positions on European integration?', *Comparative Political Studies* 35: 965–89.

Kananen, J., Taylor-Gooby, P. and Larsen, T.P. (2006) 'Public attitudes and new social risk reform', in A. Klaus and G. Bonoli (eds), *The Politics of Post-Industrial Welfare States: Adapting Post-war Social Policies to New Social Risks*, New York: Routledge, pp. 83–99.

King, D. (1995) *Actively Seeking Work? The Politics of Unemployment and Welfare Policy in the United States and Great Britain*, Chicago: University of Chicago Press.

Kitschelt, H. (1994) *The Transformation of European Social Democracy*, Cambridge: Cambridge University Press.

Kitschelt, H. and Rehm, P. (2015) 'Party alignments: change and continuity', in P. Beramendi, S. Häusermann, H. Kitschelt and H. Kriesi (eds), *The Politics of Advanced Capitalism*, Cambridge: Cambridge University Press, pp. 179–201.

Mischke, M. (2014) *Public Attitudes Towards Family Policies in Europe. Linking Institutional Context and Public Opinion*, Wiesbaden: Springer VS.

Morel, N., Palier, B. and Palme, J. (2012) *Towards a Social Investment Welfare State: Ideas, Policies and Challenges*, Bristol: The Policy Press.

Pavolini, E. and Van Lancker, W. (2018) 'The Matthew effect in childcare use: a matter of policies or preferences?', *Journal of European Public Policy* 25(6): 878–893.

Rueda, D. (2005) 'Insider-outsider politics in industrialized democracies: the challenge to social democratic parties', *American Political Science Review* 99(1): 61–74.

Welkenhuysen-Gybels, J., Billiet, J. and Cambré, B. (2003) 'Adjustment for acquiescence in the assessment of the construct equivalence of Likert-type score items', *Journal of Cross-Cultural Psychology* 34(6): 702–722.

The multidimensional politics of social investment in conservative welfare regimes: family policy reform between social transfers and social investment

Silja Häusermann

ABSTRACT
While we have many studies on social investment policies and their effects, we still know fairly little about the *politics* of social investment, especially in conservative welfare states, which provide the hardest ground for these reforms. What are the key conflicts in social investment politics? How do they intersect with compensatory welfare state conflict? Which coalition potentials exist? Based on a newly collected dataset, this contribution analyses actor configurations in German family policy reform processes since 1979. It shows that the development of social investment in conservative welfare regimes can only be understood if we conceptualize its politics in a multidimensional space. Income protection and social investment can be, and oftentimes are, two distinct conflict lines. Hence, political exchange and ambiguous agreements were conducive to a hybrid policy development: income support expansion coexists with social investment reforms. The findings show how a social investment turn can happen even in a least likely case.

1. Introduction

The male breadwinner model of family policy – typical of conservative welfare state regimes – displays a number of characteristics that clash with the social needs and demands of post-industrial societies. Rising female education levels and labour market participation rates foster claims for work–care reconciliation policies; growing family instability and divorce rates raise poverty levels in single-parent households; and the traditional household pattern – i.e., an unpaid or marginally paid female caregiver and a male full-time earner – fundamentally clashes with culturally liberal values of gender equality, individualism and equal opportunities for men and women. All these structural and ideological developments put traditional family policy arrangements in conservative welfare states into question.

ⓑ Supplemental data for this article can be accessed at 10.1080/13501763.2017.1401106

In this context, the idea of a general recalibration of welfare policies has gained ground in most countries, i.e., a reorientation away from policies that compensate income loss by (passive) transfer payments towards social investment policies. Social investment policies centre on human capital development. They can be defined as 'those policies that aim at creating, mobilizing, or preserving skills' (Garritzmann et al. 2017: 37). In the field of family policy, the reconciliation of paid employment and care responsibilities refers most directly to the mobilizing aspect of social investment, while the expansion of good-quality early childcare addresses the aspect of creating human capital (Jenson 2012). The preservation of skills matters in the definition of parents' rights in the workplace (e.g., job guarantees, rights to work flexibly or part-time) during the time of parental leaves and after. A growing literature takes stock of the development of social investment policies across Europe (e.g., Morgan 2013; Nikolai 2012). However, while the literature on the extent of policy development grows, we still know fairly little about the *politics* of social investment reforms. Which political actors support or oppose social investment? What is the key conflict line in this area of welfare state change and how does this conflict pattern relate to the traditional configuration of interests in welfare politics? In welfare state research – and in particular in the field of family policy – a broad consensus has emerged that welfare politics is increasingly multidimensional, i.e., policy change is the result of complex configurations of interests in a web of intersecting conflict lines (Bonoli and Natali 2012; Häusermann 2010, 2012). There is ample reason to believe that this holds particularly true when we address the politics of *social investment*, as the very logic of social investment deviates clearly from traditional welfare policies, i.e., it seeks to enhance labour market participation, rather than decommodifying welfare recipients.

In this contribution, I thus argue that to understand social investment policy development, we need to study the politics of reform in a *multidimensional policy space* (Häusermann 2010): the configuration of actors supporting and opposing social investment differs from the configuration of actors supporting and opposing traditional, compensatory social transfers. While this contribution provides evidence of this multidimensionality at the level of collective political actors, the contribution by Garritzmann et al. (2018) does so for the individual level. Multidimensionality allows for new actor alliances or actor coalitions – understood here simply as actors supporting a same reform – via two mechanisms: *political exchange* means that different actors defend a policy package because they trade off desirable elements across the multiple dimensions (Häusermann 2010). *Ambiguous agreements* refer to the fact that actors support a same reform for different motivations (Häusermann and Kübler 2010; Palier 2005). These coalitional dynamics are key to understanding policy development. Acknowledging the importance of multidimensionality also has implications for the kind of empirical research strategy we pursue. Complex multidimensional politics highlight case studies as a key methodological tool, because they allow us to trace coalitional dynamics. Consequently, this contribution focuses on German family policy development over time. It does not adopt an explicit causal design, but traces actor positions, conflict lines and reform coalitions over time. Its aim is not to explain family policy in every detail, but to understand how actor configurations matter for the understanding of social investment reforms in family policy in a least likely case. The characterization of Germany as a least likely (and therefore crucial) case is based on both its conservative legacy, strong Christian democracy, and the high reform and austerity pressure that dominated the agenda from the 1990s onwards (see also Blome [2017] for a similar argument).

2. Theoretical framework: dimensions of family policy development

Family policies in conservative welfare states have traditionally privileged the male breadwinner model, i.e., the support of family households mainly by means of financial transfers that were linked – if at all – to the earnings of the male breadwinner. In conservative welfare states with strong Christian Democratic parties, these transfers tended to be particularly generous. While they were supposed to support families financially, they also had the (side-)effect of stabilizing traditional gender roles, i.e., male breadwinner and female caregiving. Consequently, external care infrastructure, parental leave schemes or maternity insurance have traditionally been less developed in these regimes, compared to social-democratic welfare states (Lewis 1992). Social investment policies introduce a paradigmatic change in these conservative, Christian democratic regimes, because they represent a fundamentally different logic: they focus on strengthening social security via *ex ante* mechansims, i.e., human capital development, labour market participation and employment rights. Policies such as childcare infrastructure support both human capital investment for children and labour market participation of parents. Parental and maternity leave support may allow parents to keep their job over a time of intense care commitments, thereby contributing to skill preservation (if not too long and coupled with employment rights). Since traditional financial transfers and social investment follow such fundamentally different logics, it is unlikely that they generate identical patterns of political conflict.

How can we conceptualize the key conflict lines in the field of family policy in a post-industrial context? A one-dimensional conceptualization of political conflict may consider social investment policies at one extreme, while the traditional, income-protecting family policy constitutes the other extreme. Such a perspective, however, obstructs a view on the underlying multidimensional reform dynamics. Rather, in a two-dimensional policy space, four reform directions are possible (Beramendi et al. 2015; Häusermann 2010). Figure 1 visualizes such a space for the analysis of family policy change in relation to social investment. The two axes relate to the policy instruments at stake. The vertical dimension reflects positions in favour or against the expansion of social investment policies. The horizontal dimension reflects actor positions regarding policies, which provide additional resources to families via (passive) financial transfers. In the words of Beramendi et al. (2015: 15), they follow a 'consumptive' logic, as they re-allocate material resources in a way that makes both spending and gains immediate. The positions of actors on the two dimensions capture distinct economic-distributive interests, but they also reflect different values regarding the role and organization of the family in society.[1]

Hence, the two dimensions of social investment and income protection stand for the *policy instruments* at stake. Of course, collective actors can hold more or less expansive positions on either of these policy instruments. We can think of the quadrants as *policy goals*, i.e., ideal-typical outcomes of a policy reform strategy. And since collective actors pursue goals (rather than instruments *per se*), two actors may advocate the same policy instrument while pursuing different goals ('ambiguous agreement', e.g., Häusermann and Kübler [2010]; Palier [2005]).

In theorizing the goals that actors may pursue (represented schematically by the four quadrants), the literature on different family/social policy models (Fraser 1997) and varieties of familialism (Leitner 2003) is helpful, even though these typologies are based more strongly on the goals actors pursue in terms

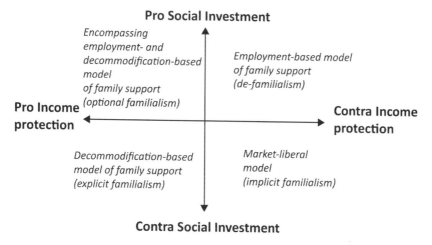

Figure 1. The policy space of post-industrial family politics.

of gender equality than in terms of employment- vs decommodification-oriented social policies, as we theorize here with regard to social investment.

The conservative welfare state has traditionally (*ante*-1980s) been characterized as a model of both low work- and low decommodification-support for families (i.e., a therefore market-liberal model), resulting in a system of breadwinner dependency, in which the (usually female) caregiver depends economically on the main breadwinner. Fraser (1997) – similarly to Sainsbury (1996)– characterizes this model as a male breadwinner approach, but Leitner's (2003: 354) characterization of 'implicit familialism' points more precisely to the resulting effect of a reform strategy that keeps state intervention generally restricted. The resulting familialism (i.e., the production of welfare via care work is relegated to the family) is implicit, rather than an explicit gender policy goal, as childcare can be bought on the market, but is not affordable for middle- and lower-class families.[2]

Actors whose preferences deviate from this liberal model of policy intervention can pursue different policy goals. If an actor advocates the extension of decommodifying support for families (via transfers), the result is a more 'explicit familialism' (Leitner 2003), which allows (and expects) families to afford the shouldering of care themselves. The gender typologies of welfare describe this model as one that relies on the separation of gender roles for men and women (Sainsbury 1996), or as 'caregiver parity' (Fraser 1997: 55), because it reduces the breadwinner dependency by compensating care work financially. However, actors may also pursue expansive income protection policies for purely de-commodifying (redistributive or status-preserving) reasons.

If actors advocate the expansion of social investment policies only (while adopting restrictive positions regarding passive benefits), they extend the support for families via skill formation, mobilization and preservation – i.e., via support of employment prospects (for either parents or children in the longer run). The goal pursued here is predominantly activation, enhancing the labour market as a source of welfare provision. The extension of childcare infrastructure is the key instrument in this respect, but leave policies that incentivize labour market participation (skill preservation over some time of leave) also count among the policy instruments that support the employment-based model, if they are not accompanied by generous income replacement policies. Such a strategy is most clearly 'defamilializing', as it lifts the care provision from the families. In terms of gender relations, such a policy strategy results in female work biographies aligning on male patterns and in a 'universal breadwinner' (Fraser 1997: 52) model.

Finally, actors who support both active and passive policy instruments in the field of family policy promote reforms in the direction of an 'optional familialism' (Leitner 2003: 354), because families do have a choice in allocating time and resources to either care or employment. Since both men and women do have a choice in being present in both the workplace and the family, the model has also been labelled 'individual earner-carer' model (Sainsbury 1996: 81).

My argument in this contribution is that this combinatory typology is useful not only to characterize policies and regimes, but also to assess political actor positions and coalitions. When locating actors in this space, we can identify coalitional potentials that drive policies towards social investment or away from it.

3. Design, data and methods

3.1. Case selection

In order to study actors' positions, actual coalition-building and policy development over time, I examine actor configurations since the late 1970s. I include all family policy reform processes at the national level between 1979 and 2013 in our sample. During this time,[3] 18 reform processes with 50 reform issues have taken place in Germany. One case is defined as a *reform issue* in a German family policy reform process. Hence, most reforms comprise several policy instruments. I analyse the positions of political actors on all 50 reform issues over time. The detailed content of all reforms is presented in the supplemental material. As to the selection of actors, I adopt an empirical approach: I include *all* organized actors in our sample that have made statements on the reform (either in consultations, hearings, in press statements or in Parliament). The number of actors hence also reflects the saliency of family policy reforms on the political agenda over time.

3.2. Data and methods

In order to analyse the development of family policy, I have retraced the issues and debates of all 18 reforms in detailed chronologies by means of secondary literature and primary sources (in particular governmental reports, parliamentary debates and reports on consultation procedures). In order to ensure that the inventory of reforms was complete and to understand actor motivations in (more recent) reforms, I have also conducted interviews with 12 family policy scholars and representatives of relevant organizations (see supplemental material for details). In order to trace actor positions and coalitional dynamics, I coded actor positions on all 50 reform issues. The unit of analysis is one actor's position on a specific reform issue. All actors' positions were coded on three aspects: (1) whether the actor was favourable to state intervention in this specific issue or not; (2) whether the social policy intervention should apply to all citizens (universal coverage) or only to parts of them; (3) whether benefits/services should be high or low, generous or limited. For each reform issue and for all available actors, these positions have been coded on a scale from 0 to 2: 1 means that the actor agrees to the position of the reform bill proposal; 2 means that an actor advocates a less generous policy (non-intervention, low benefits, low range of insured people); and 0 that the actor favours a more generous solution (universal, tax-financed, high benefit levels). In order to observe the position taken at a point in time when the actors voice their preferences most freely, I have relied on documents from the early stages of the decision-making processes: the records of the parliamentary debates (first reading) and official statements in the public hearings before the parliamentary commissions. The codings on all three aspects of the reform issues are highly correlated (between 0.9 and 0.98 across the three decades). I therefore averaged the positions for each reform element over the three aspects, which provides a single position of each actor on each reform issue.

In order to identify the actor positions and overall conflict configurations on social investment and income protection, I categorized all 50 reform issues in these two categories: 'Income protection policies' (i.e., child allowances and family benefits); and 'Social investment policies' (i.e., reforms expanding universal or means-tested childcare services and parental/maternal leave schemes from the 1990s onwards). Please see the supplemental material for a detailed discussion of these categorizations. For the analysis of results, I have then averaged actor positions per policy dimension (social investment and income replacement), and per decade, which generates an average position of each actor on each dimension per decade.

4. Empirical analysis

The empirical section of this contribution is structured as follows. After a brief discussion of the development of Germany's policy agenda, we show actors' positions and their evolution over time, and we discuss the coalitional dynamics for each time period.

4.1. Family policy development in Germany

German family policy-making has always been heavily influenced by historical legacies. After the Third Reich, state intrusion in the family and natalist policies were a taboo in the political discourse (Gerlach 2004; Naumann 2005). This did not prevent the Christian Democrats from developing a generous system of financial transfers and child allowances, differentiated according to the number of children (it was only under the social–liberal coalition in 1974 that child allowances for the first child were introduced). Until the 1960s, such child allowances remained mainly financed by employers for the working population. From the 1960s onwards, however, these private financing schemes were replaced by general tax revenues, and allowances granted independently from the labour market status of parents (Gerlach 2004). Other directions of family policy, e.g., maternity insurance, parental leave schemes, etc. have not gained strong relevance until the 1970, as the system centred around a clear legal institutionalization of the male breadwinner model (Blome 2017: 81–4).

However, this changed from the late 1970s onwards: since then, policy reform issues started to diversify beyond income protection. Table 1 contains all propositions concerning family policy discussed in the Bundestag since the 1980s, which have been categorized in social investment or income replacement policies. Maternity and parental leave policies have been prominently discussed under the social–liberal coalition in the late 1970s and to some extent under the government made by the Christian Democrats (CDU–CSU) and Liberals (FDP) (1983–1998), especially in 1985. However, these issues were never framed in a skill-oriented perspective, as their aim was to create disincentives for female labour market protection and to enhance material resources more generally. Hence, I do not count them as social investment (see supplemental material for more details). As a result, there were no social investment reform issues until the end of the 1980s. In the early 1990s, childcare services became more prominent on the agenda (not least in the wake of the 'abortion compromise' [see Blome 2017: 152ff]). However, throughout the 1990s, the 'explicit familialism' remained the dominant paradigm – supported both in conservative and to a large extent also in social-democratic milieus (Blome 2017). This changed quite radically towards the end of the 1990s, when skill-oriented social investment reforms appeared on the agenda under the Social Democrats (SPD)/Green government (increased tax deductions for external child care expenditures in 2001, incentives to shorten educational leaves in 2000, support of external child care infrastructure in 2004, expansion of educational benefits especially for working women in 2000). However, income protection policies also remained salient on the agenda in the more recent years, with increased child

Table 1. Frequency of social investment vs. income protection issues on Germany's reform agenda.

	1980s	1990s	2000s
Transfers universal	4	3	5
Tax cuts universal	2	4	2
Means-tested transfers	2		
Means-tested single parent family support	2	1	2
Income protection total	**10**	**8**	**9**
Skill-preserving parental leave			5
Childcare services general		2	9
Childcare services means-tested			
Social investment total	**0**	**2**	**14**

allowances for lone parents in 1999 or increases in child allowances in 1996, 1999, 2001, 2008, 2009 and 2012.

Overall, we therefore observe an increase in reform propositions dealing with social investment policies in the last decade. However, this increase did not come at the expense of income replacement policies, but in addition to these. Therefore, since the beginning of the 2000s, Germany's family policy is heading towards a hybrid model of family policy, which contains a combination of social investment policies with an upgrading of income protection policies. This hybrid development is very much the result of political exchange and ambiguous agreements between the left and business on the one hand, and between the left and Christian Democrats on the other hand. Eventually, the hybrid model brings the policy outcomes closer to an 'optional familialism' model. But it also undermines the goals of the social investment agenda to some extent.

We now turn to tracing actor positions and coalitional dynamics over time. While discussing the different periods, we briefly present important illustrative cases of reforms that show the coalitional dynamics typical of that period.

4.2. Coalitional dynamics in the 1980s

When aggregating all reforms between 1979 and 1990 and plotting average actor positions in Figure 2, we see the alignment of actors in the one-dimensional policy space that results from the absence of explicitly skill-based policy proposals during this period.

Figure 2 contains all actors that have made explicit statements in the respective reform processes. What we see is a rather clear polarization between the new left and family organizations at the expansive end of passive, income replacement policies on the one hand, and employer organizations on the other, with the Christian Democrats taking a middle position

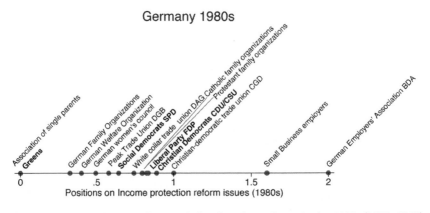

Figure 2. Actor positions in Germany's family policy reforms in the 1980s (1979–1990).

on the level of expansive passive benefits. Both the Social Democrats and the FDP (in coalition government until the early 1980s) demanded more generous income supporting policies than the Christian Democrats, especially when they were in opposition throughout the 1980s. Looking in more detail at the reforms that were discussed in this period (see the full list in the supplemental material) explains this alignment: the main focus of the early 1980s reforms (1981, 1983) was on expansive consumption transfers by the CDU/CSU and FDP government, with reforms of child allowances and family tax relieves. Both the left and the right supported such strong transfers, but differed mostly on the extent to which these should be progressive and whether they should benefit all families or only those with two or more children.

4.3. Coalitional dynamics in the 1990s: polarization over consumption policies

During the 1990s, reforms of income protection transfers continued to dominate the political agenda and preoccupations of the main parties (Blome 2017). They account for the strong polarization on the consumption axis that we see in Figure 3.

The only social investment reform of the conservative CDU/CSU/FDP government (in power until 1998) was in 1992, when reunification put pressure on adapting childcare structures in Western Germany to the more developed

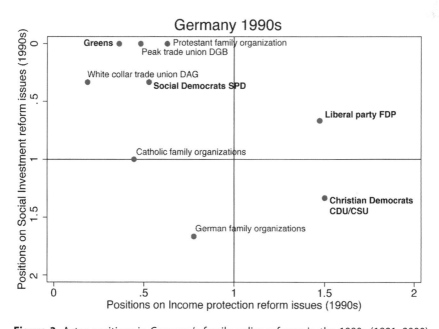

Figure 3. Actor positions in Germany's family policy reforms in the 1990s (1991–2000).

standards in Eastern Germany. The law basically introduced a legal right to childcare services, which was, however, not directly enforceable. For that reason, parts of the SPD and the Greens criticized the reform heavily. The conservative government enacted only one additional reform, in 1996, extending regressive tax cuts for higher income families and focusing child allowances on the third child. When the left came to power, they reacted in 1999 with a basically symmetrical reform that took these measures back, and also introduced an increase of tax deductions for external childcare costs (first federal law on family support 1999). Both reforms obviously increased polarization between the Left and conservatives strongly. However, the liberal party FDP supported the expansion of childcare services in 1992, thereby adopting an employment-supporting position while at the same time advocating relatively restrictive positions on additional income support. However, it is very telling that no single business organization position could at all be coded for this period: business simply did not take much interest in family policy debates in the 1990s, as hardly any of the reforms had a clear link to the labour market. It was only in the 2000s that both business organizations (mostly for reasons of enhancing female labour market participation) and Christian Democrats (mostly for demographic reasons) started to seriously consider social investment reforms.

4.4. Coalitional dynamics in the 2000s: multidimensional politics

It is only in the 2000s that the policy space became truly multidimensional, meaning that the actor configuration differed clearly between the two dimensions. Consequently, this became the most intense period of reform politics, with what some scholars have even labelled a 'transformative' change (Blome 2017: 214; Morgan 2013). Of course, it is also the period in which (in 2005) the grand coalition of SPD and CDU/CSU coalition governments starts, which facilitated broad agreements and political exchange across the reform dimensions, but it is noticeable that the multidimensional reform dynamics had started well before this change.

During the red–green government, the second law on family support in 2001 combined increases in traditional child allowances (income protection) with investments in childcare support for employed (tax reductions for childcare expenses) and to some extent also non-employed parents (flat-rate educational benefit). This package of both consumptive and investive measures allowed for political exchange between all major parties in the parliamentary debate in 2000. A similar dynamic applied to the 2000 reform of the law on educational benefits, which combined leave dispositions that should support labour market attachment with higher income replacement benefits. Similarly, the 2004 law on the support of childcare services (part of the Hartz reform package) was supported by all major parties, unions, employers and welfare organizations, as well as (through silent consent) by the CDU/CSU and FDP. While these opposition parties consented to the reforms, they did not go further with their demands (and the CDU emphasized its demand for at-home care structures via day mothers); hence, they defended relatively more restrictive positions. The 2004 reform in particular is a good example of an ambiguous agreement in this period, because it extended support for daycare centres and at the same time introduced a right to childcare for children below the age of three. Thereby, it gained approval from employers and the FDP for supporting labour market participation, and from the left for supporting women. More far-reaching reforms by the red–green government in terms of extending parental leave in 2000 and 2004, however, were not supported by the CDU/CSU, which is why it appears with a relatively more restrictive position in Figure 4. Overall, however, the first half of the first decade of the 2000s brought about a rapprochement of the main political parties.

Once the grand coalition took office, another instance of an ambiguous agreement took place: the 2007 law on parental leave and parental allowances introduced incentives for higher-income couples to share parental leave, and it received support from the government parties, but also from the greens, trade unions and employers. While employers were interested in creating labour market incentives for high-skilled women, the Greens and the left stressed the socially progressive dimension of the reform. Finally, from 2008 onwards, the government consistently pursued a hybrid reform

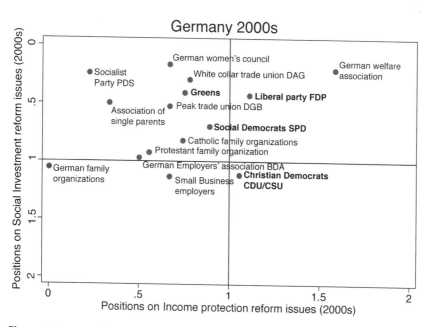

Figure 4. Actor positions in Germany's family policy reforms in the 2000s (2001–2013).

strategy: while expanding childcare services and support, it also expanded child allowances and special benefits for stay-at-home mothers. When combining both elements in one bill in 2008, the reform coalition spanned from the left to the right. This broad coalition did not, of course, agree on all elements of the reform (the left and employers opposed negative incentives for female labour market participation in 2012, and the FDP together with employers opposed means-tested benefits for low-income families in 2008), but since the overall government agenda was a package deal of expansion both in the direction of employment support and integrated support for employment and decommodification, it allowed for a paradigmatic change in the German family policy towards more social investment elements.

The ambiguity of the skill-approach that is specific of social investment (meaning that it can be read through various lenses as both gender equality policy or productivist labour market policy) has strongly contributed to the success of the social investment agenda, because it allowed to bring parts of the FDP and employers on board. In addition, the need for Christian democracy to reposition itself electorally and to attract more middle class, female votes through a more progressive agenda (Blome 2017; Fleckenstein 2011; Morgan 2013) have helped create this ambiguous support coalition for social investment that we see in Figure 4, but only the multidimensionality itself (combining social investment with transfers) has allowed to forge the broad support-base also among the conservative, Christian-democratic élites. However, not only the conservative and liberal actors have redefined their preferences over time, but also the left. Between the 1980s and the 2000s the SPD and the Greens have moved towards a more pronounced support of the employment-based model.

Hence, analysing the actors' positions over time shows that in Germany, there was no single conflict line that accounted for family policy modernization. Actor positions in Germany's family policy have indeed become more dispersed over time. In the 1980s, there was a clear left–right divide between the left and employers on matters of income protection. From the 1990s onwards, social investment and income protection have appeared on the political reform agenda simultaneously. In the 1990s, the correlation between actor positions on social investment and on income protection was still 0.5, suggesting a certain left–right association that we can also observe in Figure 3. However, these positions have become almost uncorrelated by the 2000s ($r = 0.04$), which means that the policy space has become truly multidimensional. There is no single dimension anymore that can represent family policy positions adequately. At first glance, the relative convergence of actors towards support of social investment in the 2000s may seem to contradict this finding, as it suggests an overall support coalition. But this broad coalition is precisely the result of actors being able to adopt different stances within the general paradigmatic change towards more social investment-oriented policies.

5. Conclusion

This contribution suggests a two-dimensional conceptualization of the dynamics of welfare state modernization in the field of family policy for the post-industrial age. Empirically, it analyses family policy development in the largest conservative welfare state, Germany, from the beginning of the 1980s until 2013. Germany shows – especially in the 2000s – movement towards 'optional familialism', a hybrid model of family policy reforms, where new social investment policies, i.e., childcare policies and maternity/parental insurance, are adopted alongside an expansion of traditional income protection policies.

The key argument of the contribution is that in order to understand the hybrid family policy development in Germany, we need to take the multidimensionality of reform politics seriously, and – consequently – adopt a coalitional approach to the study of policy change. Income protection and social investment are two dimensions that at least potentially divide actors in distinct ways and thereby generate possibilities for both political exchange and ambiguous agreements. Accordingly, the modernization of the conservative male breadwinner model does not follow a linear trajectory: it can go in the direction of at least two different types of policy development: optional familialism or defamilialism, depending on how social investment policies are combined with income replacement policies.

In sum, the German case shows that both reform dimensions of family policy have been salient in family policy reform debates since the 1990s, but to different extents. While income replacement dominated the political space in the 1980s and 1990s, actor positions became less linear, and by the 2000s we observed a multidimensional conflict configuration. The analysis shows that both the old and the new left, who have been supportive of social investment policies throughout the decades, are key actors for social investment reforms. But they are in need of allies either from the Christian democrats or the liberal actors (parties or employer organizations) to actually adopt social investment policies successfully. The social investment turn in Germany is mainly the result of two kinds of coalitions: ambiguous agreements between the left and employers on enhancing labour market participation, and political exchange between the left and the Christian Democrats, with the left pushing for social investment and the conservatives accompanying these reforms with parallel expansions of transfers to the traditional family model. The resulting, more converging configuration of actor positions in the 2000s has led to a combination of social investment policies with income protection measures and in consequence allowed for a 'hybrid modernization' of family policy in the direction of optional familialism. We conclude that we cannot study the development of either social investment or income protection policies in isolation. Policy development depends on the interaction of politics across both dimensions.

Notes

1. What today is often – and, from a contemporary perspective, rightfully – depicted as a patriarchal and inegalitarian system oppressing women's independence was then claimed by large parts of the women's movement itself, as Naumann (2005) shows for the German case.
2. However, family policy is made at sub-state levels, too. A study focusing on the development of policy outcomes would, of course, need to include the sub-state level reforms. For the tracing of coalitional dynamics, however, the 18 reforms provide a sufficient empirical basis.
3. This data are based on our investigation of all reform issues since the late 1970s in Germany's family policy (see supplemental material).

Acknowledgements

Previous versions of this contribution have been presented at the 2014 meeting of RC19 of the ISA in Yokohama, Japan, as well as at the Social Investment workshop in November 2016 in Lausanne, Switzerland. I am grateful to the participants of these conferences, as well as to the editors of this collection and three anonymous reviewers for helpful comments. I also would like to warmly thank Alexander Frind and Christine Zollinger for terrific research assistance.

Disclosure statement

No potential conflict of interest was reported by the author.

References

Beramendi, P., Häusermann, S., Kitschelt, H. and Kriesi, H.P. (2015) 'Introduction', in P. Beramendi, S. Häusermann, H. Kitschelt and H.P. Kriesi (eds.), *The Politics of Advanced Capitalism*, Cambridge: Cambridge University Press, pp. 1–66.

Blome, A. (2017) *The Politics of Work-Family Policies in Germany and Italy. Routledge Studies in the Political Economy of the Welfare State*, London/New York, NY: Routledge.

Bonoli, G. and Natali, D. (2012) *The Politics of the New Welfare State*, Oxford: Oxford University Press.

Fleckenstein, T. (2011) 'The politics of ideas in welfare state transformation: Christian democracy and the reform of family policy in Germany', *Social Politics International Studies in Gender, State & Society* 18(4): 543–71.

Fraser, N. (1997) *Justice Interruptus*, New York: Routledge.

Garritzmann, J., Häusermann, S., Palier, B. and Zollinger, C. (2017) 'WoPSI – The world politics of social investment', LIEPP Working Paper, n°64, March 2017.

Garritzmann, J., Busemeyer, M. and Neimanns, E. (2018) 'Public demand for social investment: new supporting coalitions for welfare state reform in Western Europe?', *Journal of European Public Policy*.

Gerlach, I. (2004) *Familienpolitik*, Wiesbaden: Verlag für Sozialwissenschaften.

Häusermann, S. (2010) *The Politics of Welfare Reform in Conservative Europe. Modernization in Hard Times*, Cambridge: Cambridge University Press.

Häusermann, S. (2012). 'The politics of new and old social risks', in G. Bonoli and D. Natali (eds.), *The Politics of the New Welfare State*, Oxford: Oxford University Press, pp. 111–33.

Häusermann, S. and Kriesi, H.P. (2015) 'Dimensions and configurations in individual-level preferences and party choice', in P. Beramendi, S. Häusermann, H. Kitschelt and H.P. Kriesi (eds.), *The Politics of Advanced Capitalism*, Cambridge: Cambridge University Press, pp. 202–230.

Häusermann, S. and Kübler, D. (2010) 'Policy frames and coalition dynamics in the recent reforms of Swiss family policy', *German Policy Studies* 6(3): 163–94.

Jenson, J. (2012) 'Redesigning citizenship regimes after neoliberalism: moving towards social investment', in N. Morel, B. Palier and J. Palme (eds.), *Towards a Social Investment Welfare State? Ideas, Policies and Challenges*, Bristol: Policy Press, pp. 61–87.

Leitner, S. (2003) 'Varieties of familialism: the caring function of the family in comparative perspective', *European Societies* 5(4): 353–75.

Lewis, J. (1992) 'Gender and the development of welfare regimes', *Journal of European Social Policy* 2(3): 159–73.

Morgan, K.J. (2013) 'Path shifting of the welfare state: electoral competition and the expansion of work-family policies in Western Europe', *World Politics* 65(1): 73–115.

Naumann, I. (2005) 'Child care and feminism in West Germany and Sweden in the 1960s and 1970s', *Journal of European Social Policy* 15(1): 47–63.

Nikolai, R. (2012) 'Towards social investment? Patterns of public policy in the OECD world', in N. Morel, B. Palier and J. Palme (eds.), *Towards a Social Investment Welfare State? Ideas, Policies and Challenges*, Bristol: The Policy Press, pp. 91–117.

Palier, B. (2005) 'Ambiguous agreement, cumulative change: French social policy in the 1990s', in W. Streeck and K. Thelen (eds.), *Beyond Continuity. Institutional Change in Advanced Political Economies*, Oxford: Oxford University Press, pp. 127–144.

Sainsbury, D. (1996) *Gender Equality and Welfare States*, Cambridge: Cambridge University Press.

The Matthew effect in childcare use: a matter of policies or preferences?

Emmanuele Pavolini and Wim Van Lancker ⓘ

ABSTRACT
Under the social investment paradigm, formal childcare services are heralded as being the policy instrument *par excellence* to combat social exclusion. However, it was shown that a Matthew effect (ME) in its use is present in almost all European countries: disadvantaged children are less likely to use childcare than more advantaged children. In this contribution we aim to uncover the cause of the ME by distinguishing between supply-side and demand-side explanations. This refers to constraints in the availability or affordability of childcare and to dominant cultural norms on motherhood. In doing so, we take due account of the role of employment. The results show that the ME in formal childcare cannot be explained by class differences in employment. Moreover, the ME is related to the supply-side and much less to the demand-side. Structural constraints in childcare provision matter everywhere and tend to limit the uptake of childcare, especially for disadvantaged children. In contrast, cultural norms on motherhood are a less important predictor of the ME in childcare use. This means that more investment in the provision of childcare services is necessary in order to achieve its ambitious policy goals.

Introduction

The social investment (SI) perspective emphasizes that social policy should not only provide a *buffer* for protection against the occurrence of social risks, but should focus on raising the *stock* of human capital and easing the *flow* of labour market integration (Hemerijck 2018). One important piece of the SI puzzle is the provision of high-quality early childhood education and care services (henceforth: formal childcare services).

At first glance, providing formal childcare services for young children is the policy instrument *par excellence* to raise the stock and ease the flow in the short term as well as over the life course. Childcare services allow for higher

---

ⓑ Supplemental data for this article can be accessed at https://doi.org/10.1080/13501763.2017.1401108

levels of maternal employment, in turn raising the family income and reducing welfare dependency at the individual level and contributing to a
balanced budget at the country level. Provided the quality of the service is sufficiently high, formal childcare contributes to child development, in turn
increasing their chances to perform well in school and in the labour market
later on. This should be beneficial in particular for children growing up in disadvantaged circumstances (Esping-Andersen *et al.* 2002).

Yet, for these beneficial outcomes to materialize, formal childcare services
need to reach those disadvantaged children. Previous research has shown
that the use of formal childcare by young children is socially stratified, with
low-income or low-skilled parents being less likely to enrol their children in
formal childcare services relative to more advantaged families (Van Lancker
2013). As a matter of fact, inequality in formal childcare use is the norm in
European countries. Such inequality in outcomes has been referred to as a
Matthew effect (ME), the observation that the benefits of government spending on social policy disproportionly accrue to middle- and upper-class relative to other social groups (Bonoli and Liechti 2018).

In this article we go beyond the state of the art by focusing on the root of
the ME in formal childcare use across 27 European member states. Hitherto,
in-depth investigations on how to understand social differentials in childcare
use were limited to single countries (Abrassart and Bonoli 2015; Krapf 2014;
Van Lancker and Ghysels 2012; Vandenbroeck *et al.* 2014). Only one exploratory study investigated how welfare state characteristics correlate with childcare inequality in a comparative way (Van Lancker and Ghysels 2016). We
propose an analytical distinction between the 'demand-side' and the
'supply-side' in explaining the ME in formal childcare use. The supply-side
refers to the availability and affordability of formal childcare, which is directly
amenable by policy, while the demand-side refers to the dominant cultural
norms on motherhood, i.e., what type of care is in the best interest of the children. Simply put: do MEs emerge because working class families face structural barriers in securing a place in formal childcare, or because they give
less preference to using formal childcare compared to middle- and upper-
class families? Looming large is the role of employment, since in particular
two-earner families have a pressing need for formal childcare services,
while household employment patterns differ across social groups (De
Wachter *et al.* 2016).

Child-centred investment and the Matthew effect

Social investment is child-centred in the sense that it is grafted on the belief
that life chances in modern economies depend on human capital accumulation in early childhood, and that societies need able, productive adults to
increase employment rates and competitiveness. Esping-Andersen and

colleagues (2002) argue that the cornerstone of any European social inclusion strategy should focus on children and their families. This argument resonated strongly in policy circles. In its 2013 Recommendation on Investing in Children, for instance, the European Commission puts the provision of high-quality childcare services centre-stage to reduce inequality and increase maternal labour market participation.

The availability of formal care services correlates strongly with maternal labour market participation (Esping-Andersen *et al.* 2002). Insofar the use of formal childcare enables mothers to engage in paid employment, this has a direct impact on the family income and, hence, on the circumstances in which their children are raised. Enrolment in formal childcare services of sufficient quality enhances cognitive and non-cognitive skills, enabling children to be better prepared for learning (Burger 2010; Leseman 2009). Given the fact that there is a strong correlation between the educational level of parents, the cognitive skills and school readiness of their children (Feinstein 2003), quality childcare helps to reduce development gaps between children from different social backgrounds (Leseman and Slot 2014).

The presence of an ME is a problem for a child-centred investment strategy. It is a process of cumulative advantage in which a favourable outcome in one institutional setting becomes a resource producing further gains in other institutional settings (DiPrete and Eirich 2006). The quality of parental care differs greatly between socioeconomic groups, and school systems in many European countries are known to reproduce or even reinforce existing inequalities (Schütz *et al.* 2008). Unequal participation in formal childcare only reinforces this pattern of accumulation of advantage and disadvantage. As such, investing in childcare services runs the risks of increasing the gap among children by the time they start school.

Analytical framework and research questions

We make an analytical distinction between three mechanisms potentially related to the ME in formal childcare use.

First of all, we expect the ME to be related to maternal employment. The availability of childcare correlates with maternal employment. Since in particular working mothers need formal childcare, the direction of causality doesn't necessarily run from childcare use to employment. Some studies have shown that the creation of additional childcare places mainly crowds out informal arrangements and in particular benefits mothers who are already employed (e.g., Havnes and Mogstad 2011). Since the increase in maternal employment observed in developed welfare states over the past few decades was a socially stratified process with higher-educated mothers being much more likely to work compared to lower-educated mothers (De Wachter *et al.* 2016), it could be the case that the ME is simply a reflection of the social gap in maternal employment. Therefore, the first research question we investigate is to what extent the ME in formal childcare use can be explained by maternal employment (RQ1).

Second, we expect the ME to be related to what we refer to as 'supply-side' factors: the availability and affordability of formal childcare services. An ME can emerge as a result of how childcare policies work, how they select (directly or indirectly) families, creating situations where middle- and upper-classes face fewer barriers to benefit from those services. In case of rationing (supply is lower than demand), the choices made by public authorities' can induce inequality. Abrassart and Bonoli (2015) focus on the institutional regulation of childcare provision in their study of a Swiss canton. Their findings suggest that differences among local authorities in the fees charged to low-income households is a significant predictor of inequality in use. The issue of availability and affordability is also related to employment. Two-earner families with stable occupations are more prevalent among middle- and upper-class families, and these families benefit more from childcare services with typical opening hours (Bihan and Martin 2004). They usually have more means to pay childcare fees (and often benefit from tax deductions) as well. In contrast, atypical, flexible and unpredictable working hours are more prevalent amongst lower social classes (Pintelon *et al.* 2013). Therefore, the second research question is to what extent supply-side constraints in terms of availability and affordability in the provision of childcare services are related to the ME in formal childcare use (RQ2).

Third, even if employment opportunities were equally distributed over social groups and no constraints in the supply of formal childcare services were at play, MEs can emerge because, on the demand-side, some parents might prefer taking care for their children themselves. This pertains to the role of culture in the relationship between care and work. Following Pfau-Effinger, culture is defined as 'the system of collective constructions of meaning by which human beings define reality and to which they orient their behaviour' (2014: 86). Previous research has shown that parents with more traditional attitudes regarding motherhood and employment are less likely to work and to use formal childcare (Steiber and Haas 2012). Few studies on childcare have given attention to the role of social class in terms of cultural norms (Duncan *et al.* 2003; Vincent *et al.* 2008). These studies show distinct class patterns in parents' decisions concerning childcare. If the dominant norm in a country offers no 'cultural support' for maternal employment and outsourcing childcare, MEs might emerge, in particular if personal preferences are in sync with the dominant norm. Therefore, the third research question is to what extent the dominant cultural norms on motherhood are related to the ME in formal childcare use (RQ3).

Finally, demand- and supply-side factors are related to each other. Policies may influence individual work–family choices, in turn changing dominant aggregated norms over time, but prevailing expectations concerning the role of motherhood may shape childcare policies as well (Brooks and Manza 2007). Moreover, demand-side and supply-side factors can reinforce or counteract each other in their impact on the ME in formal childcare use. The fourth research question is to what extent combinations of demand- and supply-side factors are related to the ME in formal childcare use (RQ4).

Research design

Data

The data used throughout this study are drawn from the 2010 European Union Labour Force Survey (EU-LFS) *ad hoc* module 'reconciliation between work and family life'. The *ad hoc* module includes information on the use of formal childcare services for young children as well as on the barriers for labour market participation connected to the availability and affordability of formal childcare services. Being an add-on to the regular EU-LFS, this provides us with the advantage of having a cross-country comparable database with larger sample sizes compared to previous research that is often based on European Union Statistics on Income and Living Conditions (EU-SILC) data.

The EU-LFS database includes 27 European member states (no data for Croatia). The analytical focus is on the level of the household (since childcare is a decision affecting all working-age adults in the household), and the sample is limited to families with a youngest child below three years old. The final sample consists of 32,643 families with young children (see Table A1 in the Online Appendix). The EU-LFS data is complemented by country-level data drawn from the European Values Study (EVS) of 2008.

Variables

The dependent variable is the *use of formal childcare services*. This includes paid childminders, preschool and childcare centres, apart from compulsory school. The respondents are asked whether they have used formal childcare services for their youngest child. The variable is dummy coded, reflecting whether families have or haven't used formal childcare for their youngest child.

The main independent variable of interest is a measure of social class of the household. In contrast with previous studies on this subject, adopting either educational level of the mother or income quintile of the household as indicators of social background, we rely on the Erikson–Goldthorpe–Portocarero (EGP) class scheme (Erikson and Goldthorpe 1992). This is more in line with political science and sociological definitions of social background, rooted in the status and characteristics of (former) participation in the labour market as measured by the International Standard Classification of Occupation 1988. We adopt a simplified version of the EGP class scheme based on three classes: (1) 'managers and professionals'; (2) 'white-collar workers'; (3) 'blue-collar workers and elementary occupations'.

To take the role of *employment* into account, we include a dummy variable measuring whether the mother in the household (or the father if no mother is present) is in paid employment. We focus on maternal employment, since previous research has made clear that childbirth negatively effects the labour supply of women, not that of men (e.g., Uunk *et al.* 2005); hence, the labour market status of the mother is relevant to understand whether families enrol their children in formal childcare. Yet, by means of robustness check, we also tested a variable measuring the work intensity of the household, operationalized by the ratio of the number of working adults to all adults in the household. The interpretation of the results (not shown) does not change.

In order to test whether supply-side or demand-side dimensions are related to social class differentials in formal childcare use, we include country-level variables measuring structural barriers to childcare participation and dominant cultural norms on motherhood. For gauging the role of structural barriers, we first draw on a set of questions included in the *ad hoc* module on the reasons why respondents with at least one child below 14 years old with young children don't work or work only part-time. Respondents that were not seeking a job or were only working part-time were asked to indicate whether this was owing to structural reasons ('suitable care services for children are not available or affordable') or that the availability or affordability of care facilities did not influence their work arrangement (which suggests a matter of choice). We calculate a country-level variable 'structural constraints' measuring the weighted proportion of respondents referring to structural reasons not to work (more).

Third, for the demand-side, we create a variable measuring dominant cultural norms on motherhood based on the question 'A pre-school child is likely to suffer if his or her mother works'. The variable measures the extent to which social norms disapprove of the mother's role in the labour market. The logic behind using this question is that if one believes that working is bad for one's child, this will affect the demand for formal childcare. We draw on the EVS wave 2008 to construct an aggregated measure of dominant norms on motherhood for all countries included in our sample, based on a subsample of respondents with children below 14 years old.

All models control for the following individual and household characteristics: highest level of education in the household (in three categories, following the International Standard Classification of Education classification

[ISCED]), age of the youngest child, number of children in the household, migration background (dummy coded: 0 = native, 1 = born in another country), being a single parent, and currently using or having used maternity or parental leave. Summary statistics of these variables are reported in Table A2 in Online Appendix.

Method

To deal with the clustered nature of our dataset (households are nested in countries) and since our dependent variable is a binary indicator, we apply multilevel logistic regression models. In particular, we estimate the probability to have used formal childcare services by means of random intercept models with country being the higher level. A multilevel design takes the hierarchical structure of the data into account and yields less biased standard errors compared to a logistic regression model with country dummies (e.g., Hox 2002). The focus of the analyses is on the ME in formal childcare use, tested by examining the relationship between social class and formal childcare use. We empirically test whether the ME can be explained by labour market participation, and whether the supply-side factors, demand-side factors or a combination of both are associated with it. The change in deviance is reported to estimate the fit of the models.

Results

Descriptive results

Panel A of Figure 1 shows the proportion of families with young children having used formal childcare services for their youngest child during a regular week, panel B shows the percentage point difference in the proportion of formal childcare use between the highest (I) and the lowest (III) social classes.

EU member states are characterized by great diversity in terms of formal childcare uptake. Differences range from 15 per cent or less in Czech Republic, Slovak Republic, Romania, Hungary, Latvia and Austria, over about 30 per cent in Finland, Germany and Ireland, to over 50 per cent in Portugal, Sweden, France, Luxemburg and Denmark. These averages conceal stark differences across social classes. Only Denmark and Malta combine high levels of formal childcare use with the absence of an ME. In Sweden, the difference is limited to less than 10 per cent. In countries such as Luxemburg, France, Portugal, Netherlands and Belgium, social class differences range between 25 and 40 per cent. It is an arithmetic regularity that percentage point differences between social classes are lower in countries reporting low levels of average formal childcare use, but even then, differences

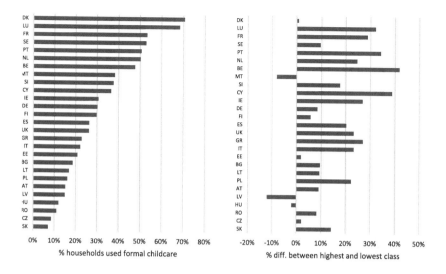

Figure 1. Average and social class differences in formal childcare use, European countries, 2010.

Note: Own calculations on EU-LFS 2010. Sample selection: households with a youngest child < three years old. Country abbreviations: DK = Denmark; LU = Luxemburg; FR = France; SE = Sweden; PT = Portugal; NL = Netherlands; BE = Belgium; MT = Malta; SI = Slovenia; CY = Cyprus; IE = Ireland; DE = Germany; FI = Finland; ES = Spain; UK = United Kingdom; GR = Greece; IT = Italy; EE = Estonia; BG = Bulgaria; LT = Lithuania; PL = Poland; AT = Austria; LV = Latvia; HU = Hungary; RO = Romania; CZ = Czech Republic; SK = Slovak Republic.

regularly amount to 10 per cent points. It is clear that the ME in formal childcare use across European Union (EU) member states is the norm rather than the exception.

Figure 2 shows how European countries score on the demand-side and supply-side dimensions of formal childcare use. The two indicators are only weakly correlated ($r = 0.18$). The scatterplot shows how countries can score high on both dimensions, on only one dimension, or score low on both dimensions. Drawing on these two dimensions, four groups of countries can be roughly distinguished. A first group consists of Ireland, Spain, Belgium and United Kingdom. In these countries, the share of respondents reporting traditional norms on motherhood is below-average, but an above-average share of respondents indicates structural constraints in childcare provision. In a second group, Bulgaria, Germany, Latvia, Poland, Greece, Romania and Austria, an above-average level of structural constraints is combined with more traditional norms on motherhood. The third group consists of Lithuania, Italy, Cyprus, Portugal, Malta, Estonia, Luxemburg and Hungary. In these countries the dominant norm on motherhood is traditional with a below-average share of people indicating supply-side problems. Finally, a fourth group comprises Denmark, Sweden, Finland and the Netherlands, as well as Slovenia, Czech Republic, France and the Slovak Republic. Here, the dominant norm is more

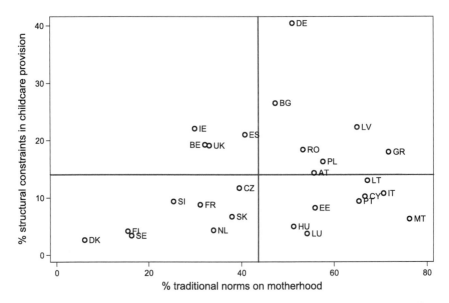

Figure 2. Supply-side and demand-side dimensions of formal childcare use, European countries, 2010.

Note: Horizontal and vertical lines represent average values of both dimensions.

progressive and structural constraints are limited. Yet, even in these countries, between 10 and 40 per cent of respondents adhere to traditional norms on motherhood, and that 30 per cent or more of families with young children haven't used formal childcare for their youngest child (cf. Figure 1).

Multivariate results

Model 1a in Table 1 shows the association between social class and formal childcare use, controlled for individual and household characteristics; Model 1b estimates whether the relationship between social class and formal child-care use is affected by maternal employment.

Model 1a confirms the significant and substantial class differentials in formal childcare use. Converting logit coefficients to probabilities, the model predicts that 35 per cent of families in the highest social class have used formal childcare for their youngest child, 30 per cent of families in the second class, and 23 per cent in the lowest class, across countries and con-trolled for individual and household characteristics. Full models showing all coefficients are reported in Table A3 in the Online Appendix. These models show that individual and household characteristics significantly influence the probability to use formal childcare.

To investigate to what extent maternal employment might explain these social class differentials in formal childcare use, model 1b adds the variable

Table 1. Multilevel logistic regression models estimating the probability to use formal childcare.

	1a		1b		2		3	
	coeff.	(se)	coeff.	(se)	coeff.	(se)	coeff.	(se)
Social class (ref. = I)								
II	−0.325***	(0.034)	−0.085	(0.060)	−0.164	(0.095)	−0.571***	(0.056)
III	−0.755***	(0.048)	−0.173**	(0.065)	0.248*	(0.119)	−0.872***	(0.088)
Maternal employment (ref. = no)			1.530***	(0.054)	1.289***	(0.033)	1.283***	(0.034)
Maternal employment* Social class								
II			−0.310***	(0.069)				
III			−0.513***	(0.090)				
Structural constraints					−0.020	(0.018)		
* Social class								
II					−0.012**	(0.004)		
III					−0.037***	(0.006)		
Traditional norms					−0.022*	(0.009)		
* Social class								
II					−0.001	(0.002)		
III					−0.004	(0.002)		
Country groups (ref = 1)								
Group 2							−0.926	(0.528)
Group 3							−0.390	(0.516)
Group 4							0.084	(0.515)
* Social class								
Group 2 * II							0.307**	(0.090)
Group 2 * III							0.106	(0.127)
Group 3 * II							0.436***	(0.090)
Group 3 * III							0.817***	(0.122)
Group 4 * II							0.501***	(0.081)
Group 4 * III							0.846***	(0.112)
Variance component								
Country	0.878***	(0.243)	0.921***	(0.254)	.618***	(0.173)	.696***	(0.194)
Model fit								
Deviance	32629.97		30969.79		30935.79		30894.19	
N(households)	32643		32643		32643		32643	
N(countries)	27		27		27		27	

Notes: Results from multilevel logistic regression models based on EU-LFS 2010. Sample: families with a youngest child below three years old. Social class categories: I = Managers/professionals; 2 = White-collar; 3 =Blue-collar/elementary occupations. Country groups: 1 = Structural constraints + progressive norms; 2 = Structural constraints + traditional norms; 3 = No structural constraints + traditional norms; 4 = No structural constraints + progressive norms. All models are controlled for age of the youngest child, number of children in the household, highest educational level of the household, country of birth, being a single parent, and leave use. Full models are reported in Table A3 in the Online Appendix. Significance levels: ***$p < 0.001$, **$p < 0.01$, *$p < 0.05$.

depicting maternal employment and its interaction with social class to the estimation. The likelihood ratio test suggests a significantly better fit. The coefficients show that in households where the mother does not work, the social class differential in formal childcare use disappears almost completely. This is expected, since households with young children where the mother stays at home are less in need of formal childcare. This points, first and foremost, to the reciprocal relationship between maternal employment and childcare use, and suggests that a social investment strategy needs to focus on increasing labour market participation in order to increase formal childcare use as well.

Yet, the interaction of social class with maternal employment is significant, suggesting that a labour market strategy alone will not suffice. Even among households with employed mothers, there are significant social class differentials in formal childcare use. Converted to probabilities, this amounts to 47 per cent of households from the highest social class predicted to have used formal childcare for their youngest child, over 39 per cent of households from the second class, to 34 per cent of the lowest class. In sum, the ME in formal childcare use cannot be readily explained by individual characteristics, nor employment status.

Let us now turn to the question how supply-side and demand-side issues are associated with social class differentials in formal childcare use. Model 2 tests the role of structural constraints (supply-side dimension) and cultural norms on motherhood (demand-side dimension) by adding cross-level interactions with social class. Cross-level interactions test whether the nature of the relationship between social class and formal childcare use changes as a function of structural constraints or cultural norms on motherhood. Model 3 tests how the interplay of structural constraints and cultural norms affects particular countries by adding the country cluster dummies identified *supra*. We tested all of these models controlling for economic development (measured as gross domestic product [GDP] per capita) and the state of the labour market (measured as the unemployment rate) at the country level, as well as with a random slope allowing the effect of social class to vary between countries. Since the results do not fundamentally change, we show the more parsimonious models without these macro-level controls (see also the warnings issued by Bryan and Jenkins [2015] about adding higher-level variables and cross-level interactions when the number of higher level observations is limited).

The results in model 2 show that the main effect of structural constraints is not significant but that the interaction effect with social class is, while the main effect of cultural norms is significant but the interaction effect with social class is not. Because cross-level interaction terms in a logit framework are notoriously difficult to interpret, Figure 3 visualizes how the supply and demand-side variables relate to social class differentials in formal childcare use. The figure reports predicted probabilities for using formal childcare by social class, over (1) the share of respondents indicating structural constraints to work related to formal childcare service, and (2) the share of the population reporting traditional norms on motherhood.

The figure shows that more traditional norms on motherhood *and* more structural constraints in childcare provision are associated with lower probabilities to use formal childcare across social classes. However, the figure shows that structural constraints in childcare provision hurt the lower social

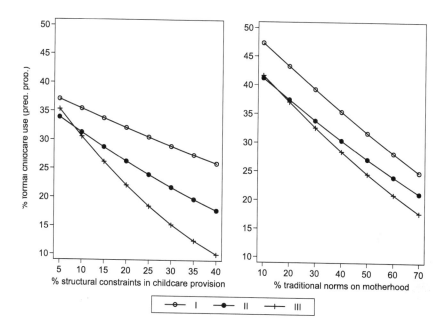

Figure 3. Predicted probabilities of formal childcare use by social class over demand-side and supply-side dimensions.

Note: Predicted probabilities based on model 2. Legend: social class I = Managers/professionals; II = White-collar; III = Blue-collar/elementary occupations.

classes relatively more. While the social class differential in formal childcare use is limited in countries where only a small share of respondents reports structural constraints, the gap widens strongly as structural constraints in childcare provision increase (RQ2). The effect of traditional norms on motherhood on social class differentials is not significant: the ME occurs in both more traditional and more progressive countries (RQ3).

It might be the case that the social gap in countries reporting high levels of structural constraints can be explained by the countries reporting high levels of traditional norms that also score high on the supply dimension, or vice versa. To test for this, we add the four groups of countries identified above to the model. Group 1 consists of countries combining higher levels of structural constraints in childcare provision with progressive norms on motherhood; group 2 combines higher levels of structural constraints with traditional norms on motherhood; group 3 includes countries with lower levels of structural constraints but traditional norms; and group 4 combines lower levels of structural constraints with progressive norms. If the supply-side dimension is more important in explaining MEs than the demand-side dimension, social class differentials should be particularly large in country groups 1 and 2; if the opposite holds, social class differentials should be larger in country groups 3 and 4. If both dimensions are important, social class differentials should be smallest in group 4. We add an interaction effect between the four country groups (which represent constructed interactions between the demand-side and supply-side indicators) and social class to model 3. Here, too, the results are visualized by means of predicted probabilities in Figure 4 to facilitate its interpretation.

Figure 4 shows that average formal childcare use is highest in countries where supply and demand are aligned, and lowest in countries where constraints in both supply and demand reinforce each other. Confirming the results from model 2, given a similar level of supply, formal childcare use tends to be lower when norms on motherhood are more traditional. Most importantly, however, differences between social classes in the probability to use formal childcare services are related to structural constraints (in groups 1 and 2), not to traditional norms on motherhood (in groups 3 and 4). Succinctly summarized: if the dominant norms on motherhood are biased against maternal employment and formal childcare use, families across classes are affected in a similar way. If the supply of childcare places is constrained, in particular families from the lower classes are hurt.

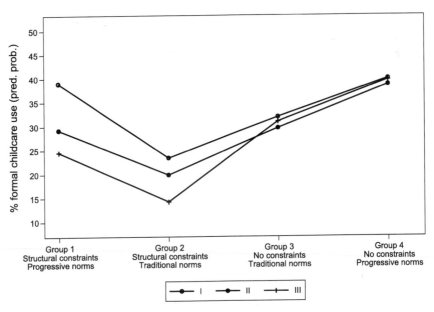

Figure 4. Predicted probabilities of formal childcare use by social class, over country groups.

Note: Predictions based on model 3. Group 1: Ireland; Spain; Belgium, and United Kingdom. Group 2: Germany; Bulgaria; Latvia; Poland; Greece; Romania; and Austria. Group 3: Lithuania; Cyprus; Estonia; Italy; Portugal; Malta; Luxemburg; and Hungary. Group 4: Denmark; Sweden; Finland; the Netherlands; Slovenia; Czech Republic; France; and Slovak Republic. Legend: social class I = Managers/professionals; II = White-collar; III = Blue-collar/elementary occupations.

Conclusion and discussion

Three conclusions stand out from our analysis. First, it is beyond doubt that the ME can be observed in formal childcare use in most European countries: both descriptive and multivariate analyses show substantial class differentials in childcare use. Second, the ME cannot be explained simply by class differentials in maternal employment. Even among households with employed mothers there are significant differences in formal childcare use between social classes. Third, the ME is related to supply-side and much less so to demand-side issues. Structural constraints in childcare provision matter everywhere and tend to limit the uptake of childcare especially for children growing up in disadvantaged circumstances. In contrast, dominant cultural norms on motherhood are a less important predictor of the ME in childcare use.

From a SI point-of-view, this is encouraging. Structural constraints in the availability or affordability are amenable by policies. This entails increasing the availability of formal childcare services, imposing quality regulations, and keeping parental fees at bay. In sum, this calls for *more* SI, and in particular higher levels of spending on childcare services, since government expenditures and childcare coverage are closely related (Van Lancker 2017).

The importance of the supply-side for mitigating the ME does not mean that cultural norms are not important to take into consideration. The probability of using formal childcare tends to be lower for all families in countries with more traditional norms, irrespective of supply-side constraints. Even in countries where the dominant norm is progressive, a substantial share of people still adheres to more traditional norms on motherhood. This means that not all families will be convinced that using formal childcare is the best thing to do, even if available and affordable. Such 'demand-side' constraint is currently not considered in the SI paradigm but should be explicitly dealt with in order to set achievable policy goals.

The ME in formal childcare means that government investment in formal childcare provision today is not likely to deliver on its promises to combat inequality in early life in the future; this might reinforce existing inequalities rather than mitigating them; the exact opposite of what the SI paradigm seeks to achieve.

Acknowledgments

The authors would like to thank Jeroen Horemans, the participants in the ESPAnet 2016 conference and in 2017 seminar 'Investing in children' in Madrid, and two anonymous referees for valuable and constructive comments and suggestions.

Disclosure statement

No potential conflict of interest was reported by the authors.

Funding

This work was supported by a postdoctoral research grant (no. 12P5215N) of the Research Foundation - Flanders (FWO).

ORCID

Wim Van Lancker ⓘ http://orcid.org/0000-0003-4071-5329

References

Abrassart, A. and Bonoli, G. (2015) 'Availability, cost or culture? obstacles to childcare services for low-income families', *Journal of Social Policy* 44(4): 787–806.

Bihan, B.L. and Martin, C. (2004) 'Atypical working hours: consequences for childcare arrangements', *Social Policy & Administration* 38(6): 565–590.

Bonoli, G. and Liechti, F. (2018) 'Good intentions and Matthew effects: access biases in participation in active labour market policies', *Journal of European Public Policy*. doi:10.1080/13501763.2017.1401105

Brooks, C. and Manza, J. (2007) *Why Welfare States Persist. The Importance of Public Opinion in Democracies*, Chicago, IL: University of Chicago Press.

Burger, K. (2010) 'How does early childhood care and education affect cognitive development? An international review of the effects of early interventions for children from different social backgrounds', *Early Childhood Research Quarterly* 25(2): 140–165.

De Wachter, D., Neels, K. Wood, J. and Vergauwen, J. (2016) 'The educational gradient of maternal employment patterns in 11 European countries', in D. Mortelmans *et al.* (ed.), *Changing Family Dynamics and Demographic Evolution*, Cheltenham, UK: Edward Elgar Publishing, pp. 140–178.

DiPrete, T.A. and Eirich, G.M. (2006) 'Cumulative advantage as a mechanism for inequality: a review of theoretical and empirical developments', *Annual Review of Sociology* 32: 271–297.

Duncan, S., Edwards, R. and Reynolds, T. (2003) 'Motherhood, paid work and partnering: values and theories', *Work, Employment & Society* 17(2): 309–330.

Erikson, R. and Goldthorpe, J.H. (1992) *The Constant Flux: A Study of Class Mobility in Industrial Societies*, Oxford: Oxford University Press.

Esping-Andersen, G., Gallie, D., Hemerijck, A. and Myles, J. (2002) *Why We Need a New Welfare State*, Oxford: Oxford University Press.

Feinstein, L. (2003) 'Inequality in the early cognitive development of British children in the 1970 cohort', *Economica* 70: 73–97.

Havnes, T. and Mogstad, M. (2011) 'Money for nothing? universal child care and maternal employment', *Journal of Public Economics* 95: 1455–1465.

Hemerijck, A. (2018) 'Social investment as a policy paradigm', *Journal of European Public Policy* doi:10.1080/13501763.2017.1401111

Hox, J.J. (2002) *Multilevel Analysis: Techniques and Applications*, London: Lawrence Erlbaum Associates.

Krapf, S. (2014) 'Who uses public childcare for 2-year-old children? coherent family policies and usage patterns in Sweden, Finland and western Germany', *International Journal of Social Welfare* 23: 25–40.

Leseman, P. (2009) 'The impact of high quality education and care on the development of young children: a review of the literature', in EACEA (ed.), *Early Childhood Education and Care: Tackling Social and Cultural Inequalities*, Brussels: EACEA, pp. 17–49.

Leseman, P. and Slot, P. (2014) 'Breaking the cycle of poverty: challenges for European early childhood education and care', *European Early Childhood Education Research Journal* 22(3): 314–326.

Pfau-Effinger, B. (2014) 'Explaining Differences in Child Care and Women's Employment across Six European Gender Arrangements', in M. Leon (ed.), *The Transformation of Care in European Societies*, Basingstoke: Palgrave, pp. 83–103.

Pintelon, O., Cantillon, B., Van den Bosch, K. and Whelan, C. (2013) 'The social stratification of social risks: the relevance of class for social investment strategies', *Journal of European Social Policy* 23(1): 52–67.

Schütz, G., Ursprung, H.W. and Wößmann, L. (2008) 'Education policy and equality of opportunity', *Kyklos* 61(2): 279–308.

Steiber, N. and Haas, B. (2012) 'Advances in explaining women's employment patterns', *Socio-Economic Review* 10(2): 343–367.

Uunk, W., Kalmijn, M. and Muffels, R. (2005) 'The impact of young children on women's labour supply: a reassessment of institutional effects in Europe', *Acta Sociologica* 48(1): 41–62.

Van Lancker, W. (2013) 'Putting the child-centred investment strategy to the test: evidence for the EU27', *European Journal of Social Security* 15(1): 4–27.

Van Lancker, W. (2017) 'Reducing inequality in childcare service use across European countries: what (if any) is the role of social spending', *Social Policy & Administration*, forthcoming.

Van Lancker, W. and Ghysels, J. (2012) 'Who benefits? The social distribution of subsidized childcare in Sweden and Flanders', *Acta Sociologica* 55(2): 125–142.

Van Lancker, W. and Ghysels, J. (2016) 'Explaining patterns of inequality in childcare service use across 31 developed economies: a welfare state perspective', *International Journal of Comparative Sociology* 57(5): 310–337.

Vandenbroeck, M., Geens, N. and Berten, H. (2014) 'The impact of policy measures and coaching on the availability and accessibility of early child care: a longitudinal study', *International Journal of Social Welfare* 23(1): 69–79.

Vincent, C., Braun, A. and Ball, S. (2008) 'Childcare, choice and social class: caring for young children in the UK', *Critical Social Policy* 28(1): 5–26.

Good intentions and Matthew effects: access biases in participation in active labour market policies

Giuliano Bonoli and Fabienne Liechti [ID]

ABSTRACT
The objective of this contribution is to investigate whether active labour market policies manage to reach the most disadvantaged individuals or are subjected to Matthew effects in the shape of access biases. We investigate this question for two typically disadvantaged groups of unemployed people: the low-skilled and immigrants. Our analysis is based on a systematic review of 87 evaluations of active labour market policies (ALMPs) covering 14 different countries and a time period of 15 years (1998–2013). We use information on participants and non-participants to ascertain whether or not access biases are present in these programmes. Our results provide evidence that a Matthew effect is present only in some programmes and in conservative welfare states but not in the Nordic countries. Our conclusion is that policies are generally explicitly targeted on the most disadvantaged (good intentions) but other factors limit their participation (Matthew effects), something which explains the mixed pattern that we observe.

Introduction

Over the last few years we have witnessed the emergence of a new orientation in social policy based on the idea that help for disadvantaged individuals should take the form of enabling interventions, that for example facilitate access to the labour market and to better jobs. This perspective, commonly referred to as 'social investment', has been rather influential in social policy debates within international organizations, academics and, especially, the European Union (EU). According to many, it represents a promising avenue to reform European welfare states, though the approach is not without problems.

The main critique that has been formulated against the social investment approach is of being biased in favour of the middle class and as a result failing to reach the most disadvantaged. Cantillon (2011), for example, has shown

ⓑ Supplemental data for this article can be accessed at https://doi.org/10.1080/13501763.2017.1401105.

that the employment gains of the pre-crisis 2000 have accrued essentially to households which already had a fair level of labour market participation. Jobless households, in contrast did not gain to any significant extent. Van Vliet and Wang (2015) found that increases in spending on social investment policies are associated with increases in poverty rates (though not in the Nordic countries). These studies suggest that social investment policies may be failing to reach those who would need them most.

This outcome is sometimes referred to as the 'Matthew effect' and is generally the result of a negative access bias to given services. Matthew Effects have been identified in public services such as health and education (Le Grand 1982) or family benefits (Deleeck *et al*. 1983), but also in typical social investment policies, such as subsidized childcare (Pavolini and Van Lancker 2017).

In this contribution, we are interested in the possible existence of access biases in a policy field that is crucial to the social investment approach: active labour market policies (ALMPs). The existing empirical evidence for access bias in ALMPs is very limited and focuses solely on specific single programmes. ALMPs play an important role in facilitating access to jobs for non-working individuals. They consist of a very diverse set of interventions, such as training or job-creation programmes, help in job search or subsidies to potential employers. ALMPs have been developed in Sweden in the 1950s, but have since spread across advanced welfare states (Bonoli 2010). Overall, ALMPs have a good reputation among both politicians and experts (Armingeon 2007). In the late 2010s, many Organization for Economic Co-operation and Development (OECD) countries spend sizable amounts on ALMPs, most of them between 0.5 per cent and 1 per cent of gross domestic product (GDP; OECD 2015).

Theoretically, we can expect ALMPs to generate both positive and negative access biases for disadvantaged people. On the one hand, ALMPs are often explicitly targeted to disadvantaged unemployed and can be expected to be relatively immune to Matthew Effects and show a positive access bias instead. On the other hand, participating in ALMPs requires some capabilities; for example, in terms of cognitive and non-cognitive skills. This requirement, in contrast, may exclude some disadvantaged individuals. Moreover, when allocating limited slots in labour market programmes, case workers may decide to give priority to individuals who are relatively close to the labour market, a practice known as 'creaming'. This tendency may be exacerbated if performance indicators that put pressure to focus on the most promising jobseekers are used.

On a pure theoretical basis, it is rather difficult to make clear cut hypotheses with regard to the presence or absence of a Matthew effect in ALMPs, as there are equally good reasons to expect positive and negative access biases. As a result, it seems appropriate to turn to empirical analysis. In this study we make use of numerous evaluations of labour market programmes. These studies in general describe the participant population and compare it to the eligible population. We collected these evaluations in a systematic way, and on the basis of the available data we assess whether or not there is an access bias in a given programme. Our dataset includes evaluation studies of all major types of ALMPs in 14 different countries over a period of 15 years (1998–2013).

We decided to focus on two known factors of labour market disadvantage as potential sources of an access bias: low-skill status and being a migrant. These two factors have been found to result in longer unemployment spells and a higher risk of labour market exclusion in several studies.[1] After discussing the presence or absence of access biases for disadvantaged individuals, we turn to the question of a possible relationship between access bias and effectiveness. In particular, we are interested in finding out whether or not the programmes that are more open to disadvantaged groups are as effective as the more selective ones.

The contribution proceeds as follows. First, we review the (limited) literature on access biases to ALMPs and formulate our expectations. Second, we present our method. Third, we discuss the access bias for low-skilled and migrants. Forth, we look at variation in access bias by welfare states. Fifth, we investigate the relationship between the types of access bias observed and programme effectiveness.

Literature and expectations

The term 'Matthew Effect'[2] is used in the social sciences to refer to situations in which initial advantages generate further advantage. The notion was first introduced in an article by Merton (1968) to describe rewards system in science. Since then the notion of 'Matthew effect' has been used in numerous publications, most of them in the field of the sociology of science, education and, of course, in social policy.

In social policy the notion of a 'Matthew effect' is used to indicate situations in which policies benefit disproportionately the middle and upper classes relative to other more disadvantaged groups (Gal 1998). This effect, which may be intended or unintended, has been identified in a large number of empirical studies. Among the first to point out this effect was Le Grand (1982: 129) in his analysis of the distributional impact of a range of public services, including health care, education, housing and transportation in the United Kingdom (UK). His verdict was unequivocal: 'Public expenditure, in about all the forms reviewed, is distributed in favour of the higher social groups.' Similar findings were obtained in Belgium by Deleeck *et al.* (1983), who found that child benefit provided a far greater advantage to middle- and upper-class families than to low-income families. Higher-income families tended to have more children and their children tended to stay longer in full-time education, a condition to receive the benefit up to the age of 25.

Research on childcare usage reaches similar conclusions. Van Lancker (2013) found that in most EU countries access to childcare is biased in favour of the middle and upper classes. A more fine-grained analysis suggests that access biases are likely be to some extent context dependent. For instance, in Sweden use of, as well as public expenditure on, childcare are rather evenly distributed among families of different social classes (Van Lancker and Ghysels 2012). In contrast, strong access biases have been uncovered in Switzerland (Abrassart and Bonoli 2015; Schlanser 2011). In a more comprehensive analysis of 27 EU countries, Pavolini and Van Lancker (2017) show that factors at the micro as well as the macro level influence the existence of a Matthew effect in childcare usage.

Overall, the evidence supports the existence of Matthew effects in social policies in general, and in social investments policies in particular. However, things may be different if we focus more narrowly on ALMPs. As already mentioned, these programmes are often targeted on disadvantaged unemployed people by design, like training for unskilled workers or job subsidies for older unemployed people. In this respect, we can expect ALMPs to be relatively immune to Matthew effects and show instead a positive access bias, because of their targeted nature. We could therefore expect a positive access bias for these groups. At the same time, however, it may also be the case that within the overall disadvantaged target population, it will be the least disadvantaged who will be most likely to benefit from these policies. This for two reasons. First, many of the interventions that go under the rubric of ALMPs require some capabilities in the first place. This is clearly the case of job-related training, which may require a fair command of the local language, or some cognitive or non-cognitive skills (e.g., Heckman 2006). Pre-existing abilities may also be a requirement for benefitting from other interventions, such as employment programmes. Since these in general require deploying a minimum of productivity and behaviour compatible with the expectation of organizations, individuals with poor social and non-cognitive skills may be excluded from participation in these programmes.

Second, since the ultimate objective of ALMPs is to put jobless people into jobs, these policies may anticipate the selectivity of the labour market. Given the fact that firms are selective, it may be the case that ALMP institutions and/or street level bureaucrats anticipate labour market selectivity and allow participation in ALMPs only to jobless people who can be seen as promising in terms of labour market re-entry (Pisoni 2015). In other words, a case worker may decide that it is not worthwhile to send an older, long-term unemployed migrant to training, because his or her chances of getting a job, even after having completed training, seem very slim. This type of mechanism has been linked to strategies such as cream-skimming that can be promoted by the use of performance indicators (Koning and Heinrich 2013; Pisoni 2015). If performance is measured by degree of success in putting people back in a job, it is possible that case workers will target resources on people who are relatively close to the labour market, while ignoring the rest.

As pointed out by Heckman and Smith (2004), gaining access to a social programme is a process that consists of several stages at which an access bias may or may not emerge.[3] Adopting a simplified version of their model, we can conceive access to labour market programmes as the result of a two stage process: eligibility and inclusion. Eligibility refers to the formal criteria that need to be fulfilled in order to be considered for participation. These tend to be favourable to disadvantaged groups as programmes are typically targeted on low-skill, long-term or older unemployed people. However, in order to be included in a programme, additional characteristics are required, such as knowledge of the local language, a given level of cognitive and/or non-cognitive skills, motivation. Unlike the first stage, this second hurdle is likely to limit access of the most disadvantaged. These features are also more difficult to target explicitly. This combination of opposing forces at different stages is found also in another study on access to ALMPs (Fertig and Osiander 2012). It has inspired the title of this piece ('Good intentions' at the eligibility stage combined with 'Matthew effects' at the inclusion stage). At the end, the result, i.e., a positive, a negative or no bias, will depend on the combined effects at these two stages.

In this respect, it would be unreasonable to expect access biases to be identical for different ALMPs. This notion, in fact, covers a very broad range of interventions which can generate different patterns of participation. Two dimensions of variation seem particularly relevant: the extent to which participation requires a given level of pre-existing skills (e.g., cognitive or language skills), and how close the interventions are to the labour market.

In particular, we expect training programmes to be more prone to a negative access bias for disadvantaged groups than job creation programmes, since the former require substantial pre-existing skills such as cognitive or language skills. We also expect a stronger negative bias for job subsidies, since these are closer to the labour market. In this situation, close contact with firms is required and jobseekers may be subjected to discrimination or anticipation of discrimination.

Finally, we can also expect the presence of an access bias to depend on the context in which a given programme operates (see also Kazepov and Ranci 2017). For example, a targeted programme operating in a context where disadvantaged people possess a fair level of cognitive skills (for example, provided by previous interventions), the positive access bias introduced at the eligibility stage is more likely to survive through the participation stage. In contrast, if the same programme operates in a completely different context, where disadvantaged individuals tend to possess lower cognitive skills, then a Matthew effect at the inclusion stage may outdo the initial positive bias of the eligibility stage. In that sense we follow Pavolini and van Lancker (2017) and argue that Matthew effects are influenced by micro-level factors such as skill-level or migration background of a person, but factors at the macro-level, such as the policy design and broader welfare states arrangements, moderate the extent to which these characteristics produce a Matthew effect.

In a further step, we assess whether the accessibility of programmes included in our sample is related to their effectiveness. We hypothesize that more effective programmes are less accessible for disadvantaged groups. Effective programmes could require a higher level of cognitive/non-cognitive skills or they may be more expensive and hence reserved to better candidates. If disadvantaged groups are not only excluded from effective programmes but are in addition sent to ineffective programmes, this could generate even further disadvantage and a stronger overall Matthew effect. Auer and Fossati (2016) have shown for the Swiss case that immigrants are often assigned to less-effective programmes than Swiss nationals.

Method

Our analysis of access biases in participation in ALMPs is based on a dataset of evaluation studies of labour market programmes. This dataset was generated by a systematic review of the large number of such studies that are available. Their main aim is to assess the programme's effectiveness in terms of employment outcome for participants. In general, however, these studies provide also information with regard to who the participants are relative to non-participants. We use this information to ascertain whether or not there is an access bias in these programmes.

This strategy has some important implications. First, we cannot use evaluation studies based on random allocation of participants and controls. In this case, since individuals are randomly allocated, by definition there will be no access bias. Second, it is difficult for us to understand the sources of a given bias, as it can originate from eligibility conditions or the inclusion in the programme. In general, these studies provide only very limited information on the selection process in the programme. On the other hand, our strategy has the big advantage of allowing us to survey a large number of studies, covering a diverse range of ALMPs. We can, as a result, gain knowledge that is quite general in relation to access biases in ALMPs and not specific to one single programme. In addition, it allows us to examine the link between access biases and effectiveness, which we do in the last part of the contribution. The following section describes the approach we have followed in order to identify the relevant studies and build or database.

As a first step we defined the type of programmes on which we are focusing. We decided to follow Kluve (2010) and included studies focusing on the four most common programme types of ALMPs. The first programme type, training, consists of both classroom training as well as on-the-job training, and can focus either on general education or specific vocational skills. The second category is job creation programmes, i.e., public work that is additional to the jobs on the actual labour. The last programme is wage subsidies, which are paid to private sector employers if they hire disadvantaged jobseekers. Note that Kluve (2010) examines a fourth type of programme, job search assistance, which we decided to drop because of an insufficient number of suitable studies.

Next, we defined the criteria for labour market disadvantage in terms of skill level and migration background. Low skilled is defined as not having completed upper-secondary education. Migration background is defined as not having the citizenship of the country of residence.

Having defined which ALMP programmes and disadvantaged groups we focus on, we now turn to the identification of the relevant studies we included in our systematic review. Up to the year 2006 we relied on meta-analyses that identified primary studies for the evaluation of labour market programmes (Card *et al.* 2010; Greenberg *et al.* 2003; Kluve 2010). To include more recent studies, we conducted a systematic search with defined key words in relevant databases and archives of institutes that evaluate labour market programmes.[4] After the exclusion of duplicates and evaluations of programmes that we are not interested in, 245 studies remained. In a second step we kept only studies that: (1) concerned training, job creation or wage subsidies programmes; (2) provided nationality and educational level for treated- and non-treated individuals that allowed calculation of an access bias; (3) provided data for the non-treated before a matched control group was calculated.

This left us with 47 of the studies that could be included in the analysis. As some studies may evaluate more than one labour market programme, this results in 87 programme evaluations, covering 14 different countries and the time period from 1998 to 2013 that can be used for our analysis.[5]

All types of welfare states regimes are represented in the 14 countries covered in our dataset. Among the conservative welfare state regime, most studies concern Germany (23 out of 87). For the social democratic welfare state regime, Denmark, Sweden, Norway and Finland are about equally represented in the sample. For the liberal and Southern welfare state regimes, we have only three studies each.

Based on this extracted information, we calculated an access bias for the two groups of interest, immigrants and the low-skilled. When the group of interest was underrepresented in the treatment group (negative access bias), this was coded as a −1. An overrepresentation in the treatment group was coded as a 1 (positive access bias), and a non-significant difference was coded as a 0. The calculation of the access bias was either based on the proportion of low-skilled and immigrants in the respective groups or the estimated probability of programme participation.[6] The first approach has the disadvantage that it cannot control for the correlation between the groups of interest.

In a second stage, we also extracted information concerning the effectiveness of the programme. Programmes were considered as effective when they had a positive effect on the participant's employment probability. Unfortunately, the time span considered by the different studies varies, and it was not possible to harmonize this time span for all studies. However, most studies reported the employment effects between one and two years after the end of the programme.

Results – access bias

In this section we present the results concerning the access bias for three different types of labour market programmes: training; job creation programmes; and job subsidies for the low-skilled and non-natives.

Training

Training programmes are likely to generate a Matthew effect as they generally require some pre-existing cognitive or language skills and motivation.

In total we included 49 programmes, of which half display no access bias for low-skilled individuals as shown in Figure 1. For the other half, a negative

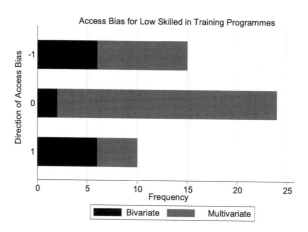

Figure 1. AB for low-skilled training. Source: Own calculation.

Note: Direction of access bias: 1 = positive access bias; 0 = no access bias; −1 = negative access bias. Bivariate: evaluation provided proportions, multivariate: estimates of the probability to participate.

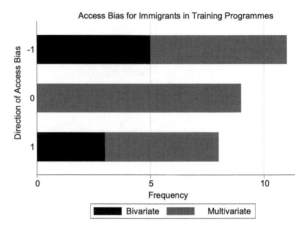

Figure 2. AB for immigrants training. Source: Own calculation.

Note: Direction of access bias: 1 = positive access bias; 0 = no access bias; −1 = negative access bias. Bivariate: evaluation provided proportions, multivariate: estimates of the probability to participate.

access bias is present more often than a positive one. For immigrants only 28 evaluations provide the numbers needed to calculate an access bias (Figure 2). Again, the number of programmes with a negative access bias exceeds the one for programmes with positive access bias. However, a third of the programmes do not display any access bias. Our results confirm the existence of both positive and negative biases in relation to both populations. However, negative biases are more frequent. This result is compatible with the hypothesis made in this contribution, that a positive bias sought by policy design may be undone by other factors, which can be subsumed under the label of Matthew effects.

Job creation programmes

These programmes are often targeted on hard-to-employ jobseekers. Since low-skilled and immigrants are overrepresented among these, we expect to find a positive access bias meaning that these two groups are overrepresented in these measures.

We identified 18 evaluations that provide details for the calculation of an access bias. The results show diverging trends between the two populations in which we are interested. While there is no negative access bias for the low-skilled (Figure 3), migrants seem considerably less likely to participate in these programmes. For them not a single programme shows a positive access bias.

More than half of the programme evaluations show that, compared to nationals, immigrants are systematically underrepresented in these programmes (Figure 4).

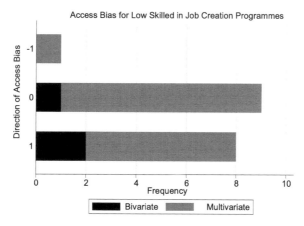

Figure 3. AB for low-skilled job creation. Source: Own calculation.

Note: Direction of access bias: 1 = positive access bias; 0 = no access bias; −1 = negative access bias. Bivariate: evaluation provided proportions, multivariate: estimates of the probability to participate.

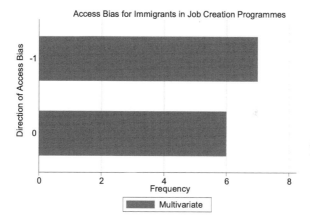

Figure 4. AB for immigrants job creation. Source: Own calculation.

Note: Direction of access bias: 1 = positive access bias; 0 = no access bias; −1 = negative access bias. Bivariate: evaluation provided proportions, multivariate: estimates of the probability to participate.

Wage subsidies

Wage subsidies are paid to private employers who agree to take on a disadvantaged unemployed person, typically defined in terms of unemployment duration, skill level or age. We would therefore expect a strong positive bias at the eligibility stage. However, the closeness to the labour market of this programme may make it more selective, and as a result a negative bias at the participation stage is to be expected.

As shown in Figure 5 it is very clear that the second, negative bias, prevails. In 6 out of 11 evaluations we find that the low-skilled are underrepresented in the treatment group relative to the non-treatment group. Only one evaluation

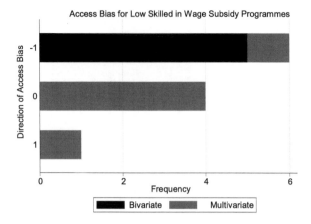

Figure 5. AB for low-skilled wage subsidy. Source: Own calculation.

Note: Direction of access bias: 1 = positive access bias; 0 = no access bias; −1 = negative access bias. Bivariate: evaluation provided proportions, multivariate: estimates of the probability to participate.

shows a positive access bias for low-skilled jobseekers, a wage subsidy programme in Germany specifically targeted on low-qualified unemployed. The other evaluations for Germany as well as those for Sweden and Norway, all provide evidence for the existence of a negative access bias. Low-skilled jobseekers were less likely to enter the programme or were underrepresented in the treatment compared to the non-treatment group. Finally, four evaluations, from Australia, New Zealand, Norway and Switzerland, found no differences in the chances of receiving a subsidy for those without, compared to those with, post-compulsory education.

The negative bias is even stronger for migrants (Figure 6). In six out of eight evaluations, immigrants had lower chances to be considered for a wage subsidy or were underrepresented in the treatment group. Only one

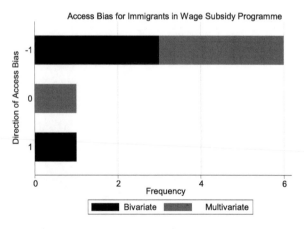

Figure 6. AB for immigrants wage subsidy. Source: Own calculation.

Note: Direction of access bias: 1 = positive access bias; 0 = no access bias; −1 = negative access bias. Bivariate: evaluation provided proportions, multivariate: estimates of the probability to participate.

evaluation of a wage subsidy in Sweden shows higher proportions of immigrants in the treatment than in the non-treatment group. Data from an evaluation conducted in Switzerland revealed no significant effect of immigrant background on the chances for programme participation. Taken together, the evaluations included in our review provide evidence for the existence of a strong negative access bias in wage subsidy schemes for both low-skilled and immigrants.

Results – variation by welfare state regime

Next we look at the influence of context on our results. We do that by relating our data on the access bias to the type of welfare state where the evaluation was carried out. More precisely, we consider separately evaluations done in conservative and in social democratic welfare states (Figures 7 and 8).[7]

Intriguingly, in spite of the small number of observations, one can clearly see that in social democratic welfare states one is more likely to find a positive access bias for both migrants and the low-skilled, while the opposite is true for the conservative welfare states.

This picture is mostly driven by training programmes, where we find most evaluations. In conservative regimes, 26 out of the 31 programmes have a negative access bias for the low-skilled. For the social democratic regime 11 out of 13 programmes have a positive or no access bias for the low-skilled. The picture is even clearer for migrants, as 16 out of 17 programmes show a negative access bias in conservative regimes while this is only the case for one out of nine programmes in the social democratic regime. But also job creation programmes show a similar picture. Three of the seven

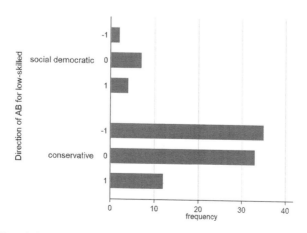

Figure 7. AB and the WFS-Regime low-skilled. Source: Own calculation.

Note: Direction of access bias: 1 = positive access bias; 0 = no access bias; −1 = negative access bias.

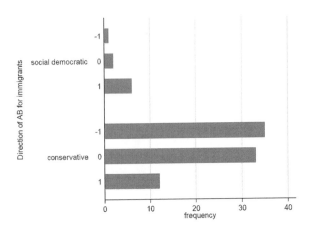

Figure 8. AB and the WFS-Regime immigrants. Source: Own calculation.

Note: Direction of access bias: 1 = positive access bias; 0 = no access bias; −1 = negative access bias.

programmes which have a negative access bias for migrants are one-Euro job programmes in Germany. Among the six evaluations that show no significant difference in the participation chances of immigrants and nationals two are from Denmark, two from Sweden and one from Switzerland and Germany each, suggesting that the context where a given programme operates might impact on the presence of a bias.

Results – access and effectiveness

The aim of ALMPs should not only be to reach the most disadvantaged groups but also to effectively increase their chances on the labour market. Our hypothesis is that disadvantaged individuals are sent to less effective programmes and tend to be excluded from the more effective ones. We therefore looked at the relationship between programme effectiveness, defined as a positive effect of the programme on the participants' employment probability, and the existence of a negative access bias.

For this analysis, we grouped all the programmes together and we also added job search assistance programmes, which were too few in our sample for a separate analysis. Training and job subsidies are more likely to be effective than job creation schemes and job search assistance.

The results are presented in Table 1. As expected, a negative access bias is more likely to occur in programmes that are more effective. The effect is significant at the 10 per cent level for the low-skilled, and not significant for migrants but clearly in the expected direction. This result can be explained in two different ways. First, disadvantaged unemployed people are sent to low-quality or less-ambitious programmes, either because they lack the cognitive skills or the motivation to participate in the more effective ones or are

106

Table 1. Relationship between programme effectiveness and access biases for low-skilled and immigrants.

	Low-skilled		Immigrants	
	No effect	Positive effect	No effect	Positive effect
Negative AB	8 (32%)	17 (68%)	11 (44%)	14 (56%)
No AB or positive AB	32 (54%)	27 (46%)	16 (65%)	9 (36%)
Total	40 (48%)	44 (53%)	27 (54%)	23 (46%)
	Pearson chi = 3.48 (Pr = 0.062)		Pearson chi = 2.01 (Pr = 0.156)	

Note: Numbers of studies, row percentage in parentheses.
Source: Own calculations

subjected to discrimination. Second, this result could come from reverse causality. Programmes that accept large numbers of highly disadvantaged people are less effective because it is more difficult to get these people back into jobs. Whatever the reason, the fact remains that disadvantaged unemployed people are less likely to participate in programmes that are effective.

Discussion and conclusion

In this contribution we investigated whether ALMPs are subject to an access bias or a Matthew effect. We expected a Matthew effect to be present in programmes that require a given level of cognitive skills, like training, and for those that are closest to the labour market, like wage subsidies. These expectations are confirmed for one of the two disadvantaged populations only, the low-skilled. The low-skilled suffer from an access bias mostly in relation to job subsidies and to a slightly lesser extent in the case of training. In contrast, insofar as job creation programmes are concerned, low-skilled unemployed are either overrepresented or at least equally represented as individuals with mid-to-high skills.

Things are different for migrants, who are underrepresented in each of the three categories of programmes we cover in this contribution. Surprisingly, however, the risk of being underrepresented is higher in job creation programme than in training. Given the low level of skill requirements for job creation programmes, we would have expected the opposite.

This result, however, is still compatible with our two-stage model of access to a labour market programme. Job creation programmes are generally not targeted on migrants, while the opposite can be true of some training programmes. As a result, migrants in job creation programmes do not benefit from the positive access bias at the eligibility stage. They are as a result tendentially excluded by the Matthew effect at the inclusion stage.

Moreover, we expected context to matter. Because of the limited number of observations, we were able to assess the frequency of access biases only in social democratic and conservative welfare states. The results are nonetheless insightful. Essentially, the observed negative access bias for both groups concerns only programmes in conservative welfare states (essentially in Germany). In the Nordic countries, training seems to be much more inclusive. This can be owing to several reasons. First, it could be the case that programme design differs systematically between the two welfare regimes, and the Nordic countries are simply more successful in designing programmes that are accessible to the most disadvantaged. Moreover, different welfare states focus on different ALMPs and differ with regard to other social policies which might have a spill over effect on the accessibility and effectiveness of ALMPs. Alternatively, this result may be owing to the fact that the average disadvantaged person in the Nordic countries possesses better cognitive (and non-cognitive) skills than this is the case in a conservative welfare state. Studies on the cognitive skills of the adult population have shown that the low-educated in the Nordic countries possess higher level of cognitive skills than in other regions (Abrassart 2013; Nelson and Stephens 2012), possibly because of a more egalitarian school system. The same training programme may lead to a bigger or smaller access bias depending on the average level of cognitive skills possessed by the target population. We need further research to disentangle these effects. Ideally, one would compare similar programmes in different countries and analyse at what stage, eligibility or inclusion, of the programme access biases emerge. This would allow us to investigate to what extent factors at the micro and macro level contribute to the emergence of Matthew effects. In the second part of the contribution we focused on the relationship between access bias and programme effectiveness. While the small N of our sample does not allow us to produce robust results, it is clear that effective programmes are more likely to exclude low-skilled and migrant unemployed people. Disadvantaged unemployed tend to be assigned to lower-quality programmes that are more distant from the labour market and as a result less likely to produce a positive effect.

Our analysis has shown that unlike other social investment policies, in particular childcare (see Pavolini and Van Lancker, 2017) Matthew effects are not inevitable when it comes to ALMPs. Particularly, in the Nordic countries, labour market programmes are less likely to exclude disadvantaged unemployed people than they are in conservative welfare states. We have also shown that migrants are more exposed to the risk being underrepresented in most programmes. This may be owing to the fact that migrant status is seldom an eligibility factor, except perhaps for language training and a few other programmes. According to our two stage models, migrants do not benefit from a positive bias at the eligibility stage, but suffer from the Matthew effect as other disadvantaged populations. As a result, they are more likely to be excluded form labour market programmes than the low-skilled, who are more often explicitly targeted at the eligibility stage.

Notes

1. On the labour market disadvantages suffered by the low-skilled, see, for example, Abrassart (2013); DiPrete (2005); Solga (2002). On the disadvantages suffered by migrants, see Auer *et al.* (2017); Heath and Cheung (2007).
2. The reference is to a verse in the Gospel of Matthew: 'For to everyone who has, more will be given, and he will have an abundance. But from the one who has not, even what he has will be taken away' (Matthew 25:29, English standard version)
3. Heckman and Smith (2004) have argued that the process of participating in a labour market programme is made up of a number of stages: eligibility; awareness; application; acceptance; and enrolment. Access biases at different stages may reinforce or, on the contrary, offset each other. The programme they study is voluntary, and in order to be eligible one must be considered as 'economically disadvantaged'. Interestingly, this highly targeted programme combines both positive and negative access biases for disadvantaged people. Low-skilled people, for example, are overrepresented at the eligibility stage, but their advantage is largely offset by underrepresentation at the stage of awareness, application and acceptance (Heckman and Smith 2004: 245).
4. See the Online Appendix for a more detailed description of the systematic review.
5. The extracted variables for each study can be found in the Online Appendix.
6. See the Online Appendix for a more detailed description of the calculation of the access bias.
7. Conservative welfare states include Germany (13 evaluations), Austria (1) and Switzerland (1). Social democratic welfare states include Sweden (3), Norway (2) and Denmark (3). For a theoretical justification of the notion of welfare regimes, see Esping-Andersen (1990).

Acknowledgements

We would like to thank Emmanuele Pavolini, Delia Pisoni, Flavia Fossati, Daniel Auer and the three anonymous reviewers for their helpful comments and suggestions. A special thank goes to the editors of this collection for their valuable feedback whilst writing this contribution.

Disclosure statement

No potential conflict of interest was reported by the authors.

ORCID

Fabienne Liechti 🄳 http://orcid.org/0000-0001-5509-3353

References

Abrassart, A. (2013) 'Cognitive skills matter: the employment disadvantage of low-educated workers in comparative Perspective', *European Sociological Review* 29(4): 707–19.

Abrassart, A. and Bonoli, G. (2015) 'Availability, cost or culture? obstacles to childcare services for low-income families', *Journal of Social Policy* 44(4): 787–806.

Armingeon, K. (2007) 'Active labour market policy, international organizations and domestic politics', *Journal of European Public Policy* 14(6): 905–32.

Auer, D., Bonoli, G. and Fossati, F. (2017) 'Why do immigrants have longer periods of unemployment? Swiss evidence', *International Migration* 55(1): 157–74.

Auer, D. and Fossati, F. (2016) 'Efficiency or equality : immigrants' access bias to active labour market policies', Paper presented at the nccr-on the move summer school meauring discrimination, University of Neuchâtel.

Bonoli, G. (2010) 'The political economy of active labor-market policy', *Politics & Society* 38(4): 435–57.

Cantillon, B. (2011) 'The paradox of the social investment state: growth, employment and poverty in the Lisbon era', *Journal of European Social Policy* 21(5): 432–49.

Card, D., Kluve, J. and Weber, A. (2010) 'Active labour market policy evaluations: a meta-analysis', *The Economic Journal* 120: F452–77.

Deleeck, H., Huybrechs, J. and Cantillon, B. (1983) *Het Mattüseffect*, Antwerpen: Kluwer.

DiPrete, T. A. (2005) 'Labor markets, inequality, and change: a european perspective', *Work and Occupations* 32(2): 119–39.

Esping-Andersen, G. (1990) *The Three Worlds of Welfare Capitalism*, Princeton: Princeton University Press.

Fertig, M. and Osiander, C. (2012) 'Selektivität beim Zugang in Weiterbildungsmaßnahmen', *IAB Discussion Paper* 19: 1–41.

Gal, J. (1998) 'Formulating the Matthew principle: on the role of the middle classes in the welfare state', *Scandinavian Journal of Social Welfare* 7(1): 42–55.

Greenberg, D.H., Michalopoulos, C. and Robins, P.K. (2003) 'A meta-analysis of government-sponsored training programs', *Industrial and Labor Relations Review* 57(1): 31–53.

Heath, A. and Cheung, S.Y. (2007) 'The comparative study of ethnic minority disadvantage', in A. Heath and S.Y. Cheung (eds), *Unequal Chances: Ethnic Minorities in Western Labour Markets*, Oxford: Oxford University Press, pp. 1–44.

Heckman, J.J. (2006) 'Skill formation and the economics of investing in disadvantaged children', *Science* 312: 1900–002.

Heckman, J.J. and Smith, J.A. (2004) 'The determinants of participation in a social program: evidence from a prototypical job training program', *Journal of Labor Economics* 22(2): 243–98.

Kazepov, Y. and Ranci, C. (2017) 'Is every country fit for social investment? Italy as an adverse case', *Journal of European Social Policy* 27(1): 90–104.

Kluve, J. (2010) 'The effectiveness of European active labor market programs', *Labour Economics* 17(6): 904–18.

Koning, P. and Heinrich, C.J. (2013) 'Cream-Skimming, parking and other intended and unintended effects of high-powered, performance-based Contracts', *Journal of Policy Analysis and Management* 32(3): 461–83.

Le Grand, J. (1982) *The Strategy of Equality: Redistribution and the Social Services*, London: Allen & Unwin.

Merton, R.K. (1968) 'The matthew effect in science: the reward and communication systems of science are considered', *Science* 159(3810): 56–63.

Nelson, M. and Stephens, J.D. (2012) 'Do social investment policies produce more and better jobs?', in N. Morel, B. Palier, and J. Palme (eds), *Towards a Social Investment Welfare State?: Ideas, Policies and Challenges*, Bristol: The Policy Press, pp. 205–34.

OECD (2015) 'Employment and labour market statistics', available at http://www.oecd-ilibrary.org/employment/data/oecd-employment-and-labour-market-statistics/labour-market-programmes-expenditure-and-participants_data-00312-en?isPartOf=/content/datacollection/lfs-data-en (accessed 19 February 2015)

Pavolini, E. and Van Lancker, W. (2017) 'Matthew effects in child care: looking for micro and macro factors', *Journal of European Public Policy* doi:10.1080/13501763.2017.1401108.

Pisoni, D. (2015) '*Matthew effect in training interventions for disadvantaged unemployed youth? A street-level bureaucracy analysis*', Paper presented at conference street level research in the employment and social policy area, Alborg University, 18–19, November.

Schlanser, R. (2011) *Qui utilise les crèches en Suisse ? Logiques sociales du recours pour la petite enfance*, Lausanne: Cahier de l'IDHEAP 264.

Solga, H. (2002) '"Stigmatization by negative selection": explaining less-educated people's decreasing employment opportunities', *European Sociological Review* 18 (2): 159–78.

Van Lancker, W. (2013) 'Putting the child-centred investment strategy to the test: evidence for the EU27', *European Journal of Social Security* 15(1): 4–27.

Van Lancker, W. and Ghysels, J. (2012) 'Who benefits? The social distribution of subsidized childcare in Sweden and flanders', *Acta Sociologica* 55(2): 125–42.

Van Vliet, O. and Wang, C. (2015) 'Social investment and poverty reduction: a comparative analysis across fifteen European countries', *Journal of Social Policy* 44(3): 611–38.

Political participation in European welfare states: does social investment matter?

Paul Marx and Christoph Giang Nguyen

ABSTRACT

The role of the welfare state has expanded beyond passive assistance and decommodificaton. In many countries, social investment policies now actively encourage (re)integration into the labour market. While the effectiveness of these policies is debated, we know even less about their broader social and political effects. In this contribution, we explore the impact of social investment policies on one key aspect of social life: political participation. Combining insights from social psychology with institutional analysis, we investigate the impact of three social investment policies (early childhood education, secondary education, active labour market policies) on two disadvantaged groups: young individuals from low-skill backgrounds; and single parents. Combining the European Social Survey with data on social investment, we find that these risk groups have reduced political efficacy and political participation. Social investment policies can alleviate these participation gaps in some cases, but not all.

Introduction

It is a disconcerting observation that those who need public policies most are least likely to make their voices heard in politics (Piven and Cloward 1989). A growing body of research shows that, instead of voicing demands for social protection and redistribution, socio-economically disadvantaged citizens tend to be politically disengaged (Brody and Sniderman 1977; Erikson 2015; Jahoda *et al.* 1972; Marx 2016; Pacheco and Plutzer 2008; Rosenstone 1982). There probably are multiple reasons for this disengagement. One powerful but still under-developed explanation is based on the psychology of economic problems. Economic worries are tremendously stressful and therefore cognitively and emotionally absorbing (Mani *et al.* 2013). Through these mechanisms, they might undermine voters' willingness and capacity to acquire, process and memorize political information. Hence, economic problems could impede the cognitive and affective foundations for political efficacy and participation.

However, such a link between objective problems, subjective worries, stress and political behaviour is likely to be moderated by institutions. Modern welfare states are designed (albeit to varying extents) to reduce citizens' economic worries (Sjöberg 2010). And indeed, egalitarian societies achieve a better political inclusion of poor (Solt 2008) and unemployed voters (Marx and Nguyen 2016). Also the policy feedback literature suggests that well-designed social policies can strengthen the political involvement of disadvantaged citizens, while imposing means-testing or conditionality tends to depress it (Bruch *et al.* 2010; Mettler and Stonecash 2008; Swartz *et al.* 2009; Watson 2015).

If welfare states contribute to political empowerment, this might be particularly true for countries adopting a social investment approach (Esping-Andersen 2002) by emphasizing 'policies that aim at creating, mobilizing, or preserving skills' (Busemeyer *et al.* 2018). Besides monetary support, these countries offer a range of educational and care services that (a) have a preventive character lowering the prospect of being trapped in economic problems, (b) signal society's deep commitment to assist people in overcoming their problems, (c) target groups who are particularly vulnerable in their political engagement, and (d) focus on empowerment and capacity-building. In this contribution, we therefore analyse whether social investment (SI) policies can contribute to the political engagement of socioeconomically disadvantaged citizens. While there is a growing interest in the policy preferences underlying SI reforms (Garritzmann *et al.* 2018), this more fundamental question has received limited attention so far.

Building on our earlier comparative research on the political involvement of the unemployed (Marx and Nguyen 2016), we use the European Social Survey and multilevel modelling to analyse how social investment policies influence the relationship between exposure to social risks and political involvement across European welfare states. This yields three findings that are not only socially and academically relevant, they also compliment the findings of this collection. First, on average, there is a significant and substantive 'involvement gap' for the two groups we study (single parents and youths from low-skill backgrounds).[1] This is irrespective of the aspect of political involvement we analyse (internal political efficacy and participation in elections).[2] Second, we show that the effects of SI policies can reach further than the literature has traditionally considered. By changing the effects of social risk exposure on political involvement, SI policies can drive political behaviour more generally. However, we also mirror concerns about Matthew effects outlined in this collection and show that some policies are more beneficial to relatively privileged groups than to disadvantaged ones.

Economic disadvantage and political involvement

One general argument for why socioeconomic disadvantage depresses political involvement relates to stress and distraction induced by economic problems (Rosenstone 1982). Material deprivation comes with concrete experiences that force people to focus on the private domain rather than on abstract social and political issues: the need to raise money for paying bills, worries about job loss and its consequences, straining working conditions and related health issues, living in unsafe neighbourhoods, exhausting family obligations because of unaffordable care services, or struggles to provide decent education for one's children. This does not even include the stress of (not) keeping up in a society that awards status based on consumption. Psychologically, economic problems then create various demands and distractions that contribute to 'cognitive load' (Mani *et al.* 2013). As a result, economically disadvantaged people *inter alia* allocate less attention to non-economic matters, show poorer intellectual performance and have a compromised short-term memory (Deck and Jahedi 2015; Gennetian and Shafir 2015). Experienced or anticipated financial strain also forces people to constantly exercise self-control (fight impulses, delay gratification), which further contributes to depleting mental resources (Vohs 2013). These mechanisms are exacerbated if social problems carry a stigma. Efforts to cope with stigmatization and to sustain self-worth absorb additional cognitive resources (Hall *et al.* 2013; Spencer *et al.* 2016).

Cognitive load can, in principle, stem from neutral or even pleasant tasks that are appraised as a challenge, but the demands and distractions economically disadvantaged citizens typically face are powerful and unpleasant stressors (Haushofer and Fehr 2014). Concretely, this means that they tend to perceive their problems as aversive and uncontrollable (Lachman and Weaver 1998) and respond with negative emotions such as anxiety and helplessness (Gallo and Matthews 2003). One consequence of intense stress can be rumination, that is, a dysfunctional fixation on a problem that impedes thinking about other aspects as well as regulation of negative emotion (Curci *et al.* 2013; Roger 2016). Generally, the physiological response to intense and persistent stress is known to undermine important cognitive functions (Sandi 2013).

Taken together, there is strong evidence that exposure to economic problems absorbs attention as well as cognitive and emotional resources. It thereby undermines the proper functioning of citizens' minds and lowers their self-control and efficacy. Based on these mechanisms, we expect to observe lower cognitive, affective, and behavioural engagement with politics among groups that are, on average, disproportionately exposed to economic problems. Concretely, we expect a lack of attention to politics (Rosenstone 1982). As Hassell and Settle (2017: 536) put it: 'every minute spent engaging in politics is time not spent addressing other financial or personal problems'. Social problems should hence limit exposure and attention to political information as well as the capacity to process them. In addition, it might be that the lack of perceived self-control associated with many social problems spills-over into depressed internal political efficacy (Marx and Nguyen 2016). In any case, based on the discussed mechanisms, we would clearly expect groups with high exposure to economic problems to be less politically efficacious and less likely to participate in politics.

H1: Socioeconomically disadvantaged groups on average have a lower political efficacy and a lower propensity to vote.

If economic problems impede political involvement through stress and emotional and cognitive absorption, a generous welfare state should, in principle, be able to alleviate these effects (Marx and Nguyen 2016; Shore 2014). However, there is little comparative research on the political integration of disadvantaged groups across different welfare states. It is our goal to fill this gap.

Theoretically, there are at least two ways in which welfare states alleviate the outlined mechanisms underlying cognitive and emotional absorption (and political disengagement). First, generous welfare states diminish experienced and anticipated material hardship, thereby lowering stress, worries, the need for absorbing coping strategies, and cognitive load. This function of welfare states has been demonstrated in comparative research on happiness and well-being (DiTella *et al.* 2003; Pacek and Radcliff 2008) – especially for economically vulnerable citizens (Anderson 2009; Anderson and Hecht 2015; Carr and Chung 2014; Sjöberg 2010; Wulfgramm 2014). Second, welfare generosity contributes to lower stigmatization because it gives legitimacy to welfare receipt as a social right. This should further reduce the stress of experiencing economic disadvantage. Hence, welfare states should make social problems less absorbing and distracting and therefore less detrimental to political involvement.

However, we are interested here in a particular aspect of the welfare state. Welfare states differ not only in their overall generosity, but also in how spending is used. As a response to a post-industrial economy and new social risks, there has been much debate in recent years about whether welfare states should move from traditional compensatory to SI policies (Bonoli 2007; Esping-Andersen 2002), which focus more explicitly on skill building, mobilization, and the (re)integration of disadvantaged citizens into the labour (Kuitto 2016). In this way, the SI turn is intended to benefit groups whose risks and problems are covered insufficiently by traditional welfare states: low-skilled, young, or non-standard workers with difficulties to enter the labour market as well as (single-)parents struggling with reconciling work and family life (Busemeyer *et al.* 2018). Could this difference between compensation and investment influence political involvement? For a number of reasons, SI policies might be particularly facilitating in this regard.

First, SI should have the potential to foster social and economic inclusion of groups that are not reached by traditional welfare states (Rovny 2014). For example, passive benefits should not necessarily help adolescents from disadvantaged families to experience upward mobility or single parents to take up work. Active labour market policies (ALMP), education spending and public childcare should be more effective. Second, the focus on intervention early in the life-course leads SI to target groups with still fragile political inclusion, because of incomplete political socialization. Young people are disproportionately affected by labour market problems. In addition, these problems should be particularly harmful for political participation, because unlike older workers they cannot rely on the habitual political engagement (Hassell and Settle 2017). Early exposure to hardship could also yield negative long-term effects, because economic problems impede socialization through (stressed) parents (Pacheco and Plutzer 2008) or in the workplace (Emmenegger *et al.* 2017). With its early human-capital-oriented interventions aiming at better labour market integration, SI could counter such problems.

Third, SI policies could be interpreted as signal of a societal and political commitment not to leave any citizen behind. On the one hand, this means concrete organizational support in tasks that would otherwise exhaust physical, emotional, and cognitive resources (e.g., job search and care). On the other hand, SI could contribute to a less stigmatizing situation. Ideally, it is perceived as the expression of an inclusive, enabling approach and solidaristic attitudes towards beneficiaries. This should be the case in particular for programmes that are designed to develop human capital in the long run or benefit recipients across class divides (such as childcare). Also the fact that beneficiaries typically become active in some sense rather than passively receiving benefits should make their status more legitimate. However, it is important to acknowledge that many SI policies do not live up to this ideal and that ALMPs in particular are often imposed on participants as a condition for benefit receipt (we return to this point in the conclusions).

Fourth, to the extent that SI policies succeed in bringing disadvantaged people into work, they can benefit from the latent function of employment such as activity, status, time structure and social contacts (Jahoda 1982) instead of suffering latent deprivation of these factors as it would occur during receipt of passive benefits. These latent functions are likely to spill over into stronger political efficacy (Marx and Nguyen 2016).

H2: The negative association between socioeconomic disadvantage internal efficacy and voting is weakened by SI policies.

However, we also recognize that SI policies are no panacea. If they do not reach vulnerable groups, for example, their effects may be muted. In fact, if vulnerable populations do not feel included in these policy frameworks, they could add to the very exclusion they are supposed to address. Moreover, the patterns of uptake and inclusion will likely differ depending on the social group and the type of policy. These Matthew effects can be a problem for both education (Pavolini and Van Lancker 2018) and ALMP (Bonoli and Liechti 2018).

To explore our hypotheses, we study the political involvement of two groups that have a relatively high risk of experiencing socioeconomic disadvantage and that figure prominently in the SI literature: (single) parents; and youth with low-skilled family background. Both groups generally have a relatively high poverty risk and face various every-day problems related to economic scarcity that should make engagement with politics difficult. At the same time, they should benefit more from SI policies such as education, care services and ALMP than from passive benefits. Without claiming to be exhaustive, we therefore believe these two groups are a plausible choice to explore effects of SI on political involvement.

However, both groups differ in their risks and needs. For single parents, the most facilitating policies should be childcare and education. There should be little doubt that it is extremely hard to care for children while being the sole breadwinner. The extent to which the state takes over care responsibilities should directly translate into more time and fewer distracting worries (about organizing everyday life, but also about the education of children and about being a good parent).

H2a: The gap between single parents and other household types in efficacy and voting is smaller in countries with generous childcare and school systems.

In the context of globalization and the knowledge economy, it has become harder for low-skilled workers to find decent jobs. Particularly young people without experience face difficulties in the labour market. A key component of SI is therefore to invest in the human capital of young people particularly from families with low education (we focus on family background because personal education is an *effect of SI*). This can be done through ALMPs, but should ideally start earlier in school or childcare already. The effect on political involvement should work through two links. First, the higher chance of having a decent job should translate into fewer worries and exposure to latent benefit of employment (see above). Second, better education should directly socialize young people into politics.

H2b: The gap between youth with low-skill family background and other age and skill groups is smaller in countries with more expansive childcare, school systems, and ALMPs.

Data and methodology

We explore how SI policies moderate the (presumably negative) relationship between membership in our risk groups and political engagement. Our micro-level data is drawn from the first four waves of the European Social Survey (ESS; 2002–2008), covering over 120,000 individual respondents in 25 European countries.[3]

To get closer to the theorized psychological mechanism, we focus on two aspects of political participation: internal political efficacy and electoral partici-pation. Internal efficacy means the subjective ability to make informed politi-cal decisions and is an important prerequisite for voters' continued political engagement. To reduce measurement error and increase cross-national concept validity (Morrell 2003), we measure internal efficacy through an addi-tive index of two items included in ESS waves 1 to 4: the perceived complexity of political reality and the ease with which respondents can make up their mind about politics. The index has been rescaled to range between 0 and 10 and is treated as a continuous variable. Actual participation is measured through a self-reported, binary indicator of whether or not respondents voted in the last national election. Using self-reported participation is proble-matic, since survey results are likely to overstate actual participation. However, this problem is not unique to the ESS, and even alternative data sources that are collected during elections, such as the Comparative Study of Electoral Systems, exhibit similar discrepancies between actual and self-reported turnout. We exclude all respondents who were not eligible to vote in the national election.

To measure membership in social risk categories, we rely on information about family composition, age, and the family's skill background. Family com-position focuses on two related sources of risk: the absence of a partner and the presence of children in the household. While we are primarily interested in single parents as a risk category, we also include singles without children and couples without children against the reference category of 'traditional' two-parent families with children.[4]

The age–family background similarly considers the intersection between two sources of political exclusion: young age and opportunities for effective socialization during ones' youth. Younger voters are usually less politically engaged (Goerres 2007). This gap should be especially pronounced for young citizens from families with low-skilled background, who on average benefit less from socialization through politically sophisticated parents with higher levels of education. The age-skill variable therefore first differentiates between young (25 and younger), prime age (26–55), and old (56 and older) respondents. In addition, it differentiates respondents based on the highest measure of parental educational, coded into low (International Stan-dard Classification of Education [ISCED] 0 to 2), medium (ISCED 3 and 4) and high (ISCED 5). This creates nine possible configurations of age and family background. Given our theoretical interests, we will focus on how the three types of young respondents compare to the reference category of prime-age individuals with a medium skill background.[5]

We include several individual-level controls that are either included directly in the ESS or derived from ESS measures. More-educated respondents are likely to have higher levels of engagement, so we include personal education level based on the ISCED. We also include measures of household income, gender, as well as measures of affiliations with trade unions, parties or religious group, who have been found to drive political engagement in previous studies (Marx and Nguyen 2016).

To measure SI policies and other country characteristics, we rely on Eurostat data.

To measure the SI context, we focus on three policies: early childhood education; secondary education; and ALMP. We measure all three through spending as a percentage of gross domestic product (GDP), but find similar results when using alternative operationalisations of SI policies (see Appendix). We also include a measure of unemployment benefits, to account for potential overlap with ALMP spending. Additionally, we control for other country-specific characteristics using the logarithm of *GDP/capita* for economic performance, the *Gini* coefficient for economic inequality, and overall *turnout* for other systemic country characteristics that influence political involvement.

Unfortunately, data availability does not allow us to reconstruct past educational spending. This is a problem, because current expenditure levels may not necessarily correspond to spending levels when respondents were actually enrolled in school. However, with little variance explained by the temporal dimension, we focus on between-country variation and average values for all second level variables to (partially) account for the difficulty of matching educational spending with social risk statuses. While this approach assumes relatively stable SI regimes, it is a necessary optimization strategy to allow for between-country comparisons. All models are either linear (internal efficacy) or logit (voting) hierarchical random-intercept models, with individuals nested within countries.

Results

Baseline models

Table 1 reports the results of our two baseline models. The dependent variables are internal efficacy and electoral participation. To facilitate model comparisons, all continuous independent variables have been mean-centred and divided by two standard deviations (Gelman 2008).

Table 1. Social risk and political engagement.

	Internal political efficacy	Vote
Family status: ref- family with children		
Single	−0.02 (0.02)	−0.42 (0.02)***
Couple, no kids	0.05 (0.02)**	−0.09 (0.02)***
Single parent	**0.01 (0.03)**	**−0.43 (0.03)***
Age–family skill background: ref – prime age/medium-skill background		
Old – high	0.37 (0.04)***	0.64 (0.07)***
Old – medium	0.18 (0.03)***	0.45 (0.04)***
Old – low	−0.10 (0.03)***	0.61 (0.03)***
Prime – high	0.12 (0.03)***	0.03 (0.03)
Prime – low	−0.22 (0.02)***	0.06 (0.03)*
Young – high	−0.13 (0.04)**	−0.32 (0.05)***
Young – medium	−0.37 (0.03)***	−0.43 (0.04)***
Young – low	**−0.66 (0.04)***	**−0.66 (0.05)***
Country level variables		
LogGDP	−0.14 (0.22)	−0.38 (0.14)**
Early childhood education	−0.17 (0.20)	−0.17 (0.13)
Secondary education	0.06 (0.15)	−0.07 (0.10)
ALMP generosity	0.31 (0.38)	0.52 (0.24)*
Passive support generosity	−0.48 (0.37)	−0.14 (0.24)
Gini	0.13 (0.19)	0.05 (0.12)
Turnout	0.42 (0.23)	1.03 (0.15)***
Num. observations	125447	125447
Num. countries	25	25
Var: country (intercept)	0.16	0.06
Var: residual	4.40	

Note: ***$p < 0.001$, **$p < 0.01$, *$p < 0.05$.
Additional control variables omitted (see Appendix). Key categories of interest are bolded.

The results of Table 1 largely support hypothesis 1 that membership in social risk categories lead to reduced political involvement. While all young voters suffer from reduced internal efficacy and a reduced probability to vote, this effect is noticeably larger for respondents from families with lower skill backgrounds. And while this table does not find a direct relationship between single-parenthood and efficacy, later analyses will show that this is an artefact because it obscures differences between low and high SI countries. Similar patterns emerge for electoral participation.

Interaction results

The results in Table 1 show a direct relationship between membership in social risk groups and political engagement. To investigate to what extent these relationships are moderated by various SI policies, we interact the two categories with the three SI indicators: spending on early childhood education, secondary education, and ALMP spending. The results of these 10 additional models are summarized in Tables 2 and 3, as well as Figures 1 and 2. (Full results can be found in the Appendix.) Figures 1 and 2 summarize graphically how SI investment policies moderate the relationship between risk groups and political participation. Each depicts the direct effect of

Table 2. Main and moderation effects for family status on political involvement.

	Internal efficacy			Electoral participation		
	Main effect	Child. educ.	Second. educ.	Main effect	Child. educ.	Second. educ.
Single	−	+	+	−	+	0
Couple, no children	+	0	+	−	0	0
Single parent	0	+	+	−	0	0

membership in a risk category, as well as the moderated effects when the listed policy variable is at 25 per cent and 75 per cent of its distribution. Tables 2 and 3 similarly summarize the main and interaction effects of risk-group membership on political involvement, in light of different SI policy configurations.

Focusing on policy moderation highlights that investigating main effects alone obscures considerable between-country heterogeneity. As Figure 1 demonstrates, for instance, the main effect of being a single parent is not associated with reduced internal efficacy. A more nuanced model, however, reveals the importance of early childhood education for single parents. All other things being equal, being a single parent in Austria (which spends roughly 0.4 per cent of its GDP on early childhood education) is associated with reduced political efficacy, while a single parent in Norway (which spends roughly 0.66 per cent of its GDP on early childhood education) no longer loses internal efficacy. As expected, this moderation effect is exclusive to single parents. Secondary education is more universally beneficial. While single parents benefit more noticeably, secondary education spending even helps childless singles.

Although internal efficacy is an important component of political engagement, electoral participation remains the most important channel to influence politics. Given the negative associations between social-risk categories and voting behaviour shown in Table 1, identifying SI policies that can alleviate

Table 3. Main and moderation effects for age-skill background on political involvement.

	Internal efficacy				Electoral participation			
	Main effect	Educ.	Second. educ.	ALMP	Main Effect	Child. educ.	Second. educ.	ALMP
Old high	+	0	0	+	+	0	0	0
Old medium	+	0	+	+	+	0	0	0
Old low	−	−	+	+	+	−	0	0
Prime high	+	+	0	0	0	+	0	0
Prime low	−	−	+	+	+	0	−	0
Young high	−	+	0	0	−	+	0	0
Young medium	−	0	0	0	−	+	−	−
Young Low	−	0	+	+	−	+	0	0

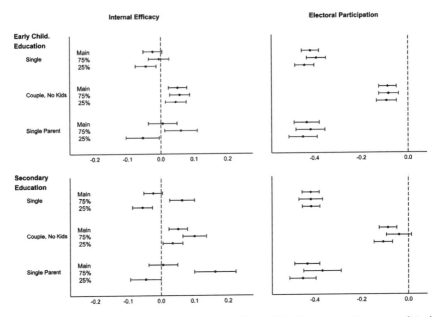

Figure 1. Coefficient comparison: marginal effect of family composition on political involvement moderated by educational policy.

this relationship is both normatively appealing and policy relevant. However, the link between SI policies and social risk is more complicated when it comes to voting. While singles, regardless of parenthood, are less likely to vote, neither form of educational support is associated with any meaningful changes in voting behaviour for single parents.

Similar patterns emerge for the intersection of age and family-skill background. Figure 2 shows vividly how crucial respondents' family background is for their sense of efficacy. While young voters from high-skilled families suffer from relatively minor decreases in efficacy, those from low-skill backgrounds exhibit a far more severe gap. However, SI policies can help alleviate this discrepancy. Both secondary education and ALMP spending do help young respondents from low-skill family backgrounds to develop a sense of internal efficacy, though they never reach the level of political efficacy of their more privileged peers or older voters. Indeed, even with very generous educational and ALMP policies, young respondents from low-skill backgrounds have considerably lower efficacy than other groups .Unfortunately, similar to the findings for family composition, these gains in efficacy do not seem to spill-over into greater electoral participation. Neither secondary education nor ALMP spending significantly improves the probability of voting for young and disadvantaged respondents. Indeed, while not central to this analysis, the results for young voters from medium-skill family backgrounds suggest that these measures may even harm young voters' likelihood to vote. However, one

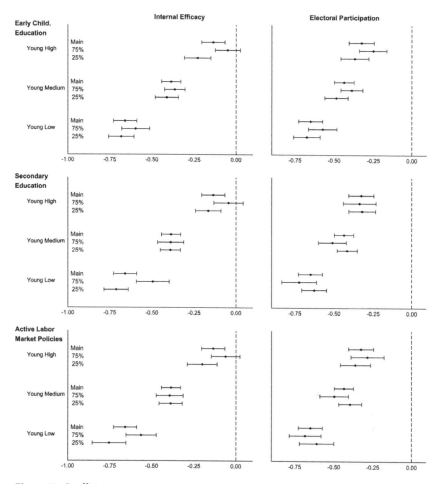

Figure 2. Coefficient comparison: marginal effect of age and family-skill background on political involvement moderated by educational policy and ALMP.

policy does consistently improve the electoral participation of young individuals. As Figure 2 shows, our results find that higher spending on early childhood education correlates with higher probability of electoral participation across all groups of young voters. Although this increase is universal, and therefore does not fully address the participatory gap among young voters from different backgrounds, it nevertheless encourages disadvantaged youths to vote.

Conclusion

In this article, we were interested in the extent to which membership in social risk groups depresses political engagement. Our hypothesis that social risk leads to lower political engagement is clearly supported. Both social risk groups we analysed, single parents and young voters from lower-skill family backgrounds, feel less confident in their ability to understand politics and are less likely to vote in national elections.

More importantly, we asked whether SI policies can make a difference in alleviating this disadvantage. Here, our results are far more mixed. While SI policies do appear to facilitate risk groups' sense of internal efficacy, this increase does not appear to translate into greater electoral participation. For instance, single parents' gap in efficacy is smaller in countries with generous SI. This is in line with our argument that SI policies can lower absorption through social problems and therefore free resources for engagement with politics (which should, in turn, lead to higher subjective capacity to make meaningful political decisions). However, to our surprise, this SI-induced efficacy boost does not also lead to a greater likelihood of voting. This is even more surprising because the single parents in SI countries should have reasons to perceive the political system as responsive to their needs. The results for young citizens' similarly show that SI policies can help build efficacy, but that this increase does not necessarily translate into greater electoral participation. Countries investing in secondary education and ALMPs have a lower efficacy gap for young citizens with low-skilled parents. However, as with single parents, this increase does not simultaneously lead to an increased likelihood that young people will actually participate in national elections.

One explanation for the non-findings on electoral participation might be that our retrospective participation variable is not ideal, because it reduces important variation through over-reporting. But given the widespread support for the relationship between internal efficacy and voting in the literature, more work is required to identify the factors that block the translation of internal efficacy into voting, and the ways in which public policies, social investment and otherwise, can be used to resolve the participation gap.

One starting point for this research may rest in early childhood education, which does appear to lower the voting gap between prime age and young citizens. Although there is less evidence that early childhood education can reduce the discrepancy among young voters, the importance of early childhood education is an important finding and certainly the one that sticks out from our analysis. If verified by future research, it would provide a strong additional justification for expanding early childhood education as a tool to increase political participation. However, more research is necessary to eliminate potential confounding factors on the macro level (such as party system characteristics, social norms to vote, etc.).

Finally, our results also highlight the dangers of relying solely on SI policies to reduce the gaps in political engagement. Our results show that in some instances, ALMP may even amplify these gaps. Two reasons might contribute to this. First, as discussed by Bonoli and Liechti 2018, ALMP could simply be channelled to other groups than our risk category of youth with low-skill background. Public employment services, for instance, might decide to prioritize training for older workers who lost their jobs and have obsolete skills. Second, ALMP spending could be coupled with strict activation measures. In the worst case, participants might even experience participation in measures as stigmatizing and degrading rather than empowering (e.g., Bruch *et al.* 2010 and Watson 2015 for similar arguments).

In sum, we could show that welfare state characteristics matter for political involvement of disadvantaged citizens, even if these gains do not always translate into actual participation. Future comparative research should go beyond our exploratory approach and zoom in on the effects of specific policies on specific groups. Finer-grained information on actual policy design could elucidate why gains in efficacy do not reliably lead to more electoral participation. Ideally, this research will rely on actual election studies with more detailed and possibly accurate information on voting behaviour. It will also be important to include mediating factors. We have argued that the stress-reducing capacity of social policies should be particularly important. While we neither had space nor appropriate data to analyse this link in the present paper, more research on mechanisms is necessary to fully understand how welfare states influence political behaviour.

Notes

1. Given the enormous importance of education and age for participation, the latter category certainly is one of the most problematic with regard to political engagement. Single motherhood is an important and growing risk factor for experiencing socioeconomic disadvantage in post-industrial societies, which is why it plays a prominent role in the SI literature. An advantage of both groups is that they are measured based on fundamental socio-structural characteristics that are not endogenous to countries' social policy approach (the risk of long-term unemployment should, for instance, depend on whether or not a SI approach is in place). However, there certainly are other disadvantaged groups whose involvement could benefit from SI and which we cannot cover in this article.
2. Internal political efficacy can be defined as citizens' subjective assessments about their ability to influence politics, which is usually seen as an important prerequisite for political participation. We include this aspect of political involvement, because it provides a plausible psychological mechanism linking social problems and participation (Marx and Nguyen 2016). This is not to suggest that other aspects, such as external efficacy, are irrelevant.
3. Specifically, we cover Austria, Belgium, Bulgaria, Cyprus, The Czech Republic, Germany, Denmark, Estonia, Spain, Finland, France, Great Britain, Greece, Croatia, Hungary, Ireland, Italy, Luxemburg, the Netherlands, Norway, Poland, Portugal, Sweden, Slovenia and Slovakia.
4. We use mutually exclusive and jointly sufficient categorical variables to allow for easier interpretation and representation of the results. However, using three-way interactions yields equivalent results.

5. For the full results that cover the moderation effects of SI policies on all age-skill groups, please consult the Appendix.

Disclosure statement

No potential conflict of interest was reported by the authors.

References

Anderson, C.J. (2009) 'The private consequences of public policies: active labor market policies and social ties in Europe', *European Political Science Review* 1(3): 341–73.

Anderson, C.J. and Hecht, J.D. (2015) 'Happiness and the welfare state: decommodification and the political economy of subjective well-being', in P. Beramendi, S. Häusermann, H. Kitschelt and H. Kriesi (eds.), *The Politics of Advanced Capitalism*, Cambridge: Cambridge University Press, pp. 357–80.

Bonoli, G. (2007) 'Time matters – postindustrialization, new social risk, and welfare state adaption in advanced industrial democracies', *Comparative Political Studies* 40(5), 495–520.

Bonoli, G. and Liechti F. (2018) 'Good intensions and the Matthew effect: access biases in participation in active labour market policies', *Journal of European Public Policy*. doi:10.1080/13501763.2017.1401105

Brody, R.A. and Sniderman, P.M. (1977) 'From life space to polling place: The relevance of personal concerns for voting behavior', *British Journal of Political Science* 7(3): 337–60.

Bruch, S.K., Ferree, M.M., and Soss, J. (2010) 'From policy to polity democracy, paternalism, and the incorporation of disadvantaged citizens', *American Sociological Review* 75(2): 205–26.

Busemeyer, M., de la Porte, C., Garritzmann, J., and Pavolini, E. (2018) 'The future of social investment: politics, policies, and outcomes', *Journal of European Public Policy*. doi:10.1080/13501763.2017.1402944

Carr, E. and Chung, H. (2014) 'Employment insecurity and life satisfaction: The moderating influence of labour market policies across Europe', *Journal of European Social Policy* 24(4): 383–99.

Curci, A., Lanciano, T., Soleti, E., and Rimé, B. (2013) 'Negative emotional experiences arouse rumination and affect working memory capacity', *Emotion* 13(5): 867–80.

Deck, C. and Jahedi, S. (2015) 'The effect of cognitive load on economic decision making: A survey and new experiments', *European Economic Review* 78(1): 97–119.

Di Tella, R., MacCulloch, R.J., and Oswald, A.J. (2003) 'The macroeconomics of happiness', *Review of Economics and Statistics* 85(4): 809–27.

Emmenegger, P., Marx, P., and Schraff, D. (2017) 'Off to a bad start: unemployment and political interest during early adulthood', *Journal of Politics* 79(1): 315–28.

Erikson, R.S. (2015) 'Income inequality and policy responsiveness', *Annual Review of Political Science* 18, 11–29.

Esping-Andersen, G. (2002) *Why We Need a New Welfare State*, Oxford: Oxford University Press.

Gallo, L.C. and Matthews, K.A. (2003) 'Understanding the association between socioeconomic status and physical health: do negative emotions play a role?', *Psychological Bulletin* 129(1): 10–51.

Garritzmann, J., Busemeyer, M., and Neimanns, E. (2018) 'Public demand for social investment: new supporting coalitions for welfare state reform in Western Europe?', *Journal of European Public Policy*. doi:10.1080/13501763.2017.1401107

Gelman, A. (2008) 'Scaling regression inputs by dividing by two standard deviations', *Statistics in Medicine* 27 (2007), 2865–2873.

Gennetian, L.A. and Shafir, E. (2015) 'The persistence of poverty in the context of financial instability: a behavioral perspective', *Journal of Policy Analysis and Management* 34(4): 904–36.

Goerres, A. (2007) 'Why are older people more likely to vote? The impact of ageing on electoral turnout in Europe', *The British Journal of Politics and International Relations* 9 (1): 90–121.

Hall, C.C., Zhao, J., and Shafir, E. (2013) 'Self-affirmation among the poor cognitive and behavioral implications', *Psychological Science* 25(2): 619–25.

Hassell, H.J. and Settle, J.E. (2017) 'The differential effects of stress on voter turnout', *Political Psychology* 38(3): 533–50.

Haushofer, J. and Fehr, E. (2014) 'On the psychology of poverty', *Science*, 344(6186), 862–867.

Jahoda, M. (1982) *Employment and Unemployment: A Social-Psychological Analysis*, Cambridge: Cambridge University Press.

Jahoda, M., Elsaesser, T., Lazarsfeld, P.F., Reginall, J., and Zeisel, H. (1972) *Marienthal: The Sociography of an Unemployed Community*, London: Tavistock Publications.

Kuitto, K. (2016) 'From social security to social investment? Compensating and social investment welfare policies in a life course perspective', *Journal of European Social Policy* 26(5): 442–59.

Lachman, M.E. and Weaver, S.L. (1998) 'The sense of control as a moderator of social class differences in health and well-being', *Journal of Personality and Social Psychology* 74(3): 763–73.

Mani, A., Mullainathan, S., Shafir, E., and Zhao, J. (2013) 'Poverty impedes cognitive function', *Science* 341(6149): 976–80.

Marx, P. (2016) 'The insider-outsider divide and economic voting: testing a new theory with German electoral data', *Socio-Economic Review* 14(1): 97–118.

Marx, P. and Nguyen, C. (2016) 'Are the unemployed less politically involved? A comparative study of internal political efficacy', *European Sociological Review* 32(5): 634–48.

Mettler, S. and Stonecash, J.M. (2008) 'Government program usage and political voice', *Social Science Quarterly* 89(2): 273–93.

Morrell, M.E. (2003). 'Survey and experimental evidence for a reliable and valid measure of internal political efficacy', *The Public Opinion Quarterly*, 67(4), 589–602.

Pacek, A.C. and Radcliff, B. (2008) 'Welfare policy and subjective well-being across nations: an individual-level assessment', *Social Indicators Research* 89(1): 179–91.

Pacheco, J.S. and Plutzer, E. (2008) 'Political participation and cumulative disadvantage: the impact of economic and social hardship on young citizens', *Journal of Social Issues* 64(3): 571–93.

Pavolini, E. and Van Lancker, W. (2018) 'The Matthew effect in childcare use: a matter of policies or preferences?', *Journal of European Public Policy*. doi:10.1080/13501763. 2017.1401108

Piven, F.F. and Cloward, R.A. (1989) 'Government statistics and conflicting explanations of nonvoting', *PS: Political Science & Politics* 22(3): 580–88.

Roger, D. (2016) 'Rumination, stress, and emotion', in G. Fink (ed.), *Stress: Concepts, Cognition, Emotion, and Behavior*, San Diego: Academic Press, pp. 261–66.

Rosenstone, S.J. (1982) 'Economic adversity and voter turnout', *American Journal of Political Science* 26(1): 25–46.

Rovny, A.E. (2014) 'The capacity of social policies to combat poverty among new social risk groups', *Journal of European Social Policy* 24(5): 405–23.

Sandi, C. (2013) 'Stress and cognition', *Wiley Interdisciplinary Reviews: Cognitive Science* 4 (3): 245–61.

Shore, J. (2014) 'How welfare states shape participatory patterns', in S. Kumlin and I. Stadelmann-Steffen (eds.), *How Welfare States Shape the Democratic Public: Policy Feedback, Participation, Voting and Attitudes*, Cheltenham: Edward Elgar, pp. 41–62.

Sjöberg, O. (2010) 'Social insurance as a collective resource: unemployment benefits, job insecurity and subjective well-being in a comparative perspective', *Social Forces* 88(3): 1281–304.

Solt, F. (2008) 'Economic inequality and democratic political engagement', *American Journal of Political Science* 52(1): 48–60.

Spencer, S.J., Logel, C., and Davies, P.G. (2016) 'Stereotype threat', *Annual Review of Psychology* 67(1): 415–37.

Swartz, T.T., Blackstone, A., Uggen, C., and McLaughlin, H. (2009) 'Welfare and citizenship: the effects of government assistance on young adults' civic participation', *The Sociological Quarterly*, 50(4), 633–665.

Vohs, K.D. (2013) 'The poor's poor mental power', *Science* 341(6149): 969–70.

Watson, S. (2015). 'Does welfare conditionality reduce democratic participation?', *Comparative Political Studies*, 48(5), 645–686.

Wulfgramm, M. (2014). 'Life satisfaction effects of unemployment in Europe: the moderating influence of labour market policy', *Journal of European Social Policy*, 24(3), 258–272.

Appendix

Dependent variable constructions

Index of political efficacy – rescaled sum of

- How often does politics seem so complicated that you can't really understand what is going on? – 5 point Likert scale
- How difficult or easy do you find it to make your mind up about political issues -5 point Likert scale

Distribution: (Mean = 4.85, median = 5 , SD = 2.33248)

Voting

Some people don't vote nowadays for one reason or another. Did you vote in the last [country] national election in [month/year]? – yes/no

Summary Statistics

Table A1. Mean values by country (continuous variables).

	Efficacy	logGDP	Early childhood education	Secondary education	ALMP %GDP	Passive support % GDP	Gini	Turnout
Austria	5.63	10.32	0.5	2.62	1.97	1.52	26.58	79.81
Belgium	4.45	10.26	0.72	2.67	2.85	3.3	27.11	90.51
Bulgaria	5.37	9.12	0.77	1.79	0.62	0.45	30.69	59.67
Cyprus	5.93	10.04	0.36	3.11	0.86	1.13	30.03	87.01
Czech Republic	4.34	9.86	0.54	2.06	0.5	0.66	25.1	62.97
Germany	5.4	10.24	0.49	2.34	2.53	1.7	28.3	75.91
Denmark	5.7	10.3	1.06	2.9	3.51	2.11	25.64	86.71
Estonia	4.74	9.57	0.41	2.41	0.55	0.36	33.49	60.44
Spain	4.26	10.07	0.56	1.74	2.86	2.57	32.59	71.66
Finland	4.67	10.23	0.36	2.66	2.58	2.23	25.79	67.55
France	4.4	10.17	0.66	2.72	2.39	1.91	28.59	62.11
Great Britain	4.84	10.23	0.35	2.49	0.58	0.64	32.93	63.15
Greece	4.73	9.93	0.16	1.33	0.64	1.06	33.69	79.31
Croatia	4.82	9.53	0.56	0.92	0.68	0.44	29.65	61.46
Hungary	5.09	9.61	0.94	2.29	0.93	0.67	26.58	65.48
Ireland	5.18	10.38	0.04	2.09	2.46	2.1	30.41	66.19
Italy	4.14	10.15	0.46	2.15	1.49	0.98	31.62	80.6
Luxemburg	5	11	0.63	1.7	1.08	1.05	27.71	90.11
Netherlands	4.87	10.38	0.4	2.2	2.62	1.35	26.69	77.46
Norway	5.17	10.63	0.66	2.25	1.04	0.61	24.77	76.79
Poland	4.6	9.48	0.51	1.89	0.96	0.54	31.59	48.31
Portugal	4.06	9.84	0.52	2.23	1.82	1.21	35.82	61.11
Sweden	4.91	10.31	0.59	2.63	2.06	1.42	24.09	82.36
Slovenia	4.79	9.9	0.54	1.48	0.87	0.69	23.25	64.01
Slovakia	4.81	9.63	0.54	1.94	0.69	0.73	25.45	64.14

Table A2. Frequencies of categorical variables.

Variable	Category	Number	%
Voting	Yes	25647	20.4
	No	99800	79.6
Family status	Family	43513	34.7
	Single	37608	30
	Couple, no kids	36613	29.2
	Single parent	7713	6.2
Age–skill nexus	Prime medium	22888	18.2
	Old high	3360	2.7
	Old medium	9649	7.7
	Old low	32414	25.8
	Prime high	11394	9.1
	Prime low	33093	26.4
	Young high	3636	2.9
	Young medium	5773	4.6
	Young low	3240	2.6
Gender	Male	58816	46.9
	Female	66631	53.1
Main activity	Paid employment	65796	52.5
	Education	6379	5.1
	Unemployed, looking for a job	4218	3.4
	Unemployed, not looking for a job	1962	1.6
	Permanently sick or disabled	3008	2.4
	Retired	29915	23.9
	Community or Military Service	163	0.1
	Housework, looking after Children	12695	10.1
	Other	1311	1
Income group	Medium	42958	34.2
	High	23989	19.1
	Low	25783	20.6
	No information	32717	26.1
Education	I: Less than lower secondary	18611	14.8
	II: Lower secondary	21946	17.5
	III: Upper secondary	50563	40.3
	IV: Advanced vocational	3109	2.5
	V–VI Tertiary	31014	24.7
	Other	204	0.2
Trade union member	Yes, currently	28403	22.6
	Yes, previously	30905	24.6
	No	66139	52.7
Party affiliation	No	60516	48.2
	Strong identifier	48956	39
	Weak identifier	15975	12.7
Religious	No	92551	73.8
	Yes	32896	26.20

Full tables for paper results

Table A3. Social risk and political engagement – full table.

	Internal political efficacy	Vote
Intercept	4.70 (0.08)***	1.41 (0.06)***
Family status: ref- family with children		
Single	−0.02 (0.02)	−0.42 (0.02)***
Couple, no kids	0.05 (0.02)**	−0.09 (0.02)***
Single parent	0.01 (0.03)	−0.43 (0.03)***
Age–family skill background: ref – prime age/medium-skill background		
Old – high	0.37 (0.04)***	0.64 (0.07)***
Old – medium	0.18 (0.03)***	0.45 (0.04)***
Old – low	−0.09 (0.03)***	0.61 (0.03)***
Prime – high	0.11 (0.03)***	0.02 (0.03)
Prime – low	−0.22 (0.02)***	0.06 (0.03)*
Young – high	−0.14 (0.04)**	−0.33 (0.05)***
Young – medium	−0.39 (0.03)***	−0.43 (0.04)***
Young – low	−0.66 (0.04)***	−0.65 (0.05)***
Female	−0.89 (0.01)***	0.07 (0.02)***
Main activity: ref – full-time employed		
Education	0.27 (0.03)***	−0.38 (0.04)***
Unemployed – looking	−0.13 (0.03)***	−0.37 (0.04)***
Unemployed – inactive	−0.25 (0.05)***	−0.45 (0.05)***
Sick or disabled	−0.26 (0.04)***	−0.35 (0.05)***
Retired	−0.18 (0.02)***	0.01 (0.03)
Community or military service	−0.17 (0.17)	0.16 (0.20)
Housework	−0.21 (0.02)***	−0.14 (0.03)***
Other activity	−0.04 (0.06)	−0.38 (0.07)***
Household income: ref – medium		
High	0.20 (0.02)***	0.23 (0.03)***
Low	−0.18 (0.02)***	−0.11 (0.02)***
Missing	−0.03 (0.02)	−0.10 (0.02)***
Education (ISCED): Ref – ISCED 2		
I: Less than lower secondary	−1.00 (0.02)***	−0.42 (0.03)***
II: Lower secondary	−0.50 (0.02)***	−0.42 (0.02)***
IV: Advanced vocational	0.27 (0.04)***	0.26 (0.05)***
V–VI: tertiary	0.64 (0.02)***	0.34 (0.02)***
Other	0.22 (0.15)	−0.22 (0.17)
Trade union: ref – yes		
Yes, previously	0.18 (0.02)***	−0.20 (0.03)***
No	0.01 (0.02)	−0.39 (0.02)***
Party affiliation		
Strong	0.80 (0.01)***	1.42 (0.02)***
Weak	0.25 (0.02)***	0.79 (0.02)***
Religious	−0.10 (0.02)***	0.37 (0.02)***
Country-level variables		
LogGDP	−0.21 (0.23)	−0.45 (0.14)**
Early childhood education	−0.19 (0.20)	−0.19 (0.13)
Secondary education	0.07 (0.15)	−0.07 (0.10)
ALMP generosity	0.28 (0.38)	0.50 (0.24)*
Passive support generosity	−0.46 (0.37)	−0.12 (0.23)
Gini	0.12 (0.19)	0.05 (0.12)
Turnout	0.42 (0.23)	1.03 (0.15)***
AIC	542300.49	106578.47
BIC	542719.29	106987.54
Log likelihood	−271107.25	−53247.24
Num. obs.	125447	125447
Num. groups: cntry	25	25
Var: cntry (intercept)	0.16	0.06
Var: residual	4.40	

Note: ***$p < 0.001$, **$p < 0.01$, *$p < 0.05$.

Interaction Results – Internal Efficacy

Table A4. Interaction: internal efficacy, family status, and education spending.

	Model 1	Model 2
Intercept	4.70 (0.08)***	4.69 (0.08)***
Family status: ref – family with children		
Single	−0.02 (0.02)	−0.02 (0.02)
Couple, no kids	0.05 (0.02)**	0.06 (0.02)***
Single parent	0.01 (0.03)	0.02 (0.03)
Age-family skill background: ref – prime age/medium-skill background		
Old – high	0.37 (0.04)***	0.37 (0.04)***
Old – medium	0.18 (0.03)***	0.18 (0.03)***
Old – low	−0.09 (0.03)***	−0.09 (0.03)***
Prime – high	0.11 (0.03)***	0.12 (0.03)***
Prime – low	−0.22 (0.02)***	−0.22 (0.02)***
Young – high	−0.14 (0.04)**	−0.14 (0.04)**
Young – medium	−0.39 (0.03)***	−0.38 (0.03)***
Young – low	−0.66 (0.04)***	−0.65 (0.04)***
Female	−0.89 (0.01)***	−0.89 (0.01)***
Main activity: ref – full-time employed		
Education	0.26 (0.03)***	0.27 (0.03)***
Unemployed – looking	−0.12 (0.03)***	−0.13 (0.03)***
Unemployed – inactive	−0.25 (0.05)***	−0.26 (0.05)***
Sick or disabled	−0.26 (0.04)***	−0.26 (0.04)***
Retired	−0.18 (0.02)***	−0.18 (0.02)***
Community or military service	−0.17 (0.17)	−0.18 (0.17)
Housework	−0.21 (0.02)***	−0.21 (0.02)***
Other activity	−0.04 (0.06)	−0.04 (0.06)
Household income: ref – medium		
High	0.20 (0.02)***	0.22 (0.02)***
Low	−0.18 (0.02)***	−0.18 (0.02)***
Missing	−0.03 (0.02)	−0.03 (0.02)
Education (ISCED): ref – ISCED 2		
I: Less than lower secondary	−1.00 (0.02)***	−1.00 (0.02)***
II: Lower secondary	−0.51 (0.02)***	−0.50 (0.02)***
IV: Advanced vocational	0.27 (0.04)***	0.27 (0.04)***
V–VI: Tertiary	0.64 (0.02)***	0.64 (0.02)***
Other	0.22 (0.15)	0.22 (0.15)
Trade union: ref – yes		
Yes, previously	0.18 (0.02)***	0.18 (0.02)***
No	0.01 (0.02)	0.01 (0.02)
Party affiliation		
Strong	0.80 (0.01)***	0.80 (0.01)***
Weak	0.25 (0.02)***	0.25 (0.02)***
Religious	−0.10 (0.02)***	−0.10 (0.02)***
Country-level variables		
logGDP	−0.20 (0.23)	−0.21 (0.23)
Early childhood education	−0.23 (0.20)	−0.19 (0.20)
Secondary education	0.07 (0.15)	−0.03 (0.16)
ALMP generosity	0.28 (0.38)	0.28 (0.38)
Passive support generosity	−0.46 (0.37)	−0.46 (0.37)
Gini	0.12 (0.19)	0.12 (0.19)
Turnout	0.42 (0.23)	0.42 (0.23)
Interaction– early childhood education		
Single	0.07 (0.03)*	
Couple, no kids	0.02 (0.03)	
Single parent	0.22 (0.05)***	

(Continued)

Table A4. Continued.

	Model 1	Model 2
Interaction – secondary education		
Single		0.18 (0.03)***
Couple, no kids		0.10 (0.03)**
Single parent		0.31 (0.05)***
AIC	542300.57	542265.78
BIC	542748.60	542713.81
Log likelihood	−271104.29	−271086.89
Num. obs.	125447	125447
Num. groups: cntry	25	25
Var: cntry (intercept)	0.16	0.16
Var: residual	4.40	4.40

Note: ***$p < 0.001$, **$p < 0.01$, *$p < 0.05$.

Table A5. Interaction: internal efficacy, age–family skill background, and skill building.

	Model 1	Model 2	Model 3
Intercept	4.69 (0.08)***	4.70 (0.09)***	4.69 (0.09)***
Family status: ref – family with children			
Single	−0.02 (0.02)	−0.04 (0.02)*	−0.03 (0.02)
Couple, no kids	0.06 (0.02)**	0.04 (0.02)*	0.05 (0.02)**
Single parent	0.01 (0.03)	0.02 (0.03)	0.01 (0.03)
Age–family skill background: ref – prime age/medium-skill background			
Old – high	0.37 (0.04)***	0.38 (0.04)***	0.36 (0.04)***
Old – medium	0.17 (0.03)***	0.18 (0.03)***	0.18 (0.03)***
Old – low	−0.09 (0.03)***	−0.09 (0.03)***	−0.08 (0.03)***
Prime – high	0.11 (0.03)***	0.14 (0.03)***	0.12 (0.03)***
Prime – low	−0.22 (0.02)***	−0.22 (0.02)***	−0.21 (0.02)***
Young – high	−0.13 (0.04)**	−0.13 (0.04)**	−0.13 (0.04)**
Young – medium	−0.39 (0.03)***	−0.39 (0.03)***	−0.39 (0.04)***
Young – low	−0.64 (0.04)***	−0.64 (0.04)***	−0.65 (0.04)***
Female	−0.89 (0.01)***	−0.89 (0.01)***	−0.88 (0.01)***
Main activity: ref – full-time employed			
Education	0.26 (0.03)***	0.26 (0.03)***	0.27 (0.03)***
Unemployed – looking	−0.12 (0.03)***	−0.13 (0.03)***	−0.12 (0.03)***
Unemployed – inactive	−0.25 (0.05)***	−0.26 (0.05)***	−0.25 (0.05)***
Sick or disabled	−0.25 (0.04)***	−0.26 (0.04)***	−0.26 (0.04)***
Retired	−0.18 (0.02)***	−0.18 (0.02)***	−0.18 (0.02)***
Community or military service	−0.17 (0.17)	−0.16 (0.17)	−0.16 (0.17)
Housework	−0.21 (0.02)***	−0.20 (0.02)***	−0.21 (0.02)***
Other activity	−0.03 (0.06)	−0.03 (0.06)	−0.04 (0.06)
Household income: ref – medium			
High	0.20 (0.02)***	0.22 (0.02)***	0.21 (0.02)***
Low	−0.18 (0.02)***	−0.17 (0.02)***	−0.18 (0.02)***
Missing	−0.03 (0.02)	−0.03 (0.02)	−0.03 (0.02)
Education (ISCED): ref – ISCED 2			
I: Less than lower secondary	−1.02 (0.02)***	−0.99 (0.02)***	−1.00 (0.02)***
II: Lower secondary	−0.50 (0.02)***	−0.50 (0.02)***	−0.50 (0.02)***
IV: Advanced vocational	0.27 (0.04)***	0.26 (0.04)***	0.27 (0.04)***
V–VI: tertiary	0.64 (0.02)***	0.64 (0.02)***	0.64 (0.02)***
Other	0.21 (0.15)	0.22 (0.15)	0.22 (0.15)
Trade union: ref – yes			
Yes, previously	0.18 (0.02)***	0.18 (0.02)***	0.19 (0.02)***
No	0.01 (0.02)	0.00 (0.02)	0.00 (0.02)

(Continued)

Table A5. Continued.

	Model 1	Model 2	Model 3
Party affiliation			
Strong	0.80 (0.01)***	0.80 (0.01)***	0.80 (0.01)***
Weak	0.25 (0.02)***	0.25 (0.02)***	0.25 (0.02)***
Religious	−0.11 (0.02)***	−0.09 (0.02)***	−0.10 (0.02)***
Country-level variables			
LogGDP	−0.20 (0.23)	−0.22 (0.23)	−0.21 (0.23)
Early childhood education	−0.14 (0.21)	−0.18 (0.21)	−0.19 (0.21)
Secondary education	0.07 (0.15)	−0.11 (0.16)	0.07 (0.16)
ALMP generosity	0.27 (0.38)	0.30 (0.38)	0.16 (0.39)
Passive support generosity	−0.45 (0.37)	−0.47 (0.38)	−0.47 (0.38)
Gini	0.12 (0.19)	0.14 (0.19)	0.13 (0.20)
Turnout	0.40 (0.23)	0.44 (0.23)	0.43 (0.24)
Interaction – early childhood education spending			
Old – high	0.03 (0.07)		
Old – medium	0.01 (0.06)		
Old – low	−0.18 (0.04)***		
Prime – high	0.12 (0.05)*		
Prime – low	−0.10 (0.04)**		
Young – high	0.34 (0.07)***		
Young – medium	0.09 (0.07)		
Young – low	0.16 (0.08)		
Interaction – secondary education spending			
Old – high		0.06 (0.09)	
Old – medium		0.13 (0.06)*	
Old – low		0.45 (0.04)***	
Prime – high		−0.07 (0.05)	
Prime – low		0.12 (0.04)**	
Young – high		0.18 (0.07)*	
Young – medium		0.00 (0.06)	
Young – Low		0.32 (0.08)***	
Interaction – ALMP spending			
Old – high			0.20 (0.07)**
Old – medium			0.16 (0.05)***
Old – low			0.22 (0.04)***
Prime – high			0.06 (0.05)
Prime – low			0.12 (0.04)**
Young – high			0.16 (0.07)*
Young – medium			−0.01 (0.06)
Young – low			0.21 (0.09)*
AIC	542242.83	542124.75	542303.81
BIC	542739.55	542621.47	542800.53
Log likelihood	−271070.42	−271011.37	−271100.91
Num. obs.	125447	125447	125447
Num. groups: cntry	25	25	25
Var: cntry (intercept)	0.15	0.16	0.16
Var: residual	4.40	4.39	4.40

Note: ***$p < 0.001$, **$p < 0.01$, *$p < 0.05$.

Interaction results – voting

Table A6. Interaction: voting, family status, and education spending.

	Model 1	Model 2
Intercept	1.41 (0.06)***	1.41 (0.06)***
Family status: ref – family with children		
Single	−0.41 (0.02)***	−0.42 (0.02)***
Couple, no kids	−0.09 (0.02)***	−0.09 (0.02)***
Single parent	−0.43 (0.03)***	−0.42 (0.03)***
Age–family skill background: ref – prime age/medium-skill background		
Old – high	0.64 (0.07)***	0.64 (0.07)***
Old – medium	0.45 (0.04)***	0.45 (0.04)***
Old – low	0.61 (0.03)***	0.61 (0.03)***
Prime – high	0.02 (0.03)	0.02 (0.03)
Prime – low	0.06 (0.03)*	0.06 (0.03)*
Young – high	−0.33 (0.05)***	−0.33 (0.05)***
Young – medium	−0.44 (0.04)***	−0.44 (0.04)***
Young – low	−0.65 (0.05)***	−0.65 (0.05)***
Female	0.07 (0.02)***	0.07 (0.02)***
Main activity: ref – full-time employed		
Education	−0.38 (0.04)***	−0.38 (0.04)***
Unemployed – looking	−0.37 (0.04)***	−0.37 (0.04)***
Unemployed – inactive	−0.45 (0.05)***	−0.45 (0.05)***
Sick or disabled	−0.35 (0.05)***	−0.35 (0.05)***
Retired	0.01 (0.03)	0.01 (0.03)
Community or military service	0.16 (0.20)	0.16 (0.20)
Housework	−0.14 (0.03)***	−0.14 (0.03)***
Other activity	−0.38 (0.07)***	−0.37 (0.07)***
Household income: ref – medium		
High	0.23 (0.03)***	0.23 (0.03)***
Low	−0.11 (0.02)***	−0.11 (0.02)***
Missing	−0.10 (0.02)***	−0.10 (0.02)***
Education (ISCED): Ref – ISCED 2		
I: Less than lower secondary	−0.42 (0.03)***	−0.42 (0.03)***
II: Lower secondary	−0.42 (0.02)***	−0.42 (0.02)***
IV: Advanced vocational	0.26 (0.05)***	0.26 (0.05)***
V–VI: Tertiary	0.34 (0.02)***	0.34 (0.02)***
Other	−0.22 (0.17)	−0.22 (0.17)
Trade union: ref – yes		
Yes, previously	−0.20 (0.03)***	−0.20 (0.03)***
No	−0.39 (0.02)***	−0.39 (0.02)***
Party affiliation		
Strong	1.42 (0.02)***	1.42 (0.02)***
Weak	0.79 (0.02)***	0.79 (0.02)***
Religious	0.37 (0.02)***	0.37 (0.02)***
Country-level variables		
LogGDP	−0.45 (0.14)**	−0.45 (0.14)**
Early childhood education	−0.23 (0.13)	−0.19 (0.13)
Secondary education	−0.07 (0.10)	−0.10 (0.10)
ALMP generosity	0.50 (0.24)*	0.50 (0.24)*
Passive support generosity	−0.12 (0.23)	−0.12 (0.23)
Gini	0.05 (0.12)	0.05 (0.12)
Turnout	1.03 (0.15)***	1.03 (0.15)***
Interaction – early childhood education		
Single	0.09 (0.04)*	
Couple, no kids	0.02 (0.05)	
Single parent	0.06 (0.07)	

(Continued)

135

Table A6. Continued.

	Model 1	Model 2
Interaction – secondary education		
Single		−0.00 (0.04)
Couple, no kids		0.10 (0.05)*
Single parent		0.12 (0.07)
AIC	106578.62	106575.83
BIC	107016.91	107014.12
Log likelihood	−53244.31	−53242.92
Num. obs.	125447	125447
Num. groups: cntry	25	25
Var: cntry (intercept)	0.06	0.06

Note: ***$p < 0.001$, **$p < 0.01$, *$p < 0.05$.

Table A7. Interaction: voting, age–family skill background, and skill building.

	Model 1	Model 2	Model 3
Intercept	1.40 (0.06)***	1.42 (0.06)***	1.41 (0.06)***
Family status: ref – family with children			
Single	−0.41 (0.02)***	−0.42 (0.02)***	−0.42 (0.02)***
Couple, no kids	−0.08 (0.02)***	−0.09 (0.02)***	−0.09 (0.02)***
Single parent	−0.43 (0.03)***	−0.43 (0.03)***	−0.43 (0.03)***
Age–family skill background: ref – prime age/medium-skill background			
Old – high	0.63 (0.07)***	0.63 (0.07)***	0.65 (0.07)***
Old – medium	0.45 (0.04)***	0.45 (0.04)***	0.45 (0.04)***
Old – low	0.60 (0.03)***	0.62 (0.03)***	0.61 (0.04)***
Prime – high	0.04 (0.03)	0.02 (0.03)	0.02 (0.03)
Prime – low	0.07 (0.03)**	0.06 (0.03)*	0.06 (0.03)*
Young – high	−0.31 (0.05)***	−0.33 (0.05)***	−0.32 (0.05)***
Young – medium	−0.43 (0.04)***	−0.45 (0.04)***	−0.45 (0.04)***
Young – low	−0.62 (0.05)***	−0.66 (0.05)***	−0.65 (0.05)***
Female	0.08 (0.02)***	0.07 (0.02)***	0.08 (0.02)***
Main activity: ref – full time employed			
Education	−0.39 (0.04)***	−0.38 (0.04)***	−0.38 (0.04)***
Unemployed – looking	−0.37 (0.04)***	−0.38 (0.04)***	−0.37 (0.04)***
Unemployed – inactive	−0.45 (0.05)***	−0.45 (0.05)***	−0.45 (0.05)***
Sick or disabled	−0.34 (0.05)***	−0.35 (0.05)***	−0.35 (0.05)***
Retired	0.02 (0.03)	0.00 (0.03)	0.01 (0.03)
Community or military service	0.15 (0.20)	0.17 (0.20)	0.17 (0.20)
Housework	−0.13 (0.03)***	−0.13 (0.03)***	−0.14 (0.03)***
Other activity	−0.37 (0.07)***	−0.37 (0.07)***	−0.38 (0.07)***
Household income: ref – medium			
High	0.23 (0.03)***	0.23 (0.03)***	0.23 (0.03)***
Low	−0.12 (0.02)***	−0.11 (0.02)***	−0.12 (0.02)***
Missing	−0.10 (0.02)***	−0.10 (0.02)***	−0.10 (0.02)***
Education (ISCED): ref – ISCED 2			
I: Less than lower secondary	−0.44 (0.03)***	−0.42 (0.03)***	−0.42 (0.03)***
II: Lower secondary	−0.42 (0.02)***	−0.42 (0.02)***	−0.42 (0.02)***
IV: Advanced vocational	0.26 (0.05)***	0.26 (0.05)***	0.27 (0.05)***
V–VI: Tertiary	0.34 (0.02)***	0.34 (0.02)***	0.34 (0.02)***
Other	−0.23 (0.17)	−0.21 (0.17)	−0.22 (0.17)
Trade union: ref – yes			
Yes, previously	−0.20 (0.03)***	−0.20 (0.03)***	−0.20 (0.03)***
No	−0.40 (0.02)***	−0.40 (0.02)***	−0.40 (0.02)***
Party affiliation			
Strong	1.42 (0.02)***	1.42 (0.02)***	1.42 (0.02)***
Weak	0.79 (0.02)***	0.79 (0.02)***	0.79 (0.02)***

(Continued)

Table A7. Continued.

	Model 1	Model 2	Model 3
Religious	0.37 (0.02)***	0.38 (0.02)***	0.37 (0.02)***
Country-level variables			
LogGDP	−0.46 (0.14)**	−0.46 (0.14)**	−0.45 (0.14)**
Early childhood education	−0.12 (0.13)	−0.19 (0.13)	−0.19 (0.13)
Secondary education	−0.07 (0.10)	−0.02 (0.10)	−0.07 (0.10)
ALMP generosity	0.48 (0.24)*	0.50 (0.24)*	0.51 (0.24)*
Passive support generosity	−0.11 (0.23)	−0.12 (0.23)	−0.11 (0.23)
Gini	0.06 (0.12)	0.05 (0.12)	0.05 (0.12)
Turnout	1.02 (0.15)***	1.04 (0.15)***	1.03 (0.15)***
Interaction – early childhood education spending			
Old – high	−0.22 (0.14)		
Old – medium	−0.16 (0.09)		
Old – low	−0.36 (0.06)***		
Prime – high	0.18 (0.07)*		
Prime – low	−0.08 (0.06)		
Young – high	0.22 (0.09)*		
Young – medium	0.19 (0.08)*		
Young – low	0.19 (0.10)*		
Interaction – secondary education spending			
Old – high		0.25 (0.16)	
Old – medium		−0.06 (0.09)	
Old – low		0.06 (0.05)	
Prime – high		−0.09 (0.08)	
Prime – low		−0.14 (0.05)**	
Young – high		−0.02 (0.09)	
Young – medium		−0.14 (0.07)*	
Young – low		−0.14 (0.09)	
Interaction – ALMP spending			
Old – high			0.22 (0.13)
Old – medium			0.01 (0.07)
Old – low			0.05 (0.05)
Prime – high			−0.06 (0.06)
Prime – low			−0.05 (0.05)
Young – high			0.09 (0.08)
Young – medium			−0.11 (0.07)
Young – low			−0.08 (0.10)
AIC	106467.94	106566.49	106580.44
BIC	106954.93	107053.47	107067.43
Log likelihood	−53183.97	−53233.24	−53240.22
Num. obs.	125447	125447	125447
Num. groups: cntry	25	25	25
Var: cntry (intercept)	0.06	0.06	0.06

Note: ***$p < 0.001$, **$p < 0.01$, *$p < 0.05$.

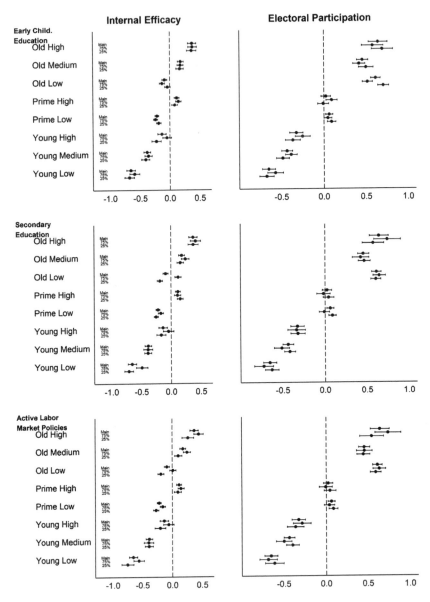

Figure A1. Full Figure – Age – Family / Skill Background

Robustness check: using alternative measure of employment and unemployment support generosity

We here replace the simple spending as percentage of GDP data with the amount spent on passive and active support measures per recipient, as a percentage of GDP. Results are consistent with our overall findings.

Table A8. Summary of results.

	Internal efficacy				Electoral participation			
	Main effect	Early childhood education	Secondary education	ALMP generosity	Main effect	Early childhood education	Secondary education	ALMP generosity
Old high	+	0	0	0	+	0	0	0
Old medium	+	0	+	+	+	0	0	0
Old low	–	–	+	+	+	–	0	0
Prime high	+	+	0	0	0	+	0	0
Prime low	–	–	+	+	+	0	–	0
Young high	–	+	0	0	–	+	0	0
Young Medium	–	0	0	–	–	+	–	–
Young low	–	0	+	+	–	+	0	0

139

Table A9. Interaction: internal efficacy, age–family skill background, and skill building.

	Model 1	Model 2	Model 3
Intercept	4.70 (0.09)***	4.71 (0.09)***	4.71 (0.09)***
Family status: ref – family with children			
Single	−0.02 (0.02)	−0.04 (0.02)*	−0.03 (0.02)*
Couple, no kids	0.06 (0.02)**	0.04 (0.02)*	0.04 (0.02)*
Single parent	0.01 (0.03)	0.02 (0.03)	0.03 (0.03)
Age–family skill background: ref – prime age/medium-skill background			
Old – high	0.37 (0.04)***	0.38 (0.04)***	0.39 (0.04)***
Old – medium	0.17 (0.03)***	0.18 (0.03)***	0.18 (0.03)***
Old – low	−0.09 (0.03)***	−0.09 (0.03)***	−0.09 (0.03)***
Prime – high	0.11 (0.03)***	0.14 (0.03)***	0.15 (0.03)***
Prime – low	−0.22 (0.02)***	−0.22 (0.02)***	−0.21 (0.02)***
Young – high	−0.13 (0.04)**	−0.13 (0.04)**	−0.11 (0.04)*
Young – medium	−0.39 (0.03)***	−0.39 (0.03)***	−0.41 (0.04)***
Young – low	−0.64 (0.04)***	−0.64 (0.04)***	−0.64 (0.04)***
Female	−0.89 (0.01)***	−0.89 (0.01)***	−0.89 (0.01)***
Main activity: ref – full time employed			
Education	0.26 (0.03)***	0.26 (0.03)***	0.27 (0.03)***
Unemployed – looking	−0.12 (0.03)***	−0.13 (0.03)***	−0.13 (0.03)***
Unemployed – inactive	−0.25 (0.05)***	−0.26 (0.05)***	−0.26 (0.05)***
Sick or disabled	−0.25 (0.04)***	−0.26 (0.04)***	−0.25 (0.04)***
Retired	−0.18 (0.02)***	−0.18 (0.02)***	−0.16 (0.02)***
Community or military service	−0.17 (0.17)	−0.16 (0.17)	−0.13 (0.16)
Housework	−0.21 (0.02)***	−0.20 (0.02)***	−0.19 (0.02)***
Other activity	−0.03 (0.06)	−0.03 (0.06)	−0.03 (0.06)
Household income: ref – medium			
High	0.20 (0.02)***	0.22 (0.02)***	0.23 (0.02)***
Low	−0.18 (0.02)***	−0.17 (0.02)***	−0.17 (0.02)***
Missing	−0.03 (0.02)	−0.03 (0.02)	−0.02 (0.02)
Education (ISCED): Ref – ISCED 2			
I: Less than lower secondary	−1.02 (0.02)***	−0.99 (0.02)***	−0.99 (0.02)***
II: Lower secondary	−0.50 (0.02)***	−0.50 (0.02)***	−0.51 (0.02)***
IV: Advanced vocational	0.27 (0.04)***	0.26 (0.04)***	0.25 (0.04)***
V–VI: Tertiary	0.64 (0.02)***	0.64 (0.02)***	0.64 (0.02)***
Other	0.21 (0.15)	0.22 (0.15)	0.21 (0.15)
Trade union: ref – yes			
Yes, previously	0.18 (0.02)***	0.18 (0.02)***	0.17 (0.02)***
No	0.01 (0.02)	0.00 (0.02)	−0.01 (0.02)
Party affiliation			
Strong	0.80 (0.01)***	0.80 (0.01)***	0.80 (0.01)***
Weak	0.25 (0.02)***	0.25 (0.02)***	0.24 (0.02)***
Religious	−0.11 (0.02)***	−0.09 (0.02)***	−0.10 (0.02)***
Country-level variables			
LogGDP	−0.19 (0.26)	−0.22 (0.26)	−0.20 (0.27)
Early childhood education	−0.09 (0.21)	−0.13 (0.21)	−0.11 (0.21)
Secondary education	0.03 (0.17)	−0.16 (0.17)	0.02 (0.17)
ALMP generosity	0.06 (0.21)	0.09 (0.21)	−0.10 (0.22)
Passive support Generosity	−0.06 (0.31)	−0.03 (0.31)	−0.05 (0.31)
Gini	0.11 (0.20)	0.13 (0.20)	0.14 (0.21)
Turnout	0.32 (0.24)	0.36 (0.24)	0.35 (0.24)
Interaction – early childhood education spending			
Old – high	0.03 (0.07)		
Old – medium	0.01 (0.06)		
Old – low	−0.18 (0.04)***		
Prime – high	0.12 (0.05)*		

(Continued)

Table A9. Continued.

	Model 1	Model 2	Model 3
Prime – low	−0.10 (0.04)**		
Young – high	0.34 (0.07)***		
Young – medium	0.09 (0.07)		
Young – low	0.16 (0.08)		
Interaction – secondary education spending			
Old – high		0.06 (0.09)	
Old – medium		0.13 (0.06)*	
Old – low		0.45 (0.04)***	
Prime – high		−0.07 (0.05)	
Prime – low		0.12 (0.04)**	
Young – high		0.18 (0.07)*	
Young – medium		0.00 (0.06)	
Young – low		0.32 (0.08)***	
Interaction – ALMP generosity			
Old – high			0.07 (0.08)
Old – medium			0.20 (0.05)***
Old – low			0.55 (0.04)***
Prime – high			−0.02 (0.05)
Prime – low			0.08 (0.04)*
Young – high			0.04 (0.07)
Young – medium			−0.13 (0.06)*
Young – low			0.24 (0.09)**
AIC	542244.96	542126.77	542010.82
BIC	542741.69	542623.49	542507.55
Log likelihood	−271071.48	−271012.38	−270954.41
Num. obs.	125447	125447	125447
Num. groups: cntry	25	25	25
Var: cntry (intercept)	0.17	0.17	0.17
Var: residual	4.40	4.39	4.39

Note: ***$p < 0.001$, **$p < 0.01$, *$p < 0.05$.

Table A10. Interaction: voting, age–family skill background, and skill building.

	Model 1	Model 2	Model 3
Intercept	1.40 (0.06)***	1.42 (0.06)***	1.41 (0.06)***
Family status: ref – family with children			
Single	−0.41 (0.02)***	−0.42 (0.02)***	−0.42 (0.02)***
Couple, no kids	−0.08 (0.02)***	−0.09 (0.02)***	−0.09 (0.02)***
Single parent	−0.43 (0.03)***	−0.43 (0.03)***	−0.43 (0.03)***
Age–family skill background: ref – prime age/medium-skill background			
Old – high	0.63 (0.07)***	0.63 (0.07)***	0.65 (0.07)***
Old – medium	0.45 (0.04)***	0.45 (0.04)***	0.45 (0.04)***
Old – low	0.60 (0.03)***	0.62 (0.03)***	0.61 (0.04)***
Prime – high	0.04 (0.03)	0.02 (0.03)	0.02 (0.03)
Prime – low	0.07 (0.03)**	0.06 (0.03)*	0.06 (0.03)*
Young – high	−0.31 (0.05)***	−0.33 (0.05)***	−0.32 (0.05)***
Young – medium	−0.43 (0.04)***	−0.45 (0.04)***	−0.45 (0.04)***
Young – low	−0.62 (0.05)***	−0.66 (0.05)***	−0.65 (0.05)***
Female	0.08 (0.02)***	0.07 (0.02)***	0.08 (0.02)***
Main activity: ref – full time employed			
Education	−0.39 (0.04)***	−0.38 (0.04)***	−0.38 (0.04)***
Unemployed – looking	−0.37 (0.04)***	−0.38 (0.04)***	−0.37 (0.04)***
Unemployed – inactive	−0.45 (0.05)***	−0.45 (0.05)***	−0.45 (0.05)***
Sick or disabled	−0.34 (0.05)***	−0.35 (0.05)***	−0.35 (0.05)***
Retired	0.02 (0.03)	0.00 (0.03)	0.01 (0.03)
Community or military service	0.15 (0.20)	0.17 (0.20)	0.17 (0.20)
Housework	−0.13 (0.03)***	−0.13 (0.03)***	−0.14 (0.03)***
Other activity	−0.37 (0.07)***	−0.37 (0.07)***	−0.38 (0.07)***
Household income: ref – medium			
High	0.23 (0.03)***	0.23 (0.03)***	0.23 (0.03)***
Low	−0.12 (0.02)***	−0.11 (0.02)***	−0.12 (0.02)***
Missing	−0.10 (0.02)***	−0.10 (0.02)***	−0.10 (0.02)***
Education (ISCED): ref – ISCED 2			
I: Less than lower secondary	−0.44 (0.03)***	−0.42 (0.03)***	−0.42 (0.03)***
II: Lower secondary	−0.42 (0.02)***	−0.42 (0.02)***	−0.42 (0.02)***
IV: Advanced vocational	0.26 (0.05)***	0.26 (0.05)***	0.27 (0.05)***
V–VI :Tertiary	0.34 (0.02)***	0.34 (0.02)***	0.34 (0.02)***
Other	−0.23 (0.17)	−0.21 (0.17)	−0.22 (0.17)
Trade union: ref – yes			
Yes, previously	−0.20 (0.03)***	−0.20 (0.03)***	−0.20 (0.03)***
No	−0.40 (0.02)***	−0.40 (0.02)***	−0.40 (0.02)***
Party affiliation			
Strong	1.42 (0.02)***	1.42 (0.02)***	1.42 (0.02)***
Weak	0.79 (0.02)***	0.79 (0.02)***	0.79 (0.02)***
Religious	0.37 (0.02)***	0.38 (0.02)***	0.37 (0.02)***
Country-level variables			
LogGDP	−0.46 (0.14)**	−0.46 (0.14)**	−0.45 (0.14)**
Early childhood education	−0.12 (0.13)	−0.19 (0.13)	−0.19 (0.13)
Secondary education	−0.07 (0.10)	−0.02 (0.10)	−0.07 (0.10)
ALMP generosity	0.48 (0.24)*	0.50 (0.24)*	0.51 (0.24)*
Passive support generosity	−0.11 (0.23)	−0.12 (0.23)	−0.11 (0.23)
Gini	0.06 (0.12)	0.05 (0.12)	0.05 (0.12)
Turnout	1.02 (0.15)***	1.04 (0.15)***	1.03 (0.15)***
Interaction – early childhood education spending			
Old – high	−0.22 (0.14)		
Old – medium	−0.16 (0.09)		
Old – low	−0.36 (0.06)***		
Prime – high	0.18 (0.07)*		
Prime – low	−0.08 (0.06)		
Young – high	0.22 (0.09)*		

(Continued)

Table A10. Continued.

	Model 1	Model 2	Model 3
Young – medium	0.19 (0.08)*		
Young – low	0.19 (0.10)*		
Interaction – secondary education spending			
Old – high		0.25 (0.16)	
Old – medium		−0.06 (0.09)	
Old – low		0.06 (0.05)	
Prime – high		−0.09 (0.08)	
Prime – low		−0.14 (0.05)**	
Young – high		−0.02 (0.09)	
Young – medium		−0.14 (0.07)*	
Young – low		−0.14 (0.09)	
Interaction – ALMP generosity			
Old – high			0.22 (0.13)
Old – medium			0.01 (0.07)
Old – low			0.05 (0.05)
Prime – high			−0.06 (0.06)
Prime – low			−0.05 (0.05)
Young – high			0.09 (0.08)
Young – medium			−0.11 (0.07)
Young – low			−0.08 (0.10)
AIC	106467.94	106566.49	106580.44
BIC	106954.93	107053.47	107067.43
Log likelihood	−53183.97	−53233.24	−53240.22
Num. obs.	125447	125447	125447
Num. groups: cntry	25	25	25
Var: cntry (intercept)	0.06	0.06	0.06

Note: ***$p < 0.001$, **$p < 0.01$, *$p < 0.05$.

Pro-elderly welfare states within child-oriented societies

Róbert Iván Gál, Pieter Vanhuysse and Lili Vargha

ABSTRACT

Families and policies both are main vehicles of intergenerational transfers. Working-age people are net contributors; children and older persons net beneficiaries. However, there is an asymmetry in socialization. Working-age people pay taxes and social security contributions to institutionalize care for older persons as a generation, but invest private resources to raise their own children, often with large *social* returns. This results in asymmetric statistical visibility. Elderly transfers are near-fully observed in National Accounts; those to children much less. Analysing ten European societies, we employ National Transfer Accounts to include public and private transfers, and National Time Transfer Accounts to value unpaid household labour. All three transfer channels combined, children receive more than twice as many per-capita resources as older persons. Europe is a continent of elderly-oriented welfare states and strongly child-oriented parents. Since children are ever-scarcer public goods in aging societies, why has investment in them not been socialized *more*?

Introduction: shining a wider light on the 'social' in investment

The contributions to this collection interpret 'social investment' nearly exclusively in terms of (productivist) *public policies* (see also Esping-Andersen 2009; Morel *et al.* 2012). Conceptually, however, social investment refers to the allocation, with the expectation of positive returns also to society, of scarce resources to the skills and human capital of (future) workers. This is a productive form of downward intergenerational transfer.[1] Incidentally, the literature on intergenerational transfers exhibits the same strong policy emphasis.[2] It puts forward three main propositions: (1) currently older generations receive more overall public transfers than in past decades (Kotlikoff and Burns 2012);

ⓑ Supplemental data for this contribution can be accessed at 10.1080/13501763.2017.1401112.

(2) older persons receive more on average than children (Vanhuysse 2013); and (3) the elderly/children public transfer ratio has been increasing (Preston 1984). Such tendencies are sometimes referred to as 'grey power', 'gerontocracy' (Sinn and Uebelmesser 2002), or 'pro-elderly bias' (Tepe and Vanhuysse 2010; Vanhuysse 2014). Some even speak of 'generational' 'storms' or 'clashes' (Kotlikoff and Burns 2012). This contribution argues that these portrayals of intergenerational transfers are misleading, since they are limited to the statistically visible world of public transfers and largely ignore intra-familial transfers (*cash*) and the household economy (*time*). Yet households and public policies both serve as vehicles of intergenerational transfers (Albertini *et al.* 2007).

For instance, a key social investment function of the cash and time parents transfer to their non-adult children is to boost children's cognitive skills and non-cognitive traits. In addition to the private returns to children, these parental transfers have significant, and often large, *social* returns later on.[3] Undoubtedly, children provide manifold private benefits to their parents and families, and part of the cost of raising them resembles pure consumption. But children are also very significantly *public* goods, predominantly paid for privately (Folbre 1994; Lee and Miller 1990). While raising children may be better described as an intrinsic commitment rather than a deliberate investment, it is a very costly and socially beneficial commitment all the same (Folbre 2008). Parents bear the lion's share of these costs – in cash and time, both directly and in terms of opportunities foregone. These private costs are in part socially imposed by socio-legal obligations for continuity of adequate care (Alstott 2004). Yet, to the extent that children subsequently become productive tax and social security paying adults, they create positive externalities that will benefit all of society. They will finance, for instance, future public pension and health and long-term care benefits – all of which will also benefit non-parents. In other words, not just are the current costs of children in part socially created but only very partially socialized. What is more, children's future social benefits are fully socialized. Society forcibly redirects some of these benefits to non-parents, thereby reducing the benefits available to parents (Olsaretti 2013).

We provide a fuller picture of the degree to which societies, not just welfare states, transfer resources between generations. We show that on their own, public transfer data offer an incomplete and biased picture of intergenerational transfers – a proverbial case of looking for a lost car key only where the streetlight shines at night. When it comes to younger age groups, the bulk of the investments in society are not by policies but by households. We thus follow the social investment and human capital literatures in viewing many resource transfers to younger citizens not as consumption but in large part as positive-return investments in productive skills. But we show that once one shines a wider light by using more complete data on all relevant forms of intergenerational transfers, a radically different picture emerges on how, and how much, societies invest. The reason is a key asymmetry in *socialization*[4] – in the forms of financing the current costs of childhood and old age. Older persons as a generation tend to rely on society, but the costs of children are predominantly borne by their own families, mostly their parents (Demeny 1987). Socialization leaves traces that public statistics can capture. Non-socialized transactions do not, leaving them much less visible (Folbre 2008).

Empirically, we make two contributions. First, we construct age profiles through National Transfer Accounts (NTAs).[5] This allows us to look not just at the allocation of primary income and its secondary distribution based on standard National Accounts (NAs), but also at the tertiary redistribution of after-tax revenues within households (e.g., parents paying for the consumption of dependent children) and between households (e.g., retired parents supporting non-cohabiting children). However, NTAs still do not cover the provision and consumption of *unpaid household labour*. Such labour, especially in the form of care for children and the fostering of their cognitive and non-cognitive human capital, is also a key form of societal investment (Esping-Andersen 2009; Folbre 1994, 2008). In a second step, we therefore provide new calculations for this key variable missing from studies of intergenerational transfers. Based on time use survey data, we estimate the value of transfers of household goods and services by age. We call these National *Time Transfer Accounts* (NTTAs; see also Donehower 2011).

We analyse all three transfer channels – public and private resources, and time – for 10 European countries spanning five welfare regime models and representing about 70 per cent of the EU population around 2005: France, Austria and Germany; Italy and Spain; Hungary and Slovenia; Finland and Sweden; and the United Kingdom (UK). Our main findings can be summarized as follows. (1) In line with the pro-elderly bias literature, European welfare states, as welfare *states*, tend to devote significantly more resources per-capita to the currently old than to the currently young. (2) However, once we take also into account private, mostly intra-familial transfers and unpaid household labour (time), the picture radically changes. All European societies, as *societies*, transfer far more per-capita resources overall to children than to older persons.

Constructing resource transfer age profiles: time is of the essence

NTAs introduce age into age-insensitive National Accounts. Whereas in NAs revenues flow among institutions (e.g., households, government and firms), NTAs recognize that the main entries of NAs' Income Account have characteristic age profiles. Labour income is minimal or zero in childhood and old age, and is largely concentrated in active age. Consumption is more uniformly distributed over the lifecycle. Public transfers are financed mostly by people in their active age and consumed mostly by people at young or old ages. Resources of households are also reallocated from the active aged to children and older persons. The lifecycle deficit (LCD) is defined as the net *balance* (difference) between consumption and labour income at any given lifecycle *stage* (Lee and Mason 2011). In rich modern societies, LCD is positive (a true deficit) in childhood and old age, when consumption is not covered by one's own labour income. LCD is negative (a surplus) in active age, when labour income exceeds consumption.

In short, NTAs redefine income flows among institutions as flows among generations. The NTA accounting standard describes age groups by: (1) how much labour income they make; (2) how much they consume; (3) how much they give to other age groups, either through public channels such as taxes, or directly, mostly among relatives; (4) how much they receive from other age groups, either as public transfers, services and public goods, or as private transfers; and (5) how much they (dis)save. This requires the extension of the usual information base of NA with income and consumption surveys as well as administrative or survey information on tax and transfer incidence. NTA analyses start by converting NA entries to the NTA aggregates of labour income (including taxes levied on labour), consumption (net of consumption related taxes) and the resulting lifecycle deficit (Lee and Mason 2011). The age profiles of these items are derived from administrative data or surveys. The profiles are adjusted to the aggregates to secure consistency between NAs and NTAs. A similar process produces the age profiles of items such as asset-based revenues, taxes and transfers and private transfers given or received, filling the gap between consumption and labour income.[6] Accordingly, panel A of Figure 1 shows the normalized per-capita age profile of LCD for our 10 countries. The LCD of older persons is on the whole higher than that of children. The highest LCD during childhood is around ages 14–16, when teenagers receive the equivalent of 59 per cent

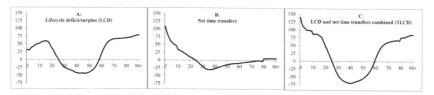

Figure 1. Per-capita lifecycle deficit, net time transfers, and total lifecycle deficit by age in Europe. Source: authors' calculation based on NTA data for LCD (www.ntaccounts.org) and on Vargha *et al.* (2016) for time transfers.

Notes: Values are population weighted averages of 10 European countries around 2005 normalized on the per-capita market labour income of persons aged 30–49 of the respective country.

of the per-capita labour income of persons aged 30–49 in their country. The same 59 per cent share is received already at age 66. Thereafter, the resource transfers received by older persons keep rising slowly.

Importantly, however, data on *unpaid household labour* are missing from both NAs and NTAs (thus from panel A). Yet such labour is a major resource transferred across generations. Sociologists have increasingly emphasized the importance of, and the changing patterns in, the time devoted to family duties and household labour (Albertini *et al.* 2007; Esping-Andersen 2015; Gershuny 2000; Lareau 2003). The equivalent of LCD in the realm of unpaid household labour is net *time* transfers. Their meaning is the same: the value of household labour consumed less the value of household labour produced. The goods and services produced and consumed here, however, are not part of the national economy, but of the household economy. We therefore created the age profile of net time transfers, in three steps (see Online Appendix 1). First, we used Harmonised European Time Use Survey (HETUS) and other time use surveys to identify the time spent on household production activities by age.[7] Second, home production was assigned to its actual consumers. Third, we imputed the value of time spent in unpaid household labour using the market wages of the person whose job is done as our reference point.

Panel B of Figure 1 presents the per-capita age profile of net time transfers, containing the estimated market value of all household work. Clearly, the shape of intergenerational transfers is radically different in the household economy (panel B) compared to the national economy (panel A). Net time transfers are highest among newborns: quite naturally, babies need the most time-intensive care. During their first year of life, European children receive on average more than the yearly per-capita prime-age labour income in their country in time transfers alone.

These time transfers subsequently decrease, but they remain substantial throughout childhood and adolescence. Five-year-olds still receive nearly 60 per cent of yearly per-capita labour income in time transfers. Time transfers still amount to more than one-third of labour income at age 10 and more than one-fifth at age 15. They only turn negative as late as age 25. The largest net time contributors are in their thirties to mid-forties – the 'rush hour of life', when most adults reach peaks of labour market stress and are also burdened with extensive household and family care duties. These duties are most time-intensive precisely during the most investment-like stage of child rearing: the first life years.

Net time transfers in panel B remain negative much longer than in panel A, becoming positive only among the oldest-old, after age 80. Active adulthood thus lasts longer in terms of unpaid household labour (from age 25 to age 79) than in terms of the national economy (from 26 to 58). This reflects the house-work, grandparenting and other civil society activities undertaken by 'young-old' Europeans in their sixties and seventies. Yet the value of such activities is comparatively small after age 70. This is because the biggest share of unpaid household labour by far is not direct person-to-person care or inter-household transfers, but rather 'intra-household public goods' produced by household members for joint consumption (e.g., cooking, cleaning gardening). But older Europeans overwhelmingly no longer live inside multigenerational households *with* their children and grandchildren. Conservatively estimated, over three-quarters of older people in our 10-country sample do not live with their children (Eurostat Census Hub data).

The *total* lifecycle deficit: Europe as a child-oriented continent

Panel C of Figure 1 combines net public transfers with LCD and net time transfers to produce the fullest description of intergenerational transfers. We call this combined picture the total lifecycle deficit (TLCD), i.e., the net balance of all resources received at any lifecycle stage. All three transfer types combined, children between birth and age nine receive between 139 and 96 per cent of per-capita labour income in their country. This is more than even the very oldest receive – those aged 90 and above. Young Europeans still receive more than three-quarters of per-capita prime-age labour income right until they reach age 17, close to voting age. Older Europeans, however, receive the same share only after they reach age 80.

Our method allows us to define lifecycle stages according to *net total resource dependency*, as opposed to chronologically, as is conventional (e.g., childhood until age 18, old age from age 65). Defined this way, TLCD-childhood in Europe lasts on average until age *25*, while TLCD-old age already starts at age *60*. Even in countries with a small higher education sector, this demarcation age for the end of childhood is still surprisingly high, as it takes young adults years to reach a level of labour productivity sufficient to compensate for increasing consumption.

Online Appendix 2 contains the per-capita values of the full transfer package in terms of prime-age labour income by transfer type flowing to children and older persons. In line with pro-elderly welfare studies (Lynch 2006; Tepe and Vanhuysse 2010; Vanhuysse 2013), older persons receive more than twice as much in net public transfers than children: 37 per cent of average prime-earnings income, compared to 15 per cent. But once private transfers are also taken into account, the picture changes. The combined public–private spheres transfer package of children (39 per cent) is slightly larger than that of older persons (34 per cent). And most importantly, if in a third step we add transfers of unpaid household labour, the original proportions are *inverted*. The children/elderly transfer ratio jumps from less than half in public transfers alone (0.39) to more than double all transfers combined (2.35).

The value of the full transfer package for a child is equivalent of 73 per cent of annual per-capita prime-age labour income. Out of this, only 15 percentage points flow through publicly recorded channels. In contrast, the public part of older persons' package is around 37 per cent of prime-age labour income, which is reduced to 31 per cent through the private transfers in cash and time older persons provide. In short, despite recent shifts from passive and/ or curative forms of welfare toward social investments, welfare states are still very much geared toward paying benefits and services in old age. The main investment during childhood, by far, is by households. Although public policies transfer more resources to the old and very old, once house-holds are taken into account Europe emerges as a *child-oriented* continent. This holds true in every one of our 10 countries, even though there is signifi-cant variance in how countries complement or crowd out working-age citi-zens in caring for dependents.

Revisiting the three channels for financing intergenerational transfers

The TLCD curve reappears in Figure 2, where we show how the gap between consumption and production is financed through three resource channels: net public transfers (mediated by government, social security or other

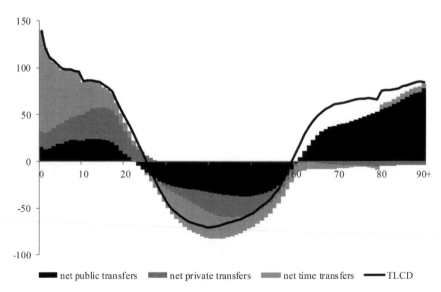

Figure 2. Per-capita public, private and time transfers and their contribution to filling the gaps of total lifecycle deficit by age in Europe. Source: Authors' calculation based on NTA data (www.ntaccounts.org) and Vargha *et al.* (2016).

Notes: Values as in Figure 1.

public actors); private transfers (within or between households, overwhelmingly among relatives); and time transfers. The enveloping curve of public transfers (including taxes and subsidies on production, taxes on income and wealth, and social contributions and benefits) shows that public policies create pro-elderly biased welfare *states*. Defined in terms of public resource dependency, childhood lasts until age 21 and old age starts at age 60. The highest net public transfer in childhood is around age 12–13, at less than one-quarter of prime-age earnings. Older Europeans receive more than this: more than half of prime-age earnings by age 77, and more than three-quarters by age 90.

However, public transfers do not cover TLCD, particularly among children. Consumption exceeds production by an equivalent of nearly 140 per cent of annual prime-age labour income for newborns, out of which public transfers cover only 15 percentage points. Other forms of inter-age transfers must fill the gap. The dark grey area shows the age profile of private transfers – flows of items that are part of the national income (e.g., services and commodities) bought by parents but consumed by their children. They are exchanged almost exclusively among relatives and overwhelmingly *within* households.[8]

The age profile of private transfers is very different. First, reflecting the typical household structure prevalent across Europe, private transfers are mostly a two-generation affair. Those up to age 27 are net receivers, and from around age 60 net private transfers become marginal. Second, while negligible in old age, private transfers are more important than public transfers at every childhood stage. Yet, large parts of the area below the TLCD curve are still uncovered. This gap is mostly filled with time transfers. Children require more time resources when small and more cash as they grow older. Second, children receive nearly one-and-a-half times as much in time transfers as in private transfers. Third, older Europeans up to age 79 are modest net providers of time.

In sum, taking the complete transfer package into account, children receive on average substantially more resources than older persons in Europe. This is rarely if ever noted in the literatures on *state* social investment, owing to the asymmetric socialization and asymmetric visibility of upward and downward transfers. Market and government transfers flow between people connected by contractual relations enforceable by law. The value of these transfers is largely set by market forces or regulation, and it is registered and accounted for. But regarding invisible transfers, the co-operation of the actors, most frequently family members, is regulated by customs and social norms (Coleman 1990; Folbre 2008). Violation of these norms is less observable, less systematically registered and, except for extreme cases, not enforceable by law. In the case of time transfers, they cannot even be measured directly because these transfers are not evaluated in the market. As a result, these transfers are largely missing from public statistics

In some sense, there is a universal functional division of labour going on between governments and families in contemporary societies. Working-age citizens pay taxes and social security contributions to care indirectly for currently older *generations* through state programmes. But they predominantly spend private time and private resources to care directly for their *own* children themselves. The resources involved in raising children remain mostly a family affair. But since working-age adults no longer tend to live with their parents, care for older generations is largely institutionalized through government programmes or markets. Transfers to older persons are easier to socialize through cash or public services provision without the intercession of a guardian. Online Appendix 3 gives further details by showing the institutional composition of transfers. Children in Europe receive nearly *half* of their net transfers in the form of unpaid household labour. Older persons are net providers of both time transfers and private transfers, but large recipients of public transfers.

Conclusions: why not *more* socialization of child investment?

Contrary to widely held perceptions, children receive more than twice as many per-capita resources as older persons in Europe. Our findings do not refute the key propositions of either the elderly bias or the social investment literatures. Welfare states, *as* welfare states, have undergone a paradigm shift towards policies aiming to boost productivity through investment in human capital and skills, while at the same time transferring more resources to older persons. But our findings do suggest that these literatures are in danger of looking for a lost car key only where the streetlight shines. Public transfer data alone offer a highly incomplete picture of what societies accomplish in terms of intergenerational transfers and investment in the human capital of (future) workers. Any apparent pro-elderly welfare state bias is the consequence of the asymmetric socialization of intergenerational transfers and their resulting asymmetric visibility in National Accounts. Once one includes also private cash and time transfers, conclusions differ radically. European societies, as *societies,* transfer more than twice as many resources on average to each child as to each older person.

Prescriptively, these findings indicate that there is much scope left for states to assist or complement families in boosting early human capital through the various education, training and work–family reconciliation policies discussed in this collection. The key role of parents points to another rationale for shining a wider light on the 'social' in investment. Only by going beyond public policies and studying how parents respond in their private investment decisions can we optimize social outcomes (Francesconi and Heckman 2016). Skill formation is characterized by dynamic complementarities: 'Skill begets skill: early learning makes later learning easier and more effective' (Carneiro and Heckman 2003: 90). While early childhood is therefore crucial, continuity is needed throughout childhood and early youth into adolescence. Effect sizes of policy interventions may go down during primary and middle school ages, but the causal mechanisms are similar. For instance, test scores, behaviours, attitudes and curriculum enrolment of middle and high school students are key predictors of later schooling, criminal and labour market outcomes (Farkas 2011). Social investment may also have a differential impact across childhood (Vanhuysse 2015). Cognitive abilities appear to be malleable predominantly during early childhood. But key non-cognitive skills seem responsive to well-designed interventions much longer, until at least late adolescence (Dweck 2012; Francesconi and Heckman 2016; Heckman 2013).

Economic models of human capital tend to focus on the emergence of intergenerational *social* policies for the young (e.g., Goldin and Katz 2008). In Becker and Murphy's (1988) account, in the absence of reliable and enforceable long-term contracts, welfare states have historically evolved in order to provide a public (cross-sectional) solution to the problem of transferring private resources from 'producers' to economically less-powerful younger 'dependents' over the life cycle. Lee (2012: 26) argues that co-operative child rearing has paved the way for the emergence of the welfare state as an institutional improvement over family care for young dependents. More generally, economic theory posits that public goods will often be undersupplied by private actors because the costs are borne by the producer, but the benefits are non-excludable. This is seen as a strong rationale for state intervention (e.g., Barr 2012). These economic models provide functionalist accounts of state policies for children. But they do not explain why, empirically, it is families, not states, who still take upon themselves the overwhelming share of resource transfers to younger generations.

Though parental (especially maternal) childrearing might appear 'natural,' rates of infanticide, abortion and orphanage have historically fluctuated according to socio-contextual determinants and have at times been substantial (Hrdy 1999). At the same time, the traditional model of private child rearing *has* reasserted itself even in the rare settings designed explicitly to strongly modify it. For instance, in a number of egalitarian collective childrearing communities founded in the 1960s–1970s, commune-member mothers ended up expressing even stronger preferences than mothers in ordinary households for caring for their own biological children (Cohen and Eiduson 1976). The originally radical Israeli kibbutzim model of collective rearing by multiple non-kin caregivers was gradually diluted over time to allow ever greater parental involvement including home sleeping, until the whole system was abandoned in the 1980s (Aviezer *et al.* 1994; Beit-Hallahmi and Rabin 1977). Hands-on child rearing thus seems unlikely to be extensively socialized.

But the question remains: why *so little* socialization of early human capital *investment*? After all, children are public goods, given the positive externalities they will later bring to all of society. More precisely still: they are *forcibly and deliberately socialized* goods whose future benefits (their taxes and other productive contributions they will make) are, technically, rival and excludable (Olsarettti 2013). This is why older persons' social rights (e.g., pensions), parents' taxation levels, and official pension ages could all, in principle, be parental investment-related and be conceived in part as private returns to earlier human capital investment (Demeny 1987; Olsaretti 2013). But empirically, social programmes explicitly and significantly internalizing the positive externalities of children by taking into account earlier child rearing efforts just cannot be observed in contemporary welfare states.

The puzzle of primary theoretical interest is why early human capital investment (not childrearing) has not been socialized much more than we observe in reality. Notwithstanding the Human Capital Twentieth Century (Goldin and Katz 2008) and the post-2000 'social investment' paradigm (Busemeyer *et al.* 2018; Hemerijck 2018), the state's role in such investment still appears very modest in most rich democracies, with the exception of Nordic Europe. Children may have become 'emotionally priceless but economically worthless' (Zelizer 1985: 3) to *parents,* but not to high-longevity, low-fertility *societies.* The productivity argument for state investment in very young children is particularly compelling, as high-quality early childhood education often displays remarkable social rates of return.[9] Yet state spending on such programmes still averaged only 0.6 per cent of gross domestic product (GDP) in the Western and 0.4 per cent in the Eastern EU member states in the first decade of the twenty-first century (Vanhuysse 2015: 277). The inherent present-bias of actors and institutions in democracies with short electoral horizons is undoubtedly one key factor (Gonzalez-Ricoy and Gosseries 2016); competing demands on tight budgets from aging voters another (Tepe and Vanhuysse 2009, 2010; Vanhuysse 2013).

There is ample evidence of 'overworked' adults (Frase and Gornick 2013) – mainly women – who spend the 'rush hour' of life in a 'time bind' at work and in their 'second shift' at home (Hochschild 1997). Our evidence only strengthens these claims. But gender, parenthood and class are the three elephants in the room here. There are additional key differences in resource contributions, most importantly between women and men, but also between parents and non-parents (Esping-Andersen 2009; Folbre 1994, 2008). Children in Europe may receive nearly half of their net transfers as unpaid household labour, but most of that is performed by *women.* Europe's small social investment *states* may be embedded within societies with larger parental investment in children, but most parental time spent on children is by women. Moreover, children face diverging destinies depending on the accident of birth (Esping-Andersen 2015; McLanahan 2004). In addition to Matthew effects in social service receipt, there is a strong, and probably increasing, class gradient to the private resources spent caring for children, which is exacerbated by higher divorce and single motherhood rates among low-socioeconomic status groups and by increasing educational homogamy in partner choice (Bonke and Esping-Andersen 2011; Lareau 2003).

Since when have transfers to children been higher per capita than to older persons? Are higher pro-elderly public transfers a form of compensation for lost private and time transfers owing to lower co-habitation levels with adult children? We do not have retrospective information describing temporal processes. Although we cannot address these questions, there is evidence that the average time spent on non-chore unpaid household labour has increased since the 1950s (Gershuny 2000). Together with the strong reduction of child mortality and the shortening of working weeks, this may have further boosted the idea that children are 'priceless' (Zelizer 1985). Time transfers have probably become more valuable in monetary terms, yet there is little evidence of productivity-driven Becker-type gender specialization. Rather, contemporary high-earning parents like to care jointly (Bonke and Esping-Andersen 2011; Esping-Andersen 2015). However, there do seem to be clear Becker-Lewis-type quantity/quality trade-offs. Lower fertility tends to increase time transfers to, and family investment in, each child (Vargha and Donehower 2016). Future research must elucidate the overall impact and the class and gender dimensions of such developments. As they stand, our results question any one-sided storyline of a creeping resource grab by older citizens. The growing public resource share toward older persons may well have gone in parallel with increasing societal resources for the young. Notwithstanding elderly bias in public spending, the twentieth century may also have been the Century of the Child, as Ellen Key (1909) predicted at its start.

Notes

1. Resource transfers are studied here among *current age groups*, not diachronically between cohorts.
2. For critical reviews, see Vanhuysse and Goerres (2012), Tepe and Vanhuysse (2009).
3. Heckman and Masterov (2007); Carneiro and Heckman (2003); Francesconi and Heckman (2016), Heckman (2013); also Esping-Andersen (2009), Vanhuysse (2015). We view transfers to *older* generations as predominantly financing consumption, not investment, as such transfers do not systematically produce significant positive returns over long temporal horizons.
4. By socialization, we mean the arrangement of intergenerational transfers by large-scale, anonymized institutions, rather than close kin or local communities. The former include governments (e.g., public child care, social security) but also non-profit organizations serving households and for-profit corporations (e.g., private schools, pension plans) (Lee and Mason 2011: 65).

5. NTA was established by Lee (1994); a manual is United Nations (2013); an intro-duction is Lee and Mason (2011).
6. Since tax-transfer systems and data sources vary across countries, technical details of producing the age profiles differ. Istenič *et al.* (2016) provide a standar-dized methodology.
7. HETUS is an effort to harmonize European time use surveys: https://www.h2.scb.se/tus/tus/default.htm
8. They are considered the balancing item between private consumption and dis-posable income communicated among family members. Estimations are based on a household sharing model and a simple set of assumptions accommodating cross-country comparison (United Nations 2013). Calculations are made on large consumption surveys; in Europe, household budget surveys.
9. See note 3.

Acknowledgements

We are grateful for comments from the editors, Kati Kuitto, Birgit Pfau-Effinger, Martin Schröder and seminar participants at the Max Planck Centre Odense, the Madrid FUNCAS workshop, Hamburg, Lausanne, Konstanz, and Pazmany Budapest univer-sities, the Hebrew University Jerusalem, the Slovak Academy, and the Canadian Parlia-ment. Gal is grateful for hospitality at Hitotsubashi University's Institute of Economic Research. We thank the following teams for providing NTA data: Bernhard Hammer (Austria), Reijo Vanne and Risto Vaittinen (Finland), Hyppolite D'Albis *et al.* (France), Fanny Kluge (Germany), Marina Zannella (Italy), Katharina Lisenkova (UK), Jože Sambt (Slovenia), Thomas Lindh *et al.* (Sweden) and Ció Patxot *et al.* (Spain). Hungarian data were produced by Gál and Vargha.

Disclosure statement

No potential conflict of interest was reported by the authors.

Funding

This contribution was written as part of the AGENTA project funded by the Seventh Framework Programme of the European Union (grant agreement no 613247) and the 'Taking Age Discrimination Seriously' project, based at the Institute of State and Law (Prague) and funded by the Grantová Agentura České Republiky (grant number 17-266295).

References

Albertini, M., Kohli, M. and Vogel, C. (2007) 'Intergenerational transfers of time and money in European families: common patterns — different regimes?', *Journal of European Social Policy* 17(17): 319–34.

Alstott, A. (2004) *No Exit*, Oxford: Oxford University Press.

Aviezer, O., van Ijzendoorn, M., Sagi, A. and Schuengel, C. (1994) '"Children of the dream" revisited: 70 years of collective early child care in Israeli kibbutzim', *Psychological Bulletin* 116(1): 99–116.

Barr, N. (2012) *Economics of the Welfare State*, 5th edition, Oxford: Oxford University Press.

Becker, G.S. and Murphy, K.M. (1988) 'The family and the state', *The Journal of Law and Economics* 31(1): 1–18.

Beit-Hallahmi, B. and Rabin, A.I. (1977) 'The kibbutz as a social experiment and as a child-rearing laboratory', *American Psychologist* 32(7): 532–41.

Bonke, J. and Esping-Andersen, G. (2011) 'Family investments in children – productivities, preferences, and parental child care', *European Sociological Review* 27(19): 43–55.

Busemeyer, M., de la Porte, C., Garritzmann, J. and Pavolini, E. (2018) 'The future of social investment: politics, policies, and outcomes', *Journal of European Public Policy* 25(6): 801–809.

Carneiro, P. and Heckman, J. (2003) 'Human capital policy', in J. Heckman and A. Krueger (eds) *Inequality in America*, Cambridge: MIT Press, pp. 77–239.

Cohen, J. and Eiduson, B. (1976) 'Changing patterns of childrearing in alternative lifestyles', in A. Davids (ed.), *Child Personality and Psychopathology Vol. 3*, New York: Wiley, pp. 25–68.

Coleman, J.S. (1990) *Foundations of Social Theory*, Cambridge: Harvard University Press.

Demeny, P. (1987) 'Re-linking fertility behavior and economic security in old age: a pronatalist reform', *Population and Development Review* 13: 128–32.

Donehower, G. (2011) 'Incorporating gender and time use into NTA', UC Berkeley. Manuscript.

Dweck, C. (2012) *Mindset*, New York: Robinson.

Esping-Andersen, G. (2009) *The Incomplete Revolution*, Cambridge: Polity Press.

Esping-Andersen, G. (2015) 'The return of the family', in P. Beramendi, S. Häusermann, H. Kitschelt and H. Kriesi (eds), *The Politics of Advanced Capitalism*, Cambridge: Cambridge University Press, pp. 157–78.

Farkas, G. (2011) 'Middle and high school skills, behaviors, attitudes, and curriculum enrolment, and their consequences', in Duncan, G. and Murnane, R. (eds), *Whither Opportunity?* New York: Russell Sage, pp. 71–90.

Folbre, N. (1994) 'Children as public goods', *American Economic Review* 84(2): 86–90.

Folbre, N. (2008) *Valuing Children*, Cambridge: Harvard University Press.

Francesconi, M. and Heckman, J. (2016) 'Child development and parental investment: Introduction', *The Economic Journal* 126: F1–F27.

Frase, P. and Gornick, J. (2013) 'The time divide in cross-national perspective: the work week, education and institutions that matter', *Social Forces* 91(3): 697–724.

Gershuny, J. (2000) *Changing Times*, Oxford: Oxford University Press.

Goldin, C. and Katz, L. (2008) *The Race Between Education and Technology*, Cambridge: Belknap Press.

Gonzalez-Ricoy, I. and Gosseries, A. (eds) (2016) *Institutions for Future Generations*, Oxford: Oxford University Press.

Heckman, J. (2013) *Giving Kids a Fair Chance*, Cambridge: MIT Press.

Heckman, J. and Masterov, J. (2007) 'The productivity argument for investing in young children', *Review of Agricultural Economics* 29(3): 446–93.

Hemerijck, A. (2018) 'Social investment as a policy paradigm', *Journal of European Public Policy* 25(6): 810–827.

Hochschild, A.R. (1997) *The Time Bind*, New York: Henry Holt.

Hrdy, S.B. (1999) *Mother Nature*, New York: Pantheon.

Istenič, T., Šeme, A., Hammer, B., Lotrič-Dolinar, A. and Sambt, J. (2016) 'European NTA manual', Manuscript.

Key, E.K.S. (1909) *The Century of the Child*, New York: Putnam.

Kotlikoff, L.J. and Burns, S. (2012) *The Clash of Generations*, Cambridge: MIT Press.

Lareau, A. (2003) *Unequal Childhoods*, Berkeley: University of California Press.

Lee, R.D. (1994) 'Population age structure, intergenerational transfer, and wealth: a new approach, with applications to the United States', *The Journal of Human Resources* 29 (4): 1027–63.

Lee, R.D. (2012) 'Intergenerational transfers, the biological life cycle, and human society', *Population and Development Review* 38: 23–35.

Lee, R.D. and Mason, A. (eds) (2011) *Population Aging and the Generational Economy*, Cheltenham: Edward Elgar.

Lee, R.D. and Miller, T. (1990) 'Population policy and externalities to childbearing', *The Annals of the American Academy of Political and Social Science* 510: 17–32.

Lynch, J. (2006) *Age in the Welfare State*, Cambridge: Cambridge University Press.

McLanahan, S. (2004) 'Diverging destinies: how children are faring under the second demographic transition,' *Demography* 41(4): 607–27.

Morel, N., Palier, B. and Palme, J. (eds) (2012) *Towards a Social Investment Welfare State?* Bristol: Policy Press.

Olsaretti, S. (2013) 'Children as public goods?', *Philosophy and Public Affairs* 41(3): 226–58.

Preston, S.H. (1984) 'Children and the elderly: divergent paths for America's dependents', *Demography* 21(4): 435–57.

Sinn, H-W., and Uebelmesser, S. (2002) 'Pensions and the path to gerontocracy in Germany', *European Journal of Political Economy* 19: 153–8.

Tepe, M. and Vanhuysse, P. (2009) 'Are aging OECD welfare states on the path to gerontocracy?' *Journal of Public Policy* 29(1): 1–28.

Tepe, M. and Vanhuysse, P. (2010) 'Elderly bias, new social risks and social spending: change and timing in eight programmes across four worlds of welfare, 1980–2003', *Journal of European Social Policy* 20(3): 217–34.

United Nations (2013) *National Transfer Accounts Manual*, New York: UN.

Vanhuysse, P. (2013) *Intergenerational Justice in Aging Societies*, Gütersloh: Bertelsmann Stiftung.

Vanhuysse, P. (2014) 'Intergenerational justice and public policy in Europe,' *European Social Observatory (OSE) Paper Series, Opinion Paper No. 16*, 17 pp.

Vanhuysse, P. (2015) 'Skills, stakes and clout: early human capital foundations for European welfare futures', in B. Manin (ed.) *The Future of Welfare in a Global Europe*, Aldershot: Ashgate, pp. 267–96.

Vanhuysse, P. and Goerres, A. (eds) (2012) *Ageing Populations in Post-Industrial Democracies*, Abingdon: Routledge.

Vargha, L. and Donehower, G. (2016) 'The quantity/quality tradeoff: a cross-country comparison of market and nonmarket investments per child in relation to fertility', Manuscript.

Vargha, L., Šeme, A., Gál, R.I., Hammer, B. and Sambt, J. (2016) *European NTA Accounts*, available at http://witt.null2.net/shiny/agenta/

Zelizer, V. (1985) *Pricing the Priceless Child*, New York: Basic Books.

Index

For Product Safety Concerns and Information please contact our EU
representative GPSR@taylorandfrancis.com Taylor & Francis Verlag GmbH,
Kaufingerstraße 24, 80331 München, Germany

Printed and bound by CPI Group (UK) Ltd, Croydon, CR0 4YY
01/05/2025
01859218-0001